D0742668

DISCARDED

RESEARCH GUIDE
TO AMERICAN LITERATURE

Postwar Literature
1945–1970

Research Guide
to American Literature

Volume 1: *Colonial Literature, 1607–1776*

Volume 2: *Early American Literature, 1776–1820*

Volume 3: *Romanticism and Transcendentalism, 1820–1865*

Volume 4: *Realism and Regionalism, 1865–1914*

Volume 5: *American Modernism, 1914–1945*

Volume 6: *Postwar Literature, 1945–1970*

Volume 7: *Contemporary Literature, 1970 to Present*

50⁰⁰

Research Guide
to American Literature

Postwar Literature
1945–1970

John Cusatis
School of the Arts, Charleston, S.C.

REF
PS
51
R47
2010
vol.6

A Bruccoli Clark Layman Book

Facts On File
An imprint of Infobase Publishing

EL CAMINO COLLEGE LIBRARY

Research Guide to American Literature: Postwar Literature, 1945–1970
Copyright © 2010 by John Cusatis

All rights reserved. No part of this book may be reproduced or utilized in any form or by any means, electronic or mechanical, including photocopying, recording, or by any information storage or retrieval systems, without permission in writing from the publisher. For information contact:

Facts On File, Inc.
An imprint of Infobase Publishing
132 West 31st Street
New York NY 10001

Library of Congress Cataloging-in-Publication Data
Research guide to American literature. — New ed.
    p. cm.
"A Bruccoli Clark Layman book."
Includes bibliographical references and index.
ISBN 978-0-8160-7861-5 (v. 1 : acid-free paper)—ISBN 978-0-8160-7862-2 (v. 2 : acid-free paper)—ISBN 978-0-8160-7863-9 (v. 3 : acid-free paper)—ISBN 978-0-8160-7864-6 (v. 4 : acid-free paper)—ISBN 978-0-8160-7865-3 (v. 5 : acid-free paper)—ISBN 978-0-8160-7866-0 (v. 6 : acid-free paper)—ISBN 978-0-8160-7867-7 (v. 7 : acid-free paper) 1. American literature—Research—Methodology—Handbooks, manuals, etc. 2. American literature—History and criticism. 3. Canon (Literature) I. Franklin, Benjamin, 1939– II. Vietto, Angela III. Habich, Robert D., 1951– IV. Quirk, Tom, 1946– V. Scharnhorst, Gary. VI. Anderson, George Parker, 1957– VII. Cusatis, John. VIII. Moser, Linda Trinh, 1964– IX. West, Kathryn, 1962– X. Facts on File, Inc.
PS51.R47 2010
810.7'2—dc22
                        2009047815

Facts On File books are available at special discounts when purchased in bulk quantities for businesses, associations, institutions, or sales promotions. Please call our Special Sales Department in New York at (212) 967-8800 or (800) 322-8755.

You can find Facts On File on the World Wide Web at http://www.factsonfile.com

Text design by Erika K. Arroyo
Composition by Bruccoli Clark Layman
Cover printed by Art Print, Taylor, PA
Book printed and bound by Maple Press, York, PA
Date printed: May 2010
Printed in the United States of America

10 9 8 7 6 5 4 3 2 1

This book is printed on acid-free paper.

Contents

Acknowledgments

This literary research guide has grown out of the input, inspiration, and support of generations of colleagues, friends, former teachers, family members and students. I am specifically grateful to Richard Layman, Philip B. Dematteis, George Parker Anderson, and everyone at Bruccoli Clark Layman. I appreciate the work of the two dozen first-rate scholars who contributed essays; each has been a pleasure to work with. Many of them helped me place unassigned entries with the most authoritative writers, who, in turn, delivered excellent work in a timely fashion. To the following individuals I extend thanks for playing a particularly pivotal role, directly or indirectly, in the genesis of this volume: John Barber, Judith Baughman, Bob Bell, Sean Bolton, Marshall Boswell, Kurt Hemmer, Ruth Kudlick, Reverend Connell McHugh, Michael Santulli, and Ken Shields. I am pleased to include the work of two members of my dissertation committee at the University of South Carolina, Keen Butterworth and William Thesing, in this volume. I am also obliged to Penn State professor Joseph Marchesani, not only for all he taught me nearly three decades ago, but also, more recently, for leading me to one of *his* former professors, science-fiction writer and scholar James Gunn, who co-wrote an entry. Thanks to colleagues and students from the School of the Arts, including Basil Kerr, Alek Mihok, Rene Miles, Caroline Rogers, Hal Ross, Bill Smyth, Susan Trott, and especially Rose Maree Myers, the school's generous founder and visionary. I am forever grateful to the late Matthew J. Bruccoli, whose impact as teacher, editor, writer, scholar, and friend is immeasurable. In addition, I value the support of my friends Grover and Martha Cleveland and Jimmy Terrell. Finally, no work could be accomplished without the inspiration and devotion of my family, particularly, my wife, Anna; our children, Giovanni, Luciano, and Annabella; my parents, Maurice and Theresa Cusatis; Matthew Cusatis; and Harold and Katie Johnson. The personal stories that my father, a veteran of World War II, has shared with my eight brothers and sisters and me over the years have heightened my interest and sharpened my understanding of the war and its aftermath, in much the same way as the works of the writers discussed within these pages.

Contributors

Series Introduction

Research Guide to American Literature is a series of handbooks for students and teachers that recommends strategies for studying literary topics and frequently taught literary works and authors. The rationale for the series is that successful study is predicated on asking the right questions and then devising a logical strategy for addressing them. The process of responsible literary investigation begins with facts and usually ends with opinions. The value of those opinions depends on the ability of the reader to gather useful information, to consider it in context, to interpret it logically, and finally to decide what the interpretation means outside the confines of the literary work. Often the answers to questions a sophisticated reader asks about a literary topic are subjective, involving a reader's perception of an author's or a character's motive; always the search for the answer to a meaningful question involves a process of self-education and, in the best of circumstances, self-awareness.

RGAL is intended as a resource to assist readers in identifying questions to ask about literature. The seven volumes in this series are organized chronologically, corresponding to generally accepted literary periods. Each volume follows this general pattern:

Part I provides the social and historical context for a literary period, explaining its historical boundaries, describing the nature of the literary output of the time, placing the literature in its social and historical contexts, identifying literary influences, and tracing the evolution of critical approaches.

Part II comprises ten study guides on general themes or topics related to the period, organized alphabetically. Each guide first provides necessary background information, then suggests questions or research topics that might be fruitfully considered, along with specific primary and secondary works that students will find useful. Each guide also includes an annotated checklist of recommended secondary works and capsule identifications of people mentioned.

Part III comprises some thirty study guides for particular literary works or authors, organized alphabetically by the author's name. Each guide begins with a brief overview of the author's career to provide context, and then suggests some half a dozen topics for discussion and research, with advice about how to begin investigating the topic. These topics are meant to facilitate classroom discussion as well as to suggest interesting ideas for research papers. Each guide includes an annotated checklist of recommended secondary works.

Part IV is an annotated general bibliography recommending the most useful general works of literary history, literary criticism, and literary reference pertinent to the period.

Part V is a glossary of terms used in the volume.

A keyword index is included in each volume.

The purpose of *RGAL* is not to tell students what literature means but to help them determine the meaning for themselves by asking significant questions and seeking answers diligently and thoughtfully. That is how learning that matters takes place. The method is as old as Socrates.

—*Richard Layman*

Part I
Overview

Boundaries of the Period

The 22 December 1946 issue of *The New Yorker* featured a short story titled "Slight Rebellion off Madison," in which the teenage protagonist explains to his bemused date that he hates school and is disgusted with society in general: "I don't get anything out of anything. I'm in bad shape. I'm in lousy shape. Look, Sally. How would you like to just beat it?" When he proposes that he and she leave New York City the next morning and escape to a remote cabin in rural New England, the girl responds, "You can't just do something like that." "Why not?" he asks. "Why the hell not?" "Because you can't," she chides. The protagonist is Holden Morrisey Caulfield, home on Christmas break from Pencey Preparatory School for Boys. The writer is J. D. Salinger, who eventually dropped the Morrisey from his protagonist's name, had him kicked out of Pencey Prep, and made him the narrator and hero of his 1951 novel, *The Catcher in the Rye*. What Holden maintains in his new role is his frustration with the adult world, which he finds unimaginative, phony, and self-centered—traits captured, for him, in the naysayer Sally. The "slight rebellion" Salinger portrays in this early glimpse of his work-in-progress foreshadows the social and cultural unrest that characterized the next two and a half decades in America, a rebelliousness to which his protagonist gives the earliest and most memorable voice.

The twenty-five years between 1945 and 1970 mark a fruitful era in American literature, and protest is the defining element in the work of its writers. The beginnings of the period could not be more clearly demarcated. On Monday, 6 August 1945, the United States dropped the first atomic bomb on Hiroshima, Japan. After a second bombing over Nagasaki on Thursday, 9 August, the Japanese officially surrendered to the Allies on 2 September 1945. After six years, World War II was over. For most Americans, not only the sixteen million who served in the military during the war, life had been put on hold. Having endured a decade of the Great Depression followed by the deadliest, most ghastly war in human history, Americans relished the return to prosperity. The war had created a booming job market, and the aftermath created increasing demand and even more jobs as military personnel took advantage of the new GI Bill, which paid for their college education and offered loans at low interest rates. Marrying, buying a home and a car, and starting a family were no longer risky or impossible ventures for most Americans. Many of the rural poor were moving into cities for work, and the middle classes began expanding into suburbs, living the comfortable, secure lives portrayed on television sets, which became ubiquitous in American households.

Yet, while a sense of complacency settled in, another bomb was ticking within the country's own borders as a restless younger generation chafed under the stronghold of the new consumer culture and its penchant for conformity. In its effort to maintain the comforts it had fought so hard to secure, the American government became increasingly vigilant regarding the "containment" of communist influences. The Soviet Union had developed its own nuclear weapons after the war, and soon the United States was involved in the Cold War, as the two nations aimed to protect their antithetical ideologies: democracy and capitalism in America, totalitarianism and communism in the Soviet Union. Many Americans detected inconsistency in their government's stance, as innocent people's lives were being disrupted by suspicions brought on by this Red Scare, as it was called. In addition, while the lives of Native Americans and African Americans were sacrificed to preserve the country's freedom during the war, these groups were denied many of the very freedoms they had fought to protect. Segregation had persisted during the war, and minority soldiers were generally placed in the most menial and often most life-threatening positions. Women, too, had assumed factory jobs during the war effort; yet, they were expected to resume lives of subservience in its wake. American prosperity was masking ugly truths, and the artists of this period, many of them minorities, began exposing the hypocrisy that troubled the young Holden Caulfield. A counter culture began to emerge as early as the late 1940s when Jack Kerouac and Neal Cassady began their adventures across North America searching for "kicks," which Kerouac spontaneously recorded in *On the Road* (1957), published nearly a decade later. General Dwight D. Eisenhower had moved from his position as Supreme Commander of the Allied Forces to the President of the United States, and the rigidity of the 1950s—captured in the crew-cut hairstyle adopted by the military and soon popular among civilians—was being countered by individuals who, like Rosa Parks, resented threats to their personal freedom. The year 1953, for example, marked both the initiation of a policy prohibiting homosexuals from holding government jobs and the debut of *Playboy* magazine. For writers, the establishment was being run by the Colonel Cathcarts of *Catch-22* (1961), the Nurse Ratcheds of *One Flew Over the Cuckoo's Nest* (1962), and the Boss Godfreys of *Cool Hand Luke* (1965), but these tyrants were being confronted by the Randle P. McMurphys, John Yossarians, and Luke Jacksons of the younger generation, whose defiance was sometimes their only weapon.

The waning of the social, cultural, and literary reaction triggered by the war and its aftermath cannot be pinpointed as neatly as its beginning; however, the claim that the end of the 1960s was the end of an era is easy to substantiate. In retrospect, there is undeniable significance in the fact that the breakup of the Beatles, whose songs and lifestyle defined the counter-culture revolution in many ways, was announced by Paul McCartney on 8 May 1970, twenty-five years to the day after Nazi Germany officially surrendered to the Allies. The breakup coincided with the release of the band's aptly titled album *Let It Be*. Some date the end of the era as 5 December 1969, when the Rolling Stones concert at Altamont, California, went awry and the Hell's Angels murdered an audience member while the group's front man, Mick Jagger, sang "Sympathy for the Devil" (1968). The year 1969 also marked a pinnacle when Neil Armstrong stepped onto the moon, fulfilling John F. Kennedy's dream during the space race with the Soviet Union. Others point to the 1968 election of Richard M. Nixon and a return to a prevailing conservatism. Some argue Nixon's election would have been impossible had not the Democratic candidate Robert Kennedy been assassinated earlier that year, only two months after Martin Luther King Jr. was murdered. Others cite the Charles Manson murders as the ultimate spoiling of 1960s idealism. Manson even cited a Beatles song, "Helter Skelter," as his inspiration. In addition, if there were any chance of a much hoped for Beatles reunion, it was spoiled when John

Lennon was assassinated in 1980 by a gunman who sat reading *The Catcher in the Rye* while waiting to be arrested for the murder of the man he believed had joined the materialistic, phony society Holden Caulfield had railed against during the dawn of the period. Finally, it is clear that the 1970s ushered in an era that encouraged self-indulgence more than self-reflection. In fact, the youth rebellion of the 1960s itself becomes a target of protest in Saul Bellow's 1970 novel, *Mr. Sammler's Planet,* in which the elderly protagonist vents his disgust with the younger generation. The influence of the postwar era certainly lingered in the work of many of its writers and their followers, just as many writers of the 1920s and 1930s such as Ernest Hemingway, William Faulkner, and John Steinbeck continued to produce enduring works and inspire young writers during the 1950s.

Dominant Genres and Literary Forms

Out of the dissidence and unrest of this quarter century blossomed many literary movements, some of which overlap, and most of which can be viewed as varieties of the predominant aesthetic movement, Postmodernism. World War II jarred the foundations of civilization, and the Postmodernists responded by subverting the foundations of its art to an even greater extent than their post–World War I Modernist predecessors. The Modernists had experimented with new approaches to writing to reflect more-complex views of mankind and its relationship to the universe. They often employed disjointed plotlines and stream-of-consciousness points of view. Like the Modernist Ezra Pound, Postmodernists were eager to "make it new" and to some extent took experimentation to a new extreme; they also opposed the now-rigid expectations of High Modernism, with its emphasis on erudition and authorial detachment. Postmodernist literature tends to be highly subjective, often self-conscious of its own form, and open-ended. Genres are frequently blended and high and popular culture fused. The Postmodern author can become a character in his fiction, as in Kurt Vonnegut's *Slaughterhouse-Five* (1969), or the title of the novel can suddenly appear as a major character, as in Richard Brautigan's *Trout Fishing in America* (1967). The composition of the work can also become the subject, as it does in both of these novels or in self-reflexive poetry such as Brautigan's "April 7, 1969," which reads, "I feel so bad today / that I want to write a poem / I don't care: any poem, this poem."

The most influential movement of the postwar period was the Beat movement, which began in New York City through the friendship of Kerouac, Allen Ginsberg, William S. Burroughs, and, later, Gregory Corso, but it blossomed in San Francisco where the East Coast Beats befriended West Coast writers such as Gary Snyder, Lawrence Ferlinghetti, Michael McClure, and Philip Whalen. The Beats shared a rejection of the establishment, which they perceived as conformist, materialistic, and hypocritical. Many sought liberation in Eastern religion, drug use, and jazz music. Their writing tended to be intuitive and spontaneous rather than intellectual and contrived, and it was marked by honesty and urgency. Connected with the Beat movement is the less aesthetically and philosophically cohesive San Francisco Renaissance, a group of experimental writers, who also emerged after the war, writing what its founder Kenneth Rexroth called "elegiac" poetry in response to a changing America. An interest in Asian language and poetry characterized many of the members of this movement, such as Brautigan, whose understated poems often resemble haiku. Many of the West Coast Beats, such as Snyder, who moved to Japan at the end of the 1950s, are included in this artistic movement, out of which grew the hippie culture of the 1960s and such psychedelic rock bands as The Grateful Dead, The Jefferson Airplane, and Big Brother and the Holding Company, and the novels of Ken Kesey and Brautigan.

Some writers associated with the San Francisco Renaissance are connected to an East Coast movement known as the Black Mountain school. Members of this school are grouped primarily due to their association with Black Mountain College, in North Carolina, and their commitment to the "projective verse," an organic open style of composition, espoused by one of the school's leading figures,

Charles Olson. Other prominent members of the group are poets Robert Creeley, Robert Duncan, and Denise Levertov. The emphasis on intuition, the subordination of form to content, and use of casual diction connects this group to another East Coast movement, the New York School, whose members include John Ashbery and Frank O'Hara. These poets, too, encouraged experimentation and sought to defy conventions, particularly the High-Modernist notion that poetry must be difficult and serious. Each of these poetic movements, with its emphasis on simplicity of form, spontaneity of composition, and precise language, owes a debt to the poet William Carlos Williams. Another group to gain prominence during this period was the confessional poets, who, like these other schools, opposed the Modernist period edict of the New Critics that a poem should be detached from its author. The work of Robert Lowell, Sylvia Plath, and Anne Sexton, for example, frankly chronicles the emotional experiences of these writers, each of whom suffered from depression. Finally, the Black Arts movement, aiming for a "black aesthetic," found a voice in poets such as Amiri Baraka (formerly LeRoi Jones) and Gwendolyn Brooks, the first African American to win the Pulitzer Prize, who modified her traditional style in the 1960s to suit the more race-conscious poetry she began writing.

A common irony that binds these writers is that while they are Postmodern in their need for new forms, their aversion to restrictions is an ancient, primal impulse. This is certainly the case with poets such as James Dickey, Robinson Jeffers, Galway Kinnell, W. S. Merwin, Theodore Roethke, Gary Snyder, and Robert Penn Warren. These poets, some of whom thrived before the war but were affected by it and remained active and relevant after it, are sometimes referred to as "modern primitives" for their concerns with humanity's over-civilization and the artist's need to draw inspiration from the natural world. Protest fills the work of these writers as much as any of those whose concerns are more urban, as they are at odds with a society that encourages man's increased separation from the natural world and, consequently, from his own essential nature. Shortly before the war Jeffers had written in "The Answer" (1937): "The greatest beauty is / Organic wholeness, the wholeness of life and things, the divine beauty of the universe. Love that, not man / Apart from that." In his postwar poetry Jeffers lamented the acquisitive, destructive impulse that began to intrude on his West Coast refuge, noting in "Carmel Point" (1954): "This beautiful place defaced with a crop of suburban houses— / How beautiful when we first beheld it, / Unbroken field of poppy and lupin walled with clean cliffs."

While poets produced some of the most enduring books of the period, such as Ginsberg's *Howl and other Poems* (1956), Ferlinghetti's *A Coney Island of the Mind* (1958), and Dickey's *Poems 1957–1967* (1967), fiction writers also dominated the era with works characterized by social and spiritual alienation. Unlike many of the movies produced during the war years, novels by writers who served in the war, such as Norman Mailer, Joseph Heller, and Vonnegut, tended to expose the horrors rather than the honors of combat. Mailer's *The Naked and the Dead* (1948) presented a realistic look at the hardships of war, while novels such as Heller's wildly original *Catch-22* (1961) and Vonnegut's science-fictive *Slaughterhouse-Five* (1969) approach the absurdity of war with black comedy. All three authors use the war as a vehicle for universal statements about oppression that characterized much of their other fiction. Salinger also fought in the war, and while his fiction also conveys a sense of moral indignation, he rarely treats war directly in his books, though a few of his protagonists are clearly disenchanted by their wartime experience and, like Heller's protagonist, with the army in general. Like Heller and Mailer, Salinger was Jewish by birth; yet, he also avoided Jewish themes in his work. Writers such as Bellow and Phillip Roth, however, charted the Jewish experience in America in several postwar novels and short stories. Roth's characters frequently struggle to reconcile their Jewish upbringing with the mores of the modern world. Bellow's characters also tend to be struggling with their identity yet often independent of their ethnic background. In this respect his work has affinities with the fiction of John Updike, whose characters' spiritual balance is often challenged by the demands of domestic life. Updike renders his tales of suburbia with deft lyricism inspired by the work of Vladimir Nabokov, the Russian writer who became a major American novelist with such works as *Lolita* (1955) and *Pale Fire* (1962). Identity is also the subject of novels by the two most prominent African American writers of the period, Ralph Ellison and James Baldwin, who in their attempts to write novels that address universal conflicts were accused of not being militant enough. Regional writing, particularly Southern literature, remained prominent during this period. Carson McCullers and Flannery O'Connor portrayed the struggles of rural misfits in the Southern Gothic tradition of William Faulkner. O'Connor and Walker Percy expressed deep religious concerns in their fiction while Harper Lee and William Styron tackled racial issues. Western writers such as Kesey and Edward Abbey produced novels that often lament the destruction of the Western frontier by developers.

Four dramatists dominated the postwar years, particularly during the late 1940s and 1950s, writing some of the best plays of the century: Arthur Miller's *Death of a Salesman* (1949), Eugene O'Neill's *Long Day's Journey into Night* (1956), and Tennessee Williams's *A Streetcar Named Desire* (1947) and *Cat on a Hot Tin Roof* (1955) are all modern Realist tragedies. Tennessee Williams, too, set his work in the South and often dealt with the changing social structure, though his themes have universal resonance. Edward Albee's plays *The Zoo Story* (1958) and *Who's Afraid of Virginia Woolf?* (1962) are more closely linked to the theatre of the absurd; yet, like his contemporaries, Albee is concerned with the conflict between honesty and the need for self-deception.

Historical and Social Context

The origins of the key historical events and dominant social issues of this period in America can be traced back to the end of World War II and the redefining of moral, social, and political objectives that evolved in its wake. While Europe and Asia attempted to rise from the rubble, America adjusted to its position as a new world power and guardian of freedom. Yet, within its borders poverty and discrimination persisted. In 1942 African Americans united to launch the "Double V Campaign," aiming for victory against the enemies of freedom not only in Europe but also at home. The first victory abroad having been achieved, the efforts of African Americans were gradually rewarded at home. In 1947 Jackie Robinson became the twentieth century's first black major-league baseball player when he signed with the Brooklyn Dodgers. Robinson was named National League Rookie of the Year that year and Most Valuable Player two years later. In 1948 President Harry S Truman ended segregation in the U.S. military. And when segregation in public schools was banned by *Brown v. Board of Education* in 1954, the Civil Rights movement was set into motion, and the battle to end racial discrimination became the most dominant social issue of the period.

Yet, the gains made during the Civil Rights movement came at a severe cost to many. First, segregation of schools was difficult to achieve harmoniously, and many school districts did not even attempt it until the end of the 1960s. In the year after the *Brown* victory, Emmett Till, a fourteen-year-old African American, was lynched in Mississippi for allegedly whistling at a white woman. His suspected murderers, who later boasted about the crime, were acquitted, and Till's mother displayed his unrecognizable body in an open casket as a testament to the cruelty of his white killers and the hatred they represented. Later that year Parks refused to relinquish her seat on an Alabama bus to a white man, triggering her arrest and the subsequent Montgomery Bus Boycott. The election of Democratic president Kennedy in 1960—the same year four African Americans staged a momentous sit-in at a Greensboro, North Carolina, Woolworth lunch counter where blacks were refused service—was an auspicious moment for civil rights, as was the admission of James Meredith to the University of Mississippi in 1962. But 1963 was one of the most distressing years of the era. In March the chief of police in Birmingham, Alabama, ordered dogs and fire hoses be used against nonviolent civil-rights protestors. On 12 June, the day after President Kennedy delivered his monumental civil-rights address, Medgar Evers, a civil-rights leader both involved in the investigation of the Till murder and instrumental in the admission of Meredith into the University of Mississippi, was murdered. His killer was arrested, tried twice before all-white juries who failed to reach a verdict, released, and brought finally to justice over thirty years later. In August, King resonantly proclaimed "I have a dream!" to over two hundred thousand gathered at the March on Washington for Jobs and Freedom, where young Bob Dylan also delivered his newly composed protest song about the Evers murder, "Only a Pawn in Their Game" (1964). This day of optimism was followed by the September bombing of a Baptist church in Birmingham, Alabama, which killed four young girls. No one was charged with the murders until the case was reopened in 2000. In November John F. Kennedy was murdered, and the assassinations of his brother Robert and of King followed less than five years later in the spring of 1968. President Kennedy's proposed civil-rights legislation, to eliminate discrimination in hiring practices in public places, was passed under President Lyndon B. Johnson. The Civil Rights Act of 1964 also addressed sexual discrimination, another issue that that was ardently argued during this era.

Like African Americans, women played a crucial role in the war effort, as captured in the image of the fictional factory worker Rosie the Riveter, a character first introduced in the 1942 song of that title. But they, too, were expected to resume inferior roles after the war ended. The term "women's liberation," later "women's lib," was coined around the time the Civil Rights Act was passed in 1964, as the struggle for women's rights began gaining momentum. In May 1960 the FDA approved the birth control pill, and in 1961 President Kennedy placed former first lady Eleanor Roosevelt in charge of the new President's Commission on the Status of Women. But it was a book written by a suburban housewife, Betty Friedan, that gave the movement perhaps its biggest boost. *The Feminine Mystique,* published 25 February 1963, attacked the traditional view that a woman's role should be confined to that of housewife and mother. The book became a *New York Times* best seller, and Friedan helped found the National Organization of Women in 1966. President Johnson's Affirmative Action Plan of 1965 helped assure that women, as well as minorities, receive educational and employment opportunities equal to those of white men. In 1969 California passed the first "no fault" divorce law.

The loosening of social restrictions on women was partly responsible for the sexual revolution, which also became vital during this period. The publication of *Sexual Behavior in the Human Male* (1948) and *Sexual Behavior in the Human Female* (1953) by Alfred C. Kinsey helped to clarify mainstream misconceptions of human sexuality, and sexual self-help manuals such as *Everything You Always Wanted to Know About Sex (But Were Afraid to Ask)* (1969), by Dr. David Reuben, began to appear frequently during the 1960s. Connected to both women's liberation and sexual liberation were the beginnings of the gay liberation movement, which gained national attention and increased support after the Stonewall riots, three days of violent protests that followed a police raid at a gay bar in Greenwich Village in June 1969. Each of these liberation movements gained ground in the following decade. In 1973, for example, the American Psychiatric Association declared that homosexuality was no longer regarded as a mental disorder.

The free love era of the 1960s was also largely inspired by the hippie movement, which marked the culmination of the protest atmosphere initiated in the early postwar years. The term "hippie" was coined in 1965, growing out of the word *hip,* an alteration of *hep,* both of which refer to one's being in tune with the latest popular cultural developments. Hippies embraced several cultural concerns, all of which were in opposition to mainstream mores, and all of which urged a return to a more primitive relationship with the earth and one another. The modern environmental movement was firmly established during this period, and again the publication of a book brought national attention to a crisis formerly understood by only a few. The book in this case was marine biologist Rachel Carson's

Silent Spring (1962), which exposed the dangers of pesticides. "As man proceeds towards his unannounced goal of the conquest of nature," Carson wrote, "he has written a depressing record of destruction, directed not only against the earth he inhabits, but against the life that shares it with him." A fire on Cleveland's oil-saturated Cuyahoga River in June 1969 further heightened national awareness of the problem.

Another major unifying concern among the hippies was the Vietnam War, one of two wars involving America during this period, both as a result of the Cold War that began at the end of World War II. As with the earlier Korean War, which lasted from 1950 to 1953, America's involvement in the Vietnam War was part of the government's effort to prevent the spread of communism. Whether they were part of the hippie movement or not, young people were the most prominent voice of protest during this era, and occasionally they died for it. Two years after police in Orangeburg, South Carolina, had opened fire on college students protesting segregation at a bowling alley, killing three people, the Ohio National Guard fired on student war protesters at Kent State University, killing four, during the spring of 1970.

The slogan "Make Love Not War," popularized in 1965, captures much of ethos of the hippie culture; however, the hippies' adversity to both the Vietnam War and to sexual repression stems from an overall antipathy toward the cultural conservatism that followed the war, which also caused them to reject material-ism, conformity, and, in activist Abbie Hoffman's words, to mistrust "anyone over thirty." Americans discerned hypocrisy not only in their government's continued tolerance of discrimination but in the House Committee on Un-American Activities interrogation of citizens suspected of having communist sympathies during the Red Scare of the 1950s. The careers of many artists, such as the highly influential black blues singer-songwriter Josh White, whose social protest songs were misconstrued as evidence of communist ideology, were ruined by these investigations. The term *McCarthyism*, referring to the demagogic Senator Joseph McCarthy, was coined to describe such unfounded accusations of subversiveness. For many during the 1960s, long hair on a male was enough to signal a threat to mainstream American values. The fact that recreational drugs were also com-monly used by hippies in their attempts to escape the banality of postwar society further alienated them from their elders. The success of the Woodstock Music & Art Fair of August 1969, attended by approximately five hundred thousand, dem-onstrated the viability of this 1960s cultural movement, the influence of which lingered into the twenty-first century.

Out of this embroiled historical and social context emerged a body of lit-erature populated by oppressed, disillusioned, and alienated characters struggling to maintain a degree of integrity and identity. Berenice, an African-American housekeeper in Carson McCullers's 1946 novella, *The Member of the Wedding*, seems to speak for the majority of literary heroes that will follow, not just blacks and females: "Everybody is caught one way or another. But they done drawn completely extra bounds around all colored people. They done squeezed us off in one corner by ourself. So we caught that first way I was telling you, as all human beings is caught. And we caught as colored people also." McCullers's novel is primarily concerned with the adolescent protagonist, Frankie, and her struggle to find "the we of me," or a way to connect with a world she finds strange and hostile. While Frankie blamed the remoteness of her Southern rural hometown for her sense of estrangement, William Carlos Williams in the same year used the city of Paterson, New Jersey, to convey the complexity and alienating effects of the modern world in his long poem *Paterson* (*Book One*, 1946; *Book Two*, 1948). Writers in all regions of the country and all genres reacted to what appeared to be a seemingly nightmarish aspect to the American dream. One writer whose voice of protest was widely heard during the postwar years was Dylan, whose songs, such as "Bob Dylan's Dream" (1963), "Motorpsycho Nightmare" (1964), and "Bob Dylan's 115th Dream" (1965), often captured the notion of a haunted promised land. On his first record, Dylan apostrophized the author of "This Land is Your Land," who was then confined to a hospital room dying of Huntington's disease, with his "Song to Woody" (1962): "Hey, hey Woody Guthrie, I wrote you a song / 'Bout a funny ol' world that's a-comin' along. / Seems sick an' it's hungry, it's tired an' it's torn, / It looks like it's a-dyin' an' it's hardly been born."

Some of the earliest expressions of the postwar zeitgeist were in response to the war itself. In 1948 two veterans of the war published novels that dealt realistically with social and moral issues involving American soldiers. Mailer's *The Naked and the Dead* explores the moral depravity among high-ranking officers, while Irwin Shaw's *The Young Lions* confronts the reality of anti-Semitism in the military. *From Here to Eternity* (1951), written by James Jones, another writer who experienced the war firsthand, also explores the abuses of power and the rebelliousness it incites among the abused.

Shaw was among the first to address the advent of McCarthyism with his second novel, *The Troubling Air* (1951), but a more memorable response came from Miller, whose 1953 drama, *The Crucible,* uses the 1692 Salem witchcraft trials as an analogue to the interrogations of those accused of having communist sympathies. Both Miller and Shaw were confronted with such allegations. During the same year Ray Bradbury published *Fahrenheit 451,* which also responds to Cold War paranoia and censorship. The following year McCarthy himself was chastised by the U.S. Senate for his overzealousness after he claimed the U.S. Army was overrun with communists. The Red Scare persisted, however, even into the 1960s. Dylan's "Talkin' John Birch Paranoid Blues" (1962) seemed to prove its point when a CBS executive would not allow him to perform it during his scheduled appearance on "The Ed Sullivan Show," causing Dylan to walk off the set.

Another protest songwriter to attack the postwar cultural climate was Melvina Reynolds, whose 1962 song, "Little Boxes," mocks the growth of suburban housing that sprang up in the 1950s. Reynolds's song was inspired by the West Lake district in the San Francisco suburb of Daly City, developed in 1947, the year before Miller's *Death of a Salesman* (1948), a tragedy concerning the moral shortsightedness of the American dream that such suburbs came to represent. Reynolds's box-like houses are filled with business executives who have "pretty children" who go to summer camp and then to the university to become business executives. In addition to Miller, many other postwar writers had begun to focus on the growth of conformity and consumerism that Reynolds's song belittles. *The Catcher in the Rye* (1951) was certainly the first major attack by a novelist regarding superficial American middle-class values. "Most people," complains the protagonist, "they're crazy about cars. They worry if they get a little scratch on them, and they're always talking about how many miles they get to the gallon, and if they get a brand new car, already they start thinking about trading it in for one that's even newer." The novel introduced the postwar popularity of the modern antihero—aloof, sensitive, disillusioned, and misunderstood.

The most resonant reaction to the consumer culture and the pressure to conform was voiced by the writers of the Beat movement, which really took shape on 7 October 1955 with Ginsberg's first public reading of his poem *Howl* (1956), the publication of which resulted in a landmark obscenity trial, as did the American appearance of *Naked Lunch* (1962), by Burroughs. These two works, along with Kerouac's *On the Road* (1957), are the three seminal Beat and early counterculture documents. The work of these iconoclastic writers is stylistically free of constraints—*Naked Lunch*, in particular, is definitively Postmodern—mirroring their antiauthoritarian concerns. The work of non-Beat writers such as Vonnegut and the labyrinthine novels of Thomas Pynchon also treat the dehumanizing consequences of a technologically advanced postwar culture.

Another non-Beat writer whose fiction responds to the decaying moral climate of the 1950s and early 1960s is the Southern novelist and short-story writer Flannery O'Connor. Yet, O'Connor's censure of modern America is also directed at the Beats. In his "Footnote to Howl" (1956) Ginsberg writes, "Everything is holy! everybody's holy! everywhere is holy!" O'Connor had no tolerance for this type of unqualified spiritual ecstasy, claiming, regarding the Beats, "holiness costs and so far as I can see they pay nothing." Like the Beats, O'Connor was outraged by a spiritually stagnating modern world. Yet, she did not see man as the measure of all things, and her characters suffer for their self-centeredness, which she perceived to be the chief moral problem of the time. Her stories also often reflect the inability of members of once-prosperous families to accept the changing, often-humbling social structure of the South, a theme treated by other Southern writers such as Tennessee Williams and illustrated best in O'Connor's story "Everything that Rises Must Converge" (1964), in which a condescending white woman is fatally assaulted after offering a black child a penny.

Race and ethnic relations in America as a whole preoccupied many of the most prominent writers of the time. Ralph Ellison's *Invisible Man* (1952) chronicles the plight of its unnamed narrator, who is stripped of his idealism while being exploited or betrayed by nearly everyone he encounters during his "rise" from the racist South. While suburban America opened its doors to the burgeoning white middle class, blacks were often prohibited from moving into these neighborhoods by housing laws, a subject treated in Lorraine Hansberry's play *A Raisin in the Sun* (1959). Many black writers responded directly to tragedies that occurred during the Civil Rights movement, such as Gwendolyn Brooks, whose "A Bronzeville Mother Loiters in Mississippi. Meanwhile, a Mississippi Mother Burns Bacon" (1960) is a reaction to the murder of Till. The urban folk music movement of the early 1960s included white songwriters reacting to many of these horrors as well.

Dylan responded to Till's murder with "The Death of Emmett Till" (1963), and his songs such as "Oxford Town" (1963), which concerns James Meredith's struggle to enroll in the University of Mississippi, and "The Lonesome Death of Hattie Carroll" (1964), about a black maid murdered by her rich employer, helped bring the causes of the Civil Rights movement to a larger audience.

The plight of other oppressed groups was the impetus for much of the poetry and prose written during this period. Plath and Sexton often wrote candidly about the constraints of domestic expectations on women, and, beginning with her 1963 collection, *Snapshots of a Daughter-in-Law,* Adrienne Rich, an early civil-rights proponent, began focusing on her identity as a woman. By the early 1970s she was at the forefront of the women's liberation movement as poet and activist. Brooks also increasingly embraced women's issues as her career developed. Responses to the women's-rights movement became more prevalent during the 1970s, and the gay-rights movement much later, although writers such as Truman Capote, Gore Vidal, and Baldwin treated homosexuality in the early postwar novels *Other Voices, Other Rooms* (1948), *The City and the Pillar* (1948), and *Giovanni's Room* (1956), respectively. As with *Naked Lunch*, Grove Press, a publisher of primarily counter-cultural literature, was brought to court on obscenity charges after they published Henry Miller's 1934 classic, *The Tropic of Cancer,* in America in 1961. Yet, the court's ruling in favor of Miller and his publishers paved the way for other sexually explicit novels such as Roth's *Portnoy's Complaint* (1969). Roth's novel also dealt with issues of cultural assimilation among Jews, a topic he first examined more earnestly in his story collection *Goodbye, Columbus* (1959), which won the National Book Award in 1960. M. Scott Momaday's Pulitzer Prize–winning novel, *House Made of Dawn* (1968), was the first major treatment of Native American concerns, a topic taken up by later writers during the 1970s. Kesey's narrator in *One Flew over the Cuckoo's Nest* is of mixed Native American and European descent, emphasizing the cultural division that frequently plagues Native Americans. Counter-culture writers such as Kesey used Native Americans and the Western frontier as symbols of an earlier, simpler, unspoiled country, and the image of the Native American became synonymous with hippie culture, as hippies not only drew inspiration from Native American values but also imitated their dress. Dickey, too, reacted to the spoiling of the American landscape by developers, and in his novel *Deliverance* (1970), he places his middle-class characters in the Georgia wilderness to convey the emasculating effects of suburban life.

The postwar era ushered in changes in publishing practices, most importantly regarding censorship. Beginning in the late 1950s, several court cases resulted in First Amendment protection of literature that by older standards could have been ruled obscene but by new standards could be considered to be of some social, intellectual, or artistic value. Technological advances led to increased production of mass-market paperbacks after the war, and movie tie-ins substantially increased book sales. One genre that benefited from this progress was science fiction, which had grown increasingly popular in the age of the atomic bomb, space exploration, and other scientific advances.

The dropping of the atomic bomb was the historical event that set the postwar era into motion, and while it gave Americans something new to fear, for the first fictional teenage cultural rebel of the era, Holden Caulfield, it served not only as a nemesis but also as a potential savior from what Jeffers called man's maniacal "self-love": "I'm sort of glad they've got the atomic bomb invented. If there's ever another war, I'm going to sit right the hell on top of it. I'll volunteer for it, I swear to God I will." Jeffers also saw in the rise of human technology and progress the seed of its destruction, which, to him, was also a strange consolation. He notes in "Carmel Point," that "the people are a tide / That swells and in time will ebb, and all their works dissolve." Man's only salvation, Jeffers claimed—and Salinger would agree—was to "uncenter our minds from ourselves," a philosophy that earned Jeffers the title of misanthrope; and in the affluence of the postwar years, one of the most powerful voices of the prewar years was considered old-fashioned, even censored by his publisher, Random House. This consensus began to change near the end of the twentieth century as the prophesies of Jeffers—as well as many of the protesting voices of the postwar years—became increasingly difficult to refute.

Literary Influences

While the social and historical events of the postwar period dramatically influenced the output of its writers, works of literature, philosophy, and religion—ranging from ancient to contemporary—also provided a shaping hand. In some cases it is difficult to determine whether one writer's work was influenced by that of another or if the works simply share an affinity. For example, existential philosophy is evident in the work of many writers during this period, but is this tendency conditioned by their having read Kierkegaard, Heidegger, Sartre, or Camus or by the fact they were living in a time in which alienation, conformity, and dread—ideas that preoccupy existentialists—abounded? Bellow, for one, disliked being labeled as part of the movement; yet, most of his work clearly expresses existential themes. In many cases, however, influence, not merely affinity, is obvious and often acknowledged by the writers themselves.

Existentialism was in vogue not just among writers and intellectuals in America during the late 1940s but even in popular culture. When its major proponent, the French philosopher and writer Jean-Paul Sartre, visited the United States in 1946, magazines such as *Newsweek, Time,* and *Life* had already introduced him to Americans. Even *Vogue,* in its June 1946 issue, included a pictorial layout titled "Portraits of Paris," featuring Sartre and Albert Camus in iconic poses. That year Sartre's play *No Exit* (1944) ran briefly on Broadway, and Camus's novel *The Stranger* (1941) was translated into English. It is easy to see how a character such as Camus' Mersault would attract postwar readers in America, many of whom could identify with his alienation and indifference to social expectations. Existentialism grew out of the nihilistic philosophy of Frederic Nietzsche, which proposed that life is inherently meaningless. For the existentialist, man is both free and condemned to give his life meaning.

Sartre summed up the founding premise of his existential thinking in three words: "existence precedes essence." That is, humans exist before they can be defined as anything. That the opposite view is generally held—that is, human behavior is and should remain largely predictable—is precisely what Camus' Mersault learns through his struggle. For Sartre, the fact that humans are subjects—not merely objects—that they can say "I am," renders them immune to definition until they begin making choices. This realization of one's subjectivity, sometimes referred to as "the existential moment," is captured frequently in the literature of the postwar period. Perhaps the most explicit expression can be found in the work of John Updike, a writer who pored over the work of the existentialists and quoted the three-word phrase above in the epigraph of his fourth novel, *Of the Farm* (1965). Updike writes in his essay "The Dogwood Tree: a Boyhood" (1962) that aside from his childhood questions regarding the existence of God, "The mystery that more puzzled me as a child was the incarnation of my ego—that omnivorous and somehow pre-existent 'I'—in a speck so specifically situated amid the billions of history. Why was I I? The arbitrariness of it astounded me; in comparison, nothing was too marvelous." The narrator of Elizabeth Bishop's late autobiographical poem, "In the Waiting Room" (1976), captures this moment as well, recalling a morning just after her seventh birthday when she, too, was suddenly astounded at the "unlikely" fact that "I had come to be here," telling herself: "you are an I, / You are an Elizabeth." And the twelve-year-old protagonist in McCullers's novel *The Member of the Wedding* asks the family's maid Berenice, "Doesn't it strike you as strange that I am I, and you are you?" To the existentialist, this realization is profound, and the way one reacts to the reality of his own subjectivity in later life will have strong moral implications. Will he choose to be autonomous or an automaton? Thus, the notion of identity is at the heart of existentialism, and existential questions pervade postwar literature: Who am I? What does it mean to live authentically? What gives life meaning?

These questions are at the core of such novels as Updike's *Rabbit, Run* (1960) and Walker Percy's *The Moviegoer* (1961), both of which were strongly influenced by the pre-existentialist writings of nineteenth-century Danish philosopher Søren Kierkegaard, specifically his concern with one's choosing between a life defined by pleasure and one based on moral duty. Ellison's *Invisible Man*, the prototypical quest novel, reveals the author's interest in the work of the French existentialist writer Andre Malraux, who wrote "All art is a revolt against man's fate," an idea Ellison's narrator upholds in the writing of the memoir that makes sense of his plight. Randle P. McMurphy of Kesey's *One Flew Over the Cuckoo's Nest* (1962) and Lloyd "Luke" Jackson of Donn Pearce's *Cool Hand Luke* (1965) are classic examples of existential characters as they refuse to surrender to the system that they know—like death—will ultimately defeat them. While Kesey's worldview was most strongly inspired by the Beats, who were themselves immersed in existentialist writings, Pearce has cited his strongest literary influence as the French writer Jean Genet, whom Sartre admired deeply, exploring what he considered Genet's prototypically existentialist life and work in his biography of the writer, *Saint Genet* (1952). The existential notion that life is absurd is certainly at the center of the works of Heller, Pynchon, and Vonnegut; yet, their protagonists, too, persist in the face of this absurdity. The work of these novelists, as well as that of many postwar Jewish writers, was influenced by the existential ideas in the work of Franz Kafka. Roth, for example, often portrays helpless characters in confounding situations that make little rational sense. A foreign writer of great influence is the Argentinean Jorges Luis Borges, whose hallucinatory fiction has been a major influence on writers such as Pynchon and John Barth.

Naturally, writers are influenced by their contemporaries or near contemporaries. For example, Roth has acknowledged Ellison's *Invisible Man* as an influence on such stories as "Defender of the Faith" (1959), which examines Jewish stereotypes in the way Ellison's novel treats African American stereotypes. In addition to existential influences, Ellison, like Baldwin and Brooks, was influenced by the work of the novelist Richard Wright. Often a clear lineage is observable among generations of writers. The impact of the free-spirited Walt Whitman continued to affect writers after World War II, and one can detect a thread running from Whitman through the Modernist Hart Crane and on to the Beat writer Ginsberg. The influence of William Carlos Williams, whose work addressed everyday occurrences in conversational language, can be seen in much of the poetry of this period, but especially in the work of the Beats, Black Mountain Poets, confessional poets, and the New York School, all of whom demonstrated a Postmodernist lack of inhibition regarding subject and style. In fiction, one can see the mark of F. Scott Fitzgerald in the short stories of Salinger, which in turn influenced Updike, each capturing the social climate and character of their time in lofty prose. And, in drama, a Naturalist strain connects four generations as Tennessee Williams's work bridges that of O'Neill and Albee, and the influence of all three can be traced in the work of the younger Sam Shepard.

While the influence of the South distinguishes Williams's plays, another French influence colors those of Albee. The impact of absurdist works by foreign playwrights Irishman Samuel Beckett and the Frenchmen Eugene Ionesco and Genet, with their existential depiction of man struggling to find meaning, value, and order in the modern world can be seen in Albee's *The Zoo Story* (1959) and *Who's Afraid of Virginia Woolf?* (1962). France was the source of other influential works, such as Simone de Beauvoir's *The Second Sex* (1949), which had a major impact on feminist writers. And the poetry of nineteenth-century French symbolists Charles Baudelaire, Arthur Rimbaud, and Paul Verlaine inspired the highly imagistic, spontaneous poetry of the Beats, particularly Ginsberg, as well as the songs of their protégé Dylan, just as it had influenced the work of the Modernists. Guillaume Apollinaire, the French Modernist who coined the term *surrealism,* was also a major influence on Ginsberg and others. Besides Crane and Williams, other Modernists continued to influence Postmodernist writers. Updike, for example, frequently reappropriated myths in the way James Joyce did, and many writers such as Heller continued Faulkner's use of a nonlinear plotline, stream-of-consciousness narration, and multiple points of view. Heller, as well as O'Connor and Albee, were all influenced by the American humorist James Thurber. And O'Connor and Brautigan acknowledged a major debt to the 1930s novelist Nathanael West and his use of the grotesque.

Like Brautigan, whose final collection of poetry *June 30th, June 30th* (1978) was written during a trip to Japan, many writers of this period were influenced by Eastern culture and poetics. Gary Snyder translated the works of the poet Hanshan in the late 1950s. Along with Ginsberg, Kerouac, and Whalen, Snyder embraced Zen Buddhism, spending fifteen years in Japan. Salinger also became immersed in Zen shortly after the publication of *The Catcher in the Rye,* an influence that lingered in his stories of the Glass family and may be partially responsible for his total withdrawal from the public. Snyder's work was also influenced by Native American culture and by Jeffers, whose poetry is steeped in the natural imagery of the Pacific Coast. All three of these influences have a common element: a view that creation is an organic whole of which man is an integral part, not a separate superior entity. Jeffers's work was also influential on other poets of this generation such as Charles Bukowski, who paid tribute with the poem "he wrote in lonely blood," (1972) and, most profoundly, William Everson (Brother Antoninus), who eulogized him with the poem "The Poet is Dead: A Memorial for Robinson Jeffers" (1964) and wrote two of the finest critical studies on Jeffers's work, *Robinson Jeffers: Fragments of an Older Fury* (1968) and *The Excesses of God: Robinson Jeffers as a Religious Figure* (1988). Finally, while Native American and Eastern religious ideas appeared frequently in the work of postwar American writers, the King James Bible remained a prominent influence.

Evolution of Critical Opinion

While a few new schools of literary criticism, such as the Chicago Critics, the Myth Critics, and Reader-Response Critics, blossomed during this period, and theories such as structuralism and deconstruction took root, the dominant critical approach remained that of the New Critics, whose approach grew out of the theories that I. A. Richards and T. S. Eliot published in the 1920s. The school established its prestige in America with the publication of John Crowe Ransom's critical volume *The New Criticism* (1941), from which it received its name, and Cleanth Brooks and Warren's textbooks *Understanding Poetry* (1938) and *Understanding Fiction* (1943).

New Criticism employs a formalist approach, as opposed to a genetic approach, to understanding literature. That is, it treats the work of literature as an autonomous form that yields its meaning independent of the circumstances of its genesis. Details regarding the author's life and the social and historical context within which he wrote have no bearing on the interpretation of a piece. Instead, literary devices such as irony, symbolism, tone, diction, and figurative language provide the basis for analysis. During the early twentieth century before the New Criticism gained prominence, the attention of critics was fixed more on the influence of political ideology than on the work of an author. The Great Depression increased the number of Americans who professed a leftist political bent, and works such as V. F. Calverton's *The Liberation of American Literature* (1932) employed Marxist principles to the analysis of literary works, an approach that gained renewed attention at the end of the postwar period. For New Critics, the background of the author was to be disregarded. Eliot wrote in one of the seminal essays out of which New Criticism developed, "Tradition and the Individual Talent" (1920): "Honest criticism and sensitive appreciation are directed not upon the poet, but upon the poetry." In their influential 1946 essay, "The Intentional Fallacy," W. K. Wimsatt and Monroe Beardsley reinforced this idea, noting that a poem should be treated as an objective reality rather than a subjective one. Equally detrimental to honest criticism was what these critics referred to as the "affective fallacy." In other words, the effect the poem has on a reader, based on the personal background he brings to his reading of it, should not inform his understanding.

In one of the most important literary critical works published during the postwar period, *The Mirror and the Lamp* (1953), an analysis of Romantic poetry, M. H. Abrams points out the four components involved in literary creation: the world, the artist, the audience, and the work. In other words, the author draws inspiration from the world and creates a work, which is then read by an audience. Various critical views place the emphasis on one or the other of these components. The earliest critical views emphasized the world, focusing on the work as mimesis, or a mirroring of reality by the writer. During the Renaissance, Abrams points out, the emphasis shifted to the audience, and a work was judged according to its ability to evoke a positive, generally cathartic effect. During the Romantic period, the writer became the dominant component, as he filtered the world through his imagination and illuminated reality for his reader, providing a "lamp" rather than a "mirror." For the New Critics, it is the work itself, independent of these other three variables, which absorbs the critic's attention.

New Criticism remained popular throughout the 1950s and 1960s for different reasons. First, poetry had increasingly become the realm of academics, and consequently, it became the fashion to write complicated poetry whose meaning only yielded itself under careful academic scrutiny. In addition, after the war the dramatic rise in college enrollment due to the GI Bill meant that undergraduate poetry classes were no longer the domain of the elite. Also, the formalist approach to poetry is highly teachable, demanding no sophisticated background in history or politics from its reader. For the New Critics, a poem is a highly integrated organic structure, a world within itself with its own linguistic rules. The critic's role is to interpret *how*, not merely *what*, the parts of this organic whole mean. New Criticism, though it was mainly concerned with poetry, which explains the prominence of poets who flourished during its reign, did not approach different genres in different ways. Another group of critics known as the Chicago School gained popularity during this period, distinguishing themselves from the more dominant school by their consideration of genre. A drama, for example, while still an autonomous form, works by a different set of rules than a short story. Aristotle had devised standards for various genres in his *Poetics*, and because the Chicago School shared this affinity with him, they were also known as neo-Aristotelians. More-drastically opposed to the approach of the New Critics were the New York Intellectuals, a group that included influential postwar critics such as Irving Howe, Alfred Kazin, Lionel Trilling, and Edmund Wilson. This school, which also predated World War II but endured through the 1960s, believed literature was inseparable from the culture within which the author wrote, and treated not only the aesthetic aspects of the work but the moral and social implications. Or, as Rene Welleck and Austin Warren distinguished the two approaches in their landmark exposition of New Criticism, *Theory of Literature* (1949), New York Intellectuals took an "extrinsic" rather than "intrinsic" approach to literary analysis, an approach the New Critics felt belonged outside the field of literature.

With the publication of "The Archetypes of Literature" in 1951 and the highly influential *Anatomy of Criticism* in 1957, critic Northrop Frye legitimized a new approach which came to be called Myth Criticism. Frye believed with the Chicago School that genre influenced the workings of literature, and he created a classification system based not only on types of literature but on universal patterns, or archetypes, that were the foundation out of which the organic parts of a work grew. Frye linked what he determined to be four general literary genres—comedy, romance, tragedy, and satire—to the four seasons: spring, summer, autumn, and winter, respectively. The work of the Swiss psychologist Carl Jung was particularly influential on Frye and the Myth Critics, as it was Jung who introduced the idea of the collective unconscious, man's innate capacity to respond to supracultural symbols. Jung viewed life as a process of "individuation," or self-realization, with innate archetypal patterns serving as guides. The mother archetype, for example, fixed in one's unconscious mind in the womb, allows an infant to recognize his mother. For Jung, the central archetype is the "self" archetype, and a satisfying life results through the uniting of this unconscious blueprint of *who* one is with a reality that matches it, a fleshing out of the archetype. For this reason, Frye sees the "quest" archetype as the most dominant in literature. As is often the case with individual growth, he notes, in literature "the heroic quest has the general shape of a descent into darkness and peril followed by a renewal of life." Thus, novels such as Salinger's *The Catcher in the Rye,* Ellison's *Invisible Man,* and O'Connor's *Wise Blood* (1952), could all be understood according to a universal pattern that reaches back through Dante, Moses, and Odysseus. Frye's system of criticism proves to be more fruitful than the New Criticism alone when applied to the work of writers such as Dickey, Jeffers, or Merwin, who embrace primitivism, as well as to the confessional poets, such as Plath, whose work is very personal.

In addition to the work of the Swiss psychologist Jung, American critical theory was also influenced by a group of thinkers from Switzerland known as the Geneva School, who espoused an approach based on the theories of the German philosophers Edmund Husserl and Martin Heidegger: phenomenology. Phenomenological criticism, like its philosophical counterpart, focused on the nature of consciousness, which Husserl contended was an "intentional" act; that is, consciousness, in a sense, endows phenomena with reality. Jung himself referred to humans with their capacity to perceive reality—unlike insentient beings—as second creators. For the phenomenologist critic, the *reader* is this second creator, as it is he who completes, or "concretizes" the work of the writer. The phenomenologist aims to discover the character of the writer's consciousness in his effort to understand the product of it and thus takes a genetic approach to interpreting literature. It is the writer's perception of the world, not the work, that is of primary importance. The writer needs the reader to flesh out the potential meaning of his work. Phenomenologist critics generally study a body of work, including notes, letters, and various drafts by the author, to understand him. Criticism, to this school of critics, is an extension of the writer's art, building on the original work.

Since consciousness is the starting point of existential philosophy, a school of existentialist critics emerged during this period as well, interpreting literary works through the tenets of that philosophy, with its emphasis on identity and personal freedom. Another related branch of critical thought, hermeneutics, places an emphasis on the intended meaning of the author, which critics such as E. D. Hirsch insisted could be determined to a degree of probability based on the analysis of the parts of a work in relation to the whole, thus refuting the "intentional fallacy" proposed by the New Critics, who argued that the author's intentions are irrelevant to literary works.

As writers of the Postmodern era continued to publish works of literature whose meaning became increasingly indeterminate and, thus, resistant to the expectations of New Criticism, a critical movement emerged in the late 1960s that minimized the importance of both the text itself and the social and historical context in which it was written. Reader-Response Criticism, which to some extent grew out of the phenomenological school of thinking that viewed the reader as a creative agent, rejected the idea that a single correct interpretation of a piece of literature exists. Rather, readers, in accord with the experience and knowledge they bring to their reading, influence, or even create, its meaning.

Determining meaning, then, is a largely subjective process. In direct opposition to the New Critics' warning of the dangers of the "affective fallacy" was the Reader-Response critics' emphasis on "affective stylistics," a term coined by the school's most prominent advocate, Stanley Fish, to highlight the role of the reader as the primary "stylist" in the process of literary communication: it is the reader whom the literature is "affecting." Reader-Response Criticism, by its very nature, does not employ a theory to interpret individual texts because it aims to prove that such theorizing occurs differently in the mind of each reader.

Like both the New Criticism and Reader-Response Criticism, structuralism, championed by such critics as Roland Barthes in the 1960s, deemphasizes the importance of the author and is thus in opposition to the phenomenologist school. Structuralism views literature as a system analogous to ordinary language, but operating with a distinct set of codes and rules. Just as native speakers of a language possess what linguists refer to as "linguistic competence," they do not need to be, and generally are not, aware of the system, or grammar, that governs the use of that language. Structuralist critics argue that literature works in the same way, and readers also gain an unconscious "literary competence" as their reading skills develop. Like linguists, structuralist critics aim to identify and classify the elements that make literary meaning possible. Thus, for these critics, the structure of the work itself and the interaction of its various "signifiers" determine its meaning.

Shortly after structuralism took hold, many of its proponents modified their position regarding the absolute meaning conveyed by these signifiers, and Poststructuralism, the critical analogue to literary Postmodernism emerged, its proponents challenging the idea that literary language is a cohesive, reliable system. The French philosopher Jacques Derrida coined the term *deconstruction* in the late 1960s, arguing that if one analyzes the system of signifiers in a literary work, he will inevitably discover contradictions, rendering a literary text open to a wide array of interpretations.

"Come writers and critics / Who prophesize with your pen," wrote Bob Dylan in 1964, "And don't speak too soon / For the wheel's still in spin." While the literary reputations of a few prominent postwar writers diminished during the final quarter of the twentieth century, only to be resurrected in recent years, others flourished. As deconstruction waned during the 1980s, "context" rather than "text" became the focus of many new literary schools, all of which grew out of expanding social consciousness of the postwar years. Consequently, as African American, postcolonial, feminist, gay and lesbian, and ecocritical schools emerged, the reputations of many postwar writers gained stature. Jeffers, whose work, like that of Brautigan and Dickey, has endured dramatic reappraisal, contended that "posthumous reputation . . . is the only kind worth considering." As many major critics, such as Harold Bloom, maintain the most abiding standard of artistic value—beauty—the work of these writers attests to the fact that, unlike the many notorious fads and fashions of the 1950s and 1960s, the literary contribution of this generation will remain indelible.

—John Cusatis

Part II
Study Guides
on General Topics

The Beat Generation

The Beat literary movement began as an underground reaction to the emerging military-industrial complex, the Cold War, and the post–World War II culture with its emphasis on conformity and consumerism. Believing that literature could change the world, the Beats aimed to evade the strictures of the dominant culture and create an environment where one could, like the nineteenth-century English poet John Keats, see the world as "a vale of Soul-making." They embraced the eighteenth-century French poet Arthur Rimbaud's "systematic derangement of the senses" by experimenting with drugs, violating sexual mores, and exploring religious and geographical terrain foreign to their upbringings. African American culture was particularly inspiring to many of the white Beats. As part of the artistic zeitgeist of the Atomic Age, which included bebop jazz (Charlie Parker, Dizzy Gillespie, and Thelonious Monk), abstract expressionist painting (Jackson Pollock, Willem de Kooning, and Franz Kline), and method acting (Montgomery Clift, Marlon Brando, and James Dean), Beat literature emphasized improvisation and spontaneity. How an artist created became as important as what he created. Being an artist was not simply something one did but something one was. The Beats formed a bridge between the Modernist writers, who dominated the American literary scene before World War II, and the Postmodernist writers, who established themselves as the country became engulfed in the Vietnam War. On the one hand, the Beat movement was allied with Romanticism, with strong ties to literary figures such as William Blake, Percy Bysshe Shelley, and Walt Whitman. On the other hand, it was a thoroughly experimental movement, following Ezra Pound's dictum to "make it new." Beat literature was meant not merely to be read but also to be heard. In an effort to take literature off the page and into the mouths of artists and the ears of audiences, the Beats used hipster slang and colloquialisms in their work. They became consummate performance artists, reading their works on the street and in bars and coffeehouses, often accompanied by jazz. Rock lyricists and musicians such as Bob Dylan, Jim Morrison, Jerry Garcia, and Janis Joplin inherited the Beat legacy in the 1960s.

The seminal texts of the Beat movement are Allen Ginsberg's *Howl and Other Poems* (1956), Jack Kerouac's *On the Road* (1957), and William S. Burroughs's *Naked Lunch* (1959). The Beat Generation began to take shape when Kerouac, Ginsberg, and Burroughs met one another through Lucien Carr in late 1943 and early 1944. Carr's killing of a friend, David Kammerer, in August 1944 led to the first literary collaboration among the Beats: Kerouac and Burroughs wrote a book about the circumstances of the killing, *And the Hippos Were Boiled in Their Tanks;* clearly a beginning effort, it was not published until 2008. The term *beat,* hipster argot for "exhausted," was introduced by a Times Square hustler named Herbert Huncke, whom Burroughs met in early 1946. Huncke became an underworld guide for this group of searchers, and through him Burroughs became acquainted with heroin. Kerouac added to *beat* the spiritual dimension of "beatitude." In a November 1948 discussion with John Clellon Holmes, another aspiring novelist, Kerouac declared theirs as a "beat generation."

Kerouac's first novel, *The Town and the City,* appeared in 1950, the same year another major figure of the movement, Gregory Corso, met Ginsberg. Holmes's *Go* was published in 1952, and Burroughs's *Junkie* appeared under the pseudonym William Lee as one half of a double Ace Books paperback in 1953; the unexpurgated version was published as *Junky* in 1977. But it was not until the 1956 publication of Ginsberg's *Howl and Other Poems* and its subsequent censorship trial that the Beats began receiving media attention. The success of *On the Road,* inspired by Kerouac's relationship with the legendary Beat hero Neal Cassady, solidified the movement as a cause célèbre.

The Beat movement began to emerge from underground when Ginsberg moved to San Francisco in 1954. There he met like-minded poets Gary Snyder, Michael McClure, and Lawrence Ferlinghetti. The Six Gallery reading on 7 October 1955, at which Ginsberg, Snyder, McClure, Philip Whalen, and Philip Lamantia read their poetry with the poet Kenneth Rexroth as the master of ceremonies and Kerouac in the audience, marked the beginning of the San Francisco Renaissance in the public imagination and the birth of the Beat Generation as a cross-continental movement.

By the time Burroughs's *Naked Lunch* (1962)—originally published as *The Naked Lunch* by the Olympia Press in Paris in 1959—was ruled not obscene by the Massachusetts Supreme Court in 1966, the Beat movement was morphing into the popular hippie counter-culture movement. Second-generation Beats, such as Ken Kesey and Ed Sanders, had strong ties to the counter culture. In January 1967 the Human Be-In at Golden Gate Park in San Francisco, with Ginsberg on the stage, signaled the passing of the torch. That June, Burroughs's face appeared in the center of The Beatles' *Sgt. Peppers Lonely Hearts Club Band* album cover.

Beat artists came from many regional, sexual, political, religious, ethnic, and racial identities. The most prominent African American Beats were Ted Joans, Bob Kaufman, and LeRoi Jones (later Amiri Baraka). And though the Beat movement has been traditionally seen as being dominated by men, recent scholarship has emphasized the central role of women such as Diane di Prima, Brenda Frazer (born Bonnie Bremser), Joyce Johnson, Hettie Jones, Lenore Kandel, Joanne Kyger, Janine Pommy Vega, Anne Waldman, and Ruth Weiss. Future research will undoubtedly complicate and illuminate the different facets of Beat identity and bring fresh insights into the various Beat literary aesthetics.

TOPICS FOR DISCUSSION AND RESEARCH

1. Beat writers often went on spiritual quests. Examine one of Kerouac's two most famous novels—*On the Road, The Dharma Bums* (1958)—or any other Beat work with a "quest" theme and analyze how the process of the quest questions post–World War II American cultural assumptions. See Nancy M. Grace's discussion of the "the quest" in relation to Kerouac's work in *Jack Kerouac and the Literary Imagination*
2. Many Beats practiced Buddhism. Choose a poem or group of poems from *Big Sky Mind: Buddhism and the Beat Generation* (1995), edited by Carole Tomkinson, or any other Beat poetry related to Buddhism, and discuss how Buddhism influ-

ences these works. See *Allen Ginsberg's Buddhist Poetics* (2007) by Tony Trigilio for a detailed discussion of the influence of Buddhism on Ginsberg's works.

3. Some of the most exciting recent scholarship in the field of Beat studies has focused on recovering the voices of Beat women. Choose a book of poetry, such as Anne Waldman's *Iovis* (1993) or di Prima's *Loba: Parts I–VIII* (as revised, 1998), or one of the memoirs written by Beat women such as Bremser's *Troia* (1969), Johnson's *Minor Characters* (1983), or Janine Pommy Vega's *Tracking the Serpent* (1997), and analyze how a female voice is constructed in these texts. *Breaking the Rule of Cool* will provide useful information.

4. The Beat writers often emphasized orality and performance as part of their aesthetic. Find recordings of Beat writers reading from their work (for example, *The Jack Kerouac Collection* [1990], *Allen Ginsberg, Holy Soul Jelly Roll: Poems and Songs 1949–1993* [1994], and *The Best of William Burroughs from Giorno Poetry Systems* [1998]) and their corresponding written texts and discuss how hearing the works performed alters and enhances our reception of them.

5. Choose a selection of poems by East Coast Beats (Ginsberg and Corso), West Coast Beats (Snyder and McClure), and African American Beats (Kaufman and Jones/Baraka) from *The Portable Beat Reader* (1992) and discuss how regional and racial identity influence the thematic content of these poets. See the important essays on African American Beats in *The Beat Generation Writers* (1996), edited by A. Robert Lee, and *Reconstructing the Beats* (2004), edited by Jennie Skerl.

RESOURCES

Primary Works

Ann Charters, ed., *The Portable Beat Reader* (New York: Viking, 1992).
An excellent collection edited by one of the most reliable scholars of Beat literature.

Carole Tomkinson, ed., *Big Sky Mind: Buddhism and the Beat Generation* (New York: Riverhead Books, 1995).
A collection of poetry, prose, letters, and interviews that demonstrates the connection promised by the title.

Biography

Ann Charters, ed., *Dictionary of Literary Biography*, volume 16: *The Beats: Literary Bohemians in Postwar America*, 2 volumes (Detroit: Gale, 1983).
Still one of the best places to become acquainted with the Beat writers, edited by one of the founding figures of Beat Studies. The entries provide excellent background information about the major figures in the Beat movement.

Interviews

Nancy M. Grace and Ronna C. Johnson, *Breaking the Rule of Cool: Interviewing and Reading Women Beat Writers* (Jackson: University Press of Mississippi, 2004).
Illuminating interviews with the most prominent Beat women.

Criticism

Nancy M. Grace, *Jack Kerouac and the Literary Imagination* (New York: Palgrave Macmillan, 2007).
An enlightening study of the spiritual elements in Kerouac's writing.

Oliver Harris, *William Burroughs and the Secret of Fascination* (Carbondale: Southern Illinois University Press, 2003).
A groundbreaking study by the leading Burroughs scholar, using archival research to illuminate understanding of Burroughs's first three novels—*Junkie* (1953), *Queer* (1985), and *The Naked Lunch* (1959)—and his collaboration with Ginsberg, *The Yage Letters* (1963).

Kurt Hemmer, ed., *Encyclopedia of Beat Literature* (New York: Facts On File, 2007).
Focuses on the works written by the Beats and those closely associated with the movement.

Tim Hunt, *Kerouac's Crooked Road: The Development of a Fiction* (Berkeley: University of California Press, 1996).
Originally published in 1981, one of the first and still one of the best scholarly studies of Kerouac. The book examines the creation of *On the Road* (1957) and *Visions of Cody* (1972).

Ronna Johnson and Grace, *Girls Who Wore Black: Women Writing the Beat Generation* (New Brunswick, N.J.: Rutgers University Press, 2002).
An important collection of essays revealing the often neglected centrality of women in the Beat movement.

William T. Lawlor, ed., *Beat Culture: Icons, Lifestyles, and Impact* (Santa Barbara, Cal.: ABC-CLIO, 2005).
As the title suggests, an ambitious effort to place the Beats in their cultural context.

A. Robert Lee, *The Beat Generation Writers* (London: Pluto Press, 1996).
Includes ten chapters, each devoted to one of the major Beat writers or groups of Beat Generation writers.

Jennie Skerl, ed., *Reconstructing the Beats* (New York: Palgrave Macmillan, 2004).
A stimulating collection of essays placing the Beats in new cultural contexts, examining neglected Beat writers, and reexamining Beat texts from new perspectives.

Matt Theado, *The Beats: A Literary Reference* (New York: Carroll & Graff, 2003).
An excellent collection of secondary material focused on Kerouac, Ginsberg, Burroughs, Cassady, Corso, Holmes, and Snyder.

Tony Trigilio, *Allen Ginsberg's Buddhist Poetics* (Carbondale: Southern Illinois University Press, 2007).
The best examination of the influence of Buddhism on Ginsberg's poetry.

PEOPLE OF INTEREST

William S. Burroughs (1914–1997)
The eminence grise of the Beat Generation, having profoundly influenced Kerouac and Ginsberg in their early days in 1940s New York and later corresponding with them through letters from Tangier, Paris, and London. Burroughs was a legendary figure in Beat circles before his most famous novel, *Naked Lunch* (1959), was published, and he was later notorious as the world's most famous junky. His most experimental work can be found in his "cut-up" trilogy: *The Soft Machine* (1961, revised 1966, revised 1968), *The Ticket That Exploded* (1962, 1967), and *Nova Express* (1964). Some of his best prose can be found in the "Red Night" trilogy: *Cities of the Red Night* (1981), *The Place of Dead Roads* (1984), and *The Western Lands* (1987).

Gregory Corso (1930–2001)
The enfant terrible of the Beats, notorious for causing stirs with his bad-boy antics wherever he appeared. Though he spent his youth in and out of reform schools, jails, and prison, he became one of the most accomplished Beat poets. He joined the Beat circle in 1950 when he met Ginsberg and became an indelible member of the movement. His most famous works are *Gasoline* (1958) and *The Happy Birthday of Death* (1960).

Diane di Prima (1934–)
Became part of the Beat inner circle in the late 1950s, was active in the underground press of the 1960s, and is now considered a major voice not just of the Beat Generation but of post–World War II American poetry in general. Di Prima's masterpiece is the still-forming *Loba* (1973–).

Lawrence Ferlinghetti (1919–)
The most famous publisher of Beat works as the driving force behind City Lights, which first published Ginsberg's *Howl and Other Poems* (1956). He is also one of the major poets to emerge from the Beat movement. His most famous collections are *Pictures of the Gone World* (1955) and *A Coney Island of the Mind* (1958), one of the most popular works of Beat poetry with over a million copies in print. He was named San Francisco's first poet laureate in 1998 and served for two years.

Allen Ginsberg (1926–1997)
The architect of the Beat Generation. Without his efforts as agent, promoter, and liaison for other Beat writers, there may not have been a Beat Generation to discuss. The publication of his first book, *Howl and Other Poems* (1956), and its subsequent censorship trial set the stage for the Beat phenomenon reaching the popular press and eventually capturing the imaginations of fellow travelers around the globe. Some scholars consider "Kaddish" (1961), an elegy for his mother, to be his masterpiece. *The Fall of America: Poems of These States, 1965–1971* (1972) won the National Book Award for Poetry. He was one of last celebrity poets, the announcement of his death finding its way onto the cover of *Rolling Stone* magazine.

Jack Kerouac (1922–1969)
The so-called "King of the Beats" and "Father of the Beat Generation." Kerouac was the author of the most famous Beat novel *On the Road* (1957), sometimes referred to as the "bible of the Beat Generation." His novels *On the Road*, *The Subterraneans* (1958), *The Dharma Bums* (1958), *Doctor Sax* (1959), *Maggie Cassidy* (1959), *Tristessa* (1960), *Big Sur* (1962), *Visions of Gerard* (1963), *Desolation Angels* (1965), *Satori in Paris* (1966), *Vanity of Duluoz* (1968), and *Visions of Cody* (1972) can be read as an extended masterpiece fictionalizing his life in what he called "the Duluoz Legend." An experimental writer, Kerouac is often associated with his idea of "spontaneous prose," which in part attempted to capture in writing what improvisation captured in bebop jazz.

Michael McClure (1932–   )
Perhaps the darkest and most interested in science of the Beat poets. His debut as a performing poet was at the famous Six Gallery reading on 7 October 1955. In the 1960s his friends included Jim Morrison, Bob Dylan, and Janis Joplin. His drama *The Beard* (1965) was one of the most notorious plays of the 1960s. In recent years he has performed his poetry accompanied by The Doors' keyboardist Ray Manzarek. His masterpiece is the anti–Vietnam War poem *Poisoned Wheat* (1965).

Gary Snyder (1930–   )
Became associated with the Beat movement at the famous Six Gallery reading on 7 October 1955 in San Francisco where Allen Ginsberg first read part 1 of "Howl." This historic event has been called the birth of the San Francisco Renaissance. Unlike the East Coast Beats, Snyder's poetry is focused much more on nature, as well as Native American and Asian cultures. He won the Pulitzer Prize in poetry with his volume *Turtle Island* (1974). He is seen as one of the most important international spokesmen for environmentalism.

Janine Pommy Vega (1942–   )
Became part of the Beat movement when she went to Greenwich Village as a teenager after reading Kerouac's *On the Road* and met Corso. While traveling around the world, Vega has managed to consistently publish her work. Her first book, *Poems to Fernando* (1968), was published by Ferlinghetti's City Lights, which also published her excellent memoir, *Tracking the Serpent: Journey to Four Continents* (1997), and her strongest collections are *Mad Dogs of Trieste: New & Selected Poems* (2000) and *The Green Piano* (2005).

—Kurt Hemmer

Literary Responses to the Civil Rights Movement and Black Power Movement

The Civil Rights movement of the 1950s, 1960s, and early 1970s has been recognized globally as the most transformative social movement of twentieth-century America. Likewise, the Black Power movement that grew out of it in the 1960s is also viewed as having a significant impact on race relations in the United States. Although both movements shared a goal to liberate black Americans from centuries-old institutionalized and socially sanctioned discrimination and racism, they had complex and differing views on integration and self-defense. Simply put, most proponents of civil rights were pro-integration and determinedly nonviolent, while the majority of black-power activists did not view integration as a prerequisite for black liberation and had no qualms about violence for the purpose of self-defense.

Students should bear in mind that there is no consensus on a timeline for the Civil Rights movement or Black Power era. Demands for civil and human rights in America can be found in various forms in every decade stretching back to the seventeenth century, when captured Africans were brought to the United States, but the seeds of the contemporary movement were firmly planted during the post–World War II years. Jackie Robinson's successful attempt to integrate Major League Baseball became a hallmark of the 1940s and of contemporary civil-rights efforts in general. In addition, sit-ins and other forms of nonviolent protest that came to symbolize the modern-day Civil Rights movement date back to at least 1943 when the Congress of Racial Equality (CORE) held a sit-in at a lunch counter in Chicago. In 1951, three years before the Supreme Court deemed segregated public educational facilities unconstitutional in the landmark case of *Brown v. Board of Education*, Barbara Johns, a sixteen-year-old Virginia high-school student, spearheaded a student protest against segregated schools. The *Brown* decision itself had roots in the *Mendez v. Westminster* case of 1946. Debate continues over the accurate starting points of the Civil Rights and Black Power movements, and many scholars view both movements as ongoing. A few of the key historical moments, in addition to issues such as housing, employment, and discrimination, that inspired creative responses are as follows, and writers responded to each of them through poetry, fiction, drama, and nonfiction:

> The murder of Emmett Till in Money, Mississippi, 1955
> The Montgomery, Alabama, bus boycott, 1955–1956
> The Little Rock, Arkansas, school desegregation, 1957–1958
> The lynching of Mack Charles Parker in Poplarville, Mississippi, 1959
> The assassination of Medgar Evers in Jackson, Mississippi, 1963
> The Sixteenth Street Baptist Church bombing in Birmingham, Alabama, 1963
> The murders of civil-rights organizers James Chaney, Andrew Goodman, and Michael Schwerner in Philadelphia, Mississippi, 1964
> The assassination of Malcolm X in New York City, 1965

The Selma to Montgomery, Alabama, Voting Rights March, 1965
The birth (and legacy) of the Black Panther Party, 1966
The assassination of Dr. Martin Luther King Jr. in Memphis, Tennessee, 1968

While it is impossible to treat the full extent of the literary responses to these issues concisely, students will benefit from exposure to a few representative works inspired by some of the most significant moments of the period.

The murder of fourteen-year-old Emmett Till in August 1955 for allegedly flirting with a married white woman in Mississippi galvanized civil-rights organizers and inspired writers as well. The poet Gwendolyn Brooks conveyed her disgust with the murder and subsequent trial in a seemingly restrained, indirect manner in "A Bronzeville Mother Loiters in Mississippi. Meanwhile, a Mississippi Mother Burns Bacon" (1960). Brooks focused on the interior and domestic life of Carolyn Bryant, the woman Till was accused of flirting with, instead of Till's murder. Furthermore, the violence described in the poem is initiated by Carolyn's husband, Roy, one of the men responsible for Till's death, and it is directed at his wife and children instead of Till. Brooks's aesthetic approach reveals Roy Bryant's propensity for anger, even toward his own family. The poem "Mississippi 1955" (1955) by Langston Hughes is one of the first poems of the era to broach the subject of terror literally. The poem calls attention to mid-twentieth-century American terrorism, the kind visited upon African Americans and white sympathizers by racist organizations and civilians. This form of terror ranged from lynchings and bombings to attempts to cripple civil-rights advocates economically, psychologically, and spiritually. The play *Blues for Mister Charlie* (1964), by James Baldwin, is heavily influenced by and based loosely on the Till murder. The play explores reactions to a similar tragedy from the perspectives of "White Town" and "Black Town."

A few months after Till's murder, Rosa Parks refused to give up her seat on a Montgomery, Alabama, bus, sparking a boycott that lasted more than a year. Dr. Martin Luther King Jr. responded to the boycott and its subsequent victory with his collection of nonfiction essays, *Stride Toward Freedom: The Montgomery Story*, in 1958.

In 1959 Lorraine Hansberry's now-classic play *A Raisin in the Sun* was produced; it was the first drama written by a black woman to appear on Broadway. The play centers on an African American family in Chicago and deals primarily with family heritage, capitalism, racism, and housing discrimination. Similarly, it provides an illustration of the difficulties of integration, conveying the idea that the burden of integration falls squarely on the shoulders of the black community. *A Raisin in the Sun* was awarded a New York Drama Critics' Circle Award and is considered a groundbreaking work of American theater.

The struggle for integration, and the opposition to it, also played a significant role in the 1963 assassination of Medgar Evers, who in 1954 became the first field secretary of the NAACP in Mississippi and was one of the state's most visible and active civil-rights leaders. Evers was instrumental in the campaign to register James Meredith as the first black student at the University of Mississippi at Oxford in 1962. Eventually, Evers became a dominant force for the rights of blacks in one of the country's most hostile and racially divided states. Among the poems that eulogized Evers after he was murdered in his driveway were Aaron Kramer's "Blues for Medgar Evers" (1964), David Ignatow's "For Medgar Evers" (1968), and Margaret Walker's "Micah" (1970). The Southern fiction writer Eudora Welty also used Evers's life and death as inspiration in her short story "Where is the Voice Coming From" (1963).

Also in 1963 Baldwin released *The Fire Next Time*, a collection of two short personal essays that addressed America's racial crisis, particularly white America's denial of past and present racial abuses. Baldwin warned that if Americans, black and white, cannot come together like "lovers" to bridge the racial divide, unrest will result in violence and destruction. He proved to be prophetic: racially charged riots later erupted in Harlem (1964), Watts (1965), and Newark and Detroit (1967). In addition, the Orangeburg Massacre occurred in South Carolina in 1968 when student attempts to enter a segregated bowling alley resulted in a riot that left three dead and twenty-eight injured. That same year hundreds of American cities devolved into chaos after the assassination of King.

In 1964 LeRoi Jones (later Amiri Baraka) produced the controversial one-act play *Dutchman*, which addressed subjects that were at the time considered taboo, such as interracial sexual desire, black middle-class identity, and violent attacks on educated black males. *Dutchman* won an Obie Award for best off-Broadway play.

The following year Malcolm X and Alex Haley published *The Autobiography of Malcolm X* (1965), addressing a range of personal and social issues, especially issues involving race relations and religion. Malcolm X was gunned down the same year by members of the Nation of Islam, a religious sect from which he had recently distanced himself. His life was remembered in poems such as Quincy Troupe's "For Malcolm Who Walks in the Eyes of Our Children" (1968), Baraka's "A Poem for Black Hearts" (1969), Sonia Sanchez's "malcolm" (1969), and Robert Hayden's "El-Hajj: Malik El-Shabazz" (1970). Dudley Randall, founder of Broadside Press, published the anthology *For Malcolm: Poems on the Life and Death of Malcolm X* (1967).

The assassination of King, the leader of America's nonviolent Civil Rights struggle, on 4 April 1968, spawned a wealth of poetic responses. Among the numerous elegies written for King were Haki Madhubuti's "Assassination" (1968), Brooks's "Riot" (1969), Lucille Clifton's "the meeting after the savior gone" (1969), Robert Lowell's "Two Walls" (1969), and Nikki Giovanni's "Reflections on April 4, 1968" (1970).

TOPICS FOR DISCUSSION AND RESEARCH

1. Literary responses to social movements often produce a certain amount of anxiety for writers. For example, a writer must decide *how* to address a given topic, such as the assassination of an inspirational leader or the murder of an ordinary citizen, as artistically as possible, without becoming trite or melodramatic. Based on a few of the responses provided above, such as works written

about Till, Evers, or King, how well have writers handled this task? How do they manage to address difficult emotional subjects in their writing? Do they, in turn, employ emotional language or aesthetics, or do they somehow distance themselves in some manner in order to address their topic? Which approach works best and why?

2. Creative responses to historical events present additional challenges as well. For example, a literary response strives to be more than a "blow-by-blow" account of the historical material, an approach better left to journalists and historians. Creative responses, which may be closely or loosely based on the facts of the events, aim to enhance a reader's understanding of the event intellectually and/or emotionally. Baldwin's *Blues for Mister Charlie*, for example, is loosely based on the murder of Till. How does the playwright honor Till while altering the facts of the case? How does the play, despite its historical inaccuracies, enhance a reader's comprehension of the crime?

3. After reading a chapter in *Voices of Freedom*, an oral-history account of the Civil Rights movement, in conjunction with a creative response, students might explore the relationship between an oral account based on personal experience and a creative response that is not required to be historically accurate. How do these pieces differ in their respective abilities to relay history to readers? For example, how do oral histories of Evers mesh with poems written in his honor? Neither account may be historically reliable, considering how faulty memories can plague oral accounts of historical moments, but both should be historically grounded and should elucidate the historical moment in some way for readers. How is this task accomplished from both creative and oral history perspectives?

4. Religion played an extremely significant role in both the Civil Rights and Black Power movements, with the former inspired by Christian theology and the latter by Islamic teachings. How are these influences represented in literary responses? For example, what role does religion play in Baldwin's *The Fire Next Time?* How does he view the two religions? Also, how does religion inform Hansberry's *A Raisin in the Sun* or Jones's *Dutchman?* Can Hansberry's play be considered pro-Christian? Why does Jones invoke Adam and Eve? Likewise, how does religion contribute to poems written for King and Malcolm X? Is religion viewed in a negative light in any of the responses? If so, how does this perspective contribute to the work's overall message?

5. After reading Jones's *Dutchman* students might analyze the significance of its ending. What is the play attempting to say about educated black males in American society by way of Lula's actions? To what extent does the play's message concerning black males apply to contemporary society?

RESOURCES

Biography

Henry Hampton and Steve Fayer, *Voices of Freedom: An Oral History of the Civil Rights Movement from the 1950s through the 1980s* (New York: Bantam, 1990).
Oral histories that track the major moments of the Civil Rights era.

Criticism

Regina Jennings, "Poetry of the Black Panther Party: Metaphors of Militancy," *Journal of Black Studies*, 29 (September 1998): 106–129.
Critical examination of the poetry, history, and rhetoric found in the organization's newspaper.

Eugene Redmond, *Drumvoices: The Mission of Afro-American Poetry, A Critical History* (Garden City, N.Y.: Anchor Press, 1976).
Critical introduction and historical overview of black poetry, ending with works produced in the 1960s and 1970s.

James Edward Smethurst, *The Black Arts Movement: Literary Nationalism in the 1960s and 1970s* (Chapel Hill: University of North Carolina Press, 2005).
Explores Black Power–era literature from historical and sociological perspectives.

Angelyn Mitchell, *Within the Circle: An Anthology of African American Literary Criticism from the Harlem Renaissance to the Present* (Durham, N.C.: Duke University Press, 1994).
Collection of critical essays that helps place civil-rights and black-power literature within the continuum of African American literature.

PEOPLE OF INTEREST

James Baldwin (1924–1987)
Was one of America's most accomplished essayists and also gained prominence as a novelist, poet, and playwright. Baldwin was a prominent literary activist, and his support of Martin Luther King Jr. and the Civil Rights movement is expressed in *The Fire Next Time* (1963). He later became disheartened by what he viewed as America's reluctance to adopt democratic principles, which is evident in *No Name in the Street* (1972).

Amiri Baraka (1934–   )
A founder of the Black Arts movement, the literary wing of the Black Power movement. He has published more than a dozen collections of poetry but has also produced fiction, drama, and essays, most of which concern the history and liberation of African Americans in the United States.

Gwendolyn Brooks (1917–2000)
The first black writer to win the Pulitzer Prize (1950) and became one of the most accomplished poets of twentieth-century America. *The Bean Eaters* (1960), *In the Mecca* (1968), and *Riot* (1969) are essential for civil-rights and black-power studies. Brooks also wrote essays and a novel, *Maud Martha* (1953).

Nikki Giovanni (1943–   )
Organized Cincinnati's first Black Arts Festival in 1967 and published two volumes of poetry, *Black Feeling, Black Talk*, and *Black Judgement*, in 1968, establishing her as a fixture of the Black Power movement. She has since published more

than three dozen collections of poetry, children's books, essays, and multimedia works.

Sonia Sanchez (1934–   )

Helped establish black-studies courses at San Francisco State University in the late 1960s at approximately the same time that she published her first two collections of poetry, *Home Coming* (1969) and *We a BaddDDD People* (1970). Sanchez has since published more than two dozen works including poetry collections, plays, children's books, anthologies, and audio works.

—Jeffrey Coleman

The Cold War and Literature

At the end of World War II the United States and the Soviet Union emerged as the most powerful and influential countries in the world. Although they were allied against the Axis powers during the war, deeply rooted ideological differences and conflicting visions for the reconstruction of Europe and the rest of the world ultimately divided the superpowers and led to an era of severe global tension known as the Cold War. Although there are no exact beginning and ending dates for the Cold War, many historians date the beginning in 1945, at the conclusion of World War II, and the ending in 1991, when Mikhail Gorbachev resigned as the Soviet president and abolished the Soviet Union. Pitted against one another in the broadest sense during the Cold War, the United States and its Western counterparts stood for democracy and representative government, while the Soviet Union and its counterparts stood for communism and the totalitarian state. The period after World War II was dominated by fierce competition for superiority between the two nations that involved a struggle for political, technological, and martial dominance on both a localized and a worldwide scale.

There are six main themes through which American literature responds to and engages with the Cold War: containment culture and the containment narrative; McCarthyism and anticommunism; widespread paranoia; conformity and the consensus culture; the rise of consumerism; and counter-cultural rebellion.

When thinking about the Cold War and literature, many scholars have examined the "containment" policy that dominated American foreign policy during the era. Containment was an idea initially articulated as a U.S. government foreign-policy initiative for containing the threat of Soviet communism. Containment policy originated in 1947 with U.S. diplomat George F. Kennan, who argued for the containment of communist influence on the grounds of the Soviet Union's inherently dangerous expansionist tendencies. Cultural and literary scholar Alan Nadel's 1995 book *Containment Culture* details what he perceives as Cold War literature's exemplification of containment. Nadel employs J. D. Salinger's *The Catcher in the Rye* (1951) as a text whose narrator, Holden Caulfield, he believes, overtly expresses the attitudes of containment in his need to expose "phonies." Holden's need to weed out phonies, Nadel argues, parallels the compulsive attempts during the 1940s and 1950s of the House Committee on Un-American Activities (HCUA) and U.S. Senator Joseph McCarthy to expose those Americans posing as patriots and upholders of democracy while potentially harboring communist sympathies.

Senator McCarthy's anticommunist campaign signified the full transformation of containment policy into the domestic realm. The idea that communists and Soviet spies were living in the United States and were employed in government positions struck fear into the American people and set the stage for the infamous HCUA hearings in which people, notably literary and motion-picture celebrities, were investigated on the basis of their alleged association with communism. Arthur Miller's 1953 play *The Crucible* allegorically represents through the lens of the Salem witch trials of 1692 the author's feelings regarding the congressional hearings and the subsequent effect on those accused of being communists, often on the basis of hearsay evidence. In Miller's play accusations of witchcraft and general hysteria sweep colonial Massachusetts and chillingly mirror the similarly widespread panic over communism that swept America in the 1950s. Miller was himself called to testify before the HCUA in 1956. Novelist Mary McCarthy presents a more lighthearted and satirical investigation of McCarthyism's effects in *The Groves of Academe* (1951). The novel focuses on the dismissal of Professor Henry Mulcahy and the attempt to uncover the true reason for his dismissal from his teaching post. Mulcahy's fitness to teach is reduced to a determination of whether he was ever a communist or affiliated with organizations harboring communist sympathies—not uncommon grounds for discharge from important positions in the 1950s.

Even after McCarthy was discredited in 1954, the American public was left with an unsettling feeling of paranoia and fear. McCarthyites exaggerated the extent of the communist threat and demonstrated the American government's less-than-democratic methods of addressing possible communist infiltration. Some people equated government practices during the height of McCarthyism with the tyranny of communism. In *The Crying of Lot 49* (1966), Thomas Pynchon reflects on paranoia, conspiracy, and dislocation as legitimate reactions to a world gone awry. The novel's protagonist, Oedipa Maas, finds herself enmeshed in what appears to be a worldwide conspiracy that relates to the death and the estate of her one-time boyfriend Pierce Inverarity. The novel's distinctly American landscape and paranoid complexity take Cold War anxieties to such an extreme that most perceptions in the novel remain elusive, uncertain, and worthy of suspicion.

Many scholars who read Cold War literature as engaged with containment policy, McCarthyism, and paranoia also read the culture and the literature of the Cold War as one expressly concerned with consensus and conformity. If rooting out and containing communism at home and abroad was a cause that every loyal American should support, then it followed logically that a "consensus culture" would evolve as an expression of patriotism. Critics have read many Cold War texts as upholding such an established consensus—one of the most significant of these being Sloan Wilson's *The Man in the Gray Flannel Suit* (1955). Wilson imagines the idea of consensus culture as it appears within the spheres of business and family. The novel's protagonist, Tom Rath, appears to readily place the needs and concerns of family, corporation, and country over his own individual aspirations. Tom Rath became an iconic representation of mainstream Cold War cultural sentiments.

The theme of consumerism functions in many ways as an extension of conformity and the consensus culture. Consumerism refers to excessive consumption of material goods and possessions—essentially, purchasing more and more goods as a means for attaining happiness and success. During the Cold War, consumerism functioned as a way to stimulate the American economy in hopes of maintaining economic supremacy over the Soviet Union. While much of the consensus culture willingly subscribed to the practice of consumerism, some writers reacted strongly against it as a force of cultural deterioration that caused Americans to identify more with material possessions than truly worthy causes or ideas. In

Lolita (1955), Vladimir Nabokov, himself a Russian-born immigrant in America, details the journey of an aristocratic European pedophile as he makes his way across America with twelve-year-old Lolita as his sexual captive. If readers place their shock and moral outrage aside, they will notice that the novel successfully enacts a penetrating satire of Cold War consumerist. Humbert Humbert, the main character, is repelled by Lolita's excessive fascination with the latest trends and realizes that he can quell her rebellious nature and continue to manipulate her by showering her with material gifts. Additionally, Nabokov comments on gaudy advertisements for products that proclaim themselves a necessity for every American.

A troubling but also artistically inspiring condition of the Cold War in the United States was its simultaneous ideological emphasis on both individual freedom on the one hand and patriotic loyalty to the collective interests of America on the other. Allen Ginsberg speaks to the immediacy of just such an inner conflict when he informs America, "I am sick of your insane demands," in his 1956 poem "America." Literary themes such as the search for and reconciliation of identity, the coming of age and maturation of the consciousness, and the assertion of individualism in the face of domineering authority took on new dimensions as Cold War cultural and ideological influences clashed. Writers sought to reconcile their own identities and situations as Americans, and these personal struggles found their way into the assorted stories and characters of American literature during the Cold War.

The three canonical male Beat writers—Ginsberg, Jack Kerouac, and William S. Burroughs—were concerned with repudiating mass movements such as containment, consensus, and consumerism. If mainstream America was a consensus culture, then the Beat Generation was an anticonsensus movement, primarily interested in rejecting mainstream Cold War society's prevailing interests and preoccupations. In "Howl" (1956) and "America" Ginsberg laments the oppressive forces of Cold War conformity and draws attention to the dislocated and marginalized figures of the time—experimental artists and musicians, bohemians, drug users, and homosexuals, among others. In *Junkie* (1953) Burroughs depicts a heroin-addicted character whose life, though unorthodox and certainly nonconformist, demonstrates a side of American culture that is entirely absent from works such as *The Man in the Gray Flannel Suit*. One of the quintessential countercultural novels of the Beat Generation is Kerouac's *On the Road* (1957), in which the protagonist, Sal Paradise, wrestles with alienation and struggles to find his place in a world indifferent to his interests that begs for him to conform. Sal ultimately rejects consumerism and conformity and sets out "on the road" to discover the inner fabric of America; he hopes to find an America that he can identify with as a patriotic but free-spirited individual.

In Ralph Ellison's *Invisible Man* (1952) the unnamed narrator finds himself caught up in an organization called The Brotherhood, which is Ellison's proxy for the Communist Party of the United States of America. The Brotherhood initially lures him in with promises of equality for all—regardless of race, religion, or other factors. Eventually, however, the narrator uncovers The

Brotherhood's scheme to use him as little more than a tool for rallying the support of the African American community. He finds it ultimately impossible to reconcile his individual personality and aspirations with those of the collective society and thus opts out of American civilization entirely and moves underground—physically and symbolically rejecting both communism and American society's institutionalized racism and oppression of blacks. Ellison powerfully represents the struggle of a young African American man to find his place in a repressive, white-dominated world.

TOPICS FOR DISCUSSION AND RESEARCH

1. After reading *The Catcher in the Rye,* students might read Nadel's essay on containment policy, which can found in Harold Bloom's *Holden Caulfield* (Philadelphia: Chelsea House, 1990). Students might analyze Nadel's reading of the novel and discuss whether his evidence adequately supports his argument. As an additional assignment, students could apply Nadel's containment-narrative methodology to *The Crucible* or other 1950s literature and argue for or against such a reading of these texts.

2. Many movies that were produced during the Cold War used metaphor, symbol, and allegory to subtly address the pervasive American fear of communism and communist infiltration. Students will benefit from viewing such movies as *Them!* (1954), *Kiss Me Deadly* (1955), *Invasion of the Body Snatchers* (1956), and *The Mouse That Roared* (1959) to identify and trace these devices.

3. The Beat writers attempted to distance themselves from mainstream American society, casting aside popular conceptions of American culture and setting out in search of their own. Beat writers also scathingly criticized American consumerism and other aspects of mainstream American culture. After studying Ginsberg's "America" or "Howl," students might consider the degree to which one might characterize Ginsberg as patriot. Perhaps the same discussion can be conducted based on the work of other Beat writers.

4. Focusing on Ellison's use of "The Brotherhood" in *Invisible Man* as a proxy for the real-world Communist Party of the United States of America, students might consider how Ellison represents the communist party and its ideologies. How does he characterize the communist party's supposed blindness to race? Students can refer to Jesse Wolfe's 2000 essay "'Ambivalent Man': Ellison's Rejection of Communism" (*African American Review,* 34, 4) for a reading of the text that asserts Ellison's criticism and condemnation of communism.

5. Many people point to the 1960s as the beginning of counter-cultural and social activist movements in the United States; however, the roots of the hippie, civil-rights and modern feminist movements all reach back at least to the 1950s. Students might examine the works produced by Kerouac, Burroughs, or Ellison during the 1950s, paying particular attention to aspects of the novels that indicate an engagement with counter-culture or social activism. How do these works represent the earlier phases of those movements?

RESOURCES
Criticism

Paul S. Boyer, *By the Bomb's Early Light: American Thought and Culture at the Dawn of the Atomic Age* (Chapel Hill: University of North Carolina Press, 1994).
A historical study of the various cultural reactions to the nuclear bomb in the years 1945–1950.

Douglas Field, ed., *American Cold War Culture* (Edinburgh: University of Edinburgh Press, 2005).
An examination of the relationship between Cold War culture and Cold War politics in the years following World War II.

Joel Foreman, *The Other Fifties: Interrogating Mid-century American Icons* (Urbana: University of Illinois Press, 1997).
A collection of essays that reexamine 1950s popular culture icons as agents of rebellion who initiated and influenced the 1960s counter-cultural movements.

Christina Klein, *Cold War Orientalism: Asia in the Middlebrow Imagination, 1945–1961* (Berkeley: University of California Press, 2003).
Opposes the dominant containment ideology used to explain American Cold War culture, emphasizing the importance of third-world nations, specifically those in Southeast Asia, and calls attention to the role of other countries outside the United States and the USSR during the Cold War.

Peter Knight, *Conspiracy Nation: The Politics of Paranoia in Postwar America* (New York: New York University Press, 2002).
A collection of essays that examine various conspiracy theories throughout the second half of the twentieth century.

Elaine Tyler May, *Homeward Bound: American Families in the Cold War Era* (New York: Basic Books, 1988).
A study that examines the increased emphasis on American family life and domesticity during the Cold War.

Lary May, ed., *Recasting America: Culture and Politics in the Age of Cold War* (Chicago: University of Chicago Press, 1989).
A collection of mainly historical essays arguing that Cold War American culture was distinctly formed and influenced by the political situation following World War II.

Leerom Medovoi, *Rebels: Youth and the Cold War Origins of Identity* (Durham, N.C.: Duke University Press, 2005).
Focuses on sources and representations of rebellion during the Cold War. Medovoi examines figures from Holden Caulfield to Elvis Presley and James Dean in an attempt to discover how rebellion formed identities during the Cold War.

Alan Nadel, *Containment Culture: American Narratives, Postmodernism, and the Atomic Age* (Durham, N.C.: Duke University Press, 1995).
Expands the political idea of containment to apply to many aspects of American culture during the Cold War, using literature and movies as illustrations.

Thomas H. Schaub, *American Fiction in the Cold War* (Madison: University of Wisconsin Press, 1991).
Provides in-depth analysis of the exchange between Cold War culture and specific pieces of literary fiction.

Ellen Schrecker, *Many Are the Crimes: McCarthyism in America* (Princeton: Princeton University Press, 1998).
A historical examination of communism in America and the McCarthy era specifically. Searches for the roots of American communism, exploring why so many Americans participated in the hysteria and paranoia associated with McCarthyism.

Stephen Whitfield, *The Culture of the Cold War* (Baltimore: Johns Hopkins University Press, 1996).
A historical study that seeks to understand the importance of the Cold War in forming a new American national identity after World War II.

PEOPLE OF INTEREST

Ralph Ellison (1914–1994)
Best known for his novel *Invisible Man* (1952), which won the National Book Award. Although Ellison did not publish another novel during his lifetime, he published critical essays on a wide variety of social, political, and literary subjects.

Mary McCarthy (1912–1989)
Critic and novelist best known for such novels as *The Company She Keeps* (1942), *The Groves of Academe* (1952), and *The Group* (1963) and for her memoir, *Memories of a Catholic Girlhood* (1957).

Arthur Miller (1915–2005)
Won the Pulitzer Prize in drama for *Death of a Salesman* (1949). Miller was forced to testify before the HCUA in 1956 and considered this event to be one of the most influential of his life.

Vladimir Nabokov (1899–1977)
Immigrated to the United States from Russia and began a career as an English-language novelist. His works include *Lolita* (1955) and *Pale Fire* (1962).

Thomas Pynchon (1937–   )
Reclusive author about whom little is known except that he graduated from Cornell University with a degree in English and spent two years in the U.S. Navy. His books include *V.* (1963), *The Crying of Lot 49* (1966), and *Gravity's Rainbow* (1973).

J. D. Salinger (1919–2010)
Reclusive author of *The Catcher in the Rye* (1951), *Nine Stories* (1953), *Franny and Zooey* (1961), and *Raise High the Roof Beam, Carpenters, Seymour: An Introduction* (1963).

Sloan Wilson (1920–2003)
American author who published fifteen novels, two of which, *The Man in the Gray Flannel Suit* (1955) and *A Summer Place* (1958), were best sellers and were adapted into motion pictures.

—*Sean P. Gerrity*

Confessional Poetry

Critic M. L. Rosenthal coined the term "confessional poetry" in his review of Robert Lowell's *Life Studies* (1959) in the 19 September 1959 issue of *The Nation*, noting that while most poets conceal themselves, "Lowell removes the mask." The term came to identify the intensely personal style wherein the "I" is essential to the inception, construction, and resonance of a poem. Subsequently, John Berryman, Sylvia Plath, Theodore Roethke, Anne Sexton, and W. D. Snodgrass were also categorized under this heading, arousing debate among critics ever since. Some argue that writers are only human and, as such, are incapable of being completely forthright, as the term suggests. Others contend that all poetry is confessional to a degree, often pointing to the sonnets of Petrarch and William Shakespeare as the first confessional poems. In the end, though, the argument should settle on one fact: the confessionalists were the first to write with such candor about what might be perceived, in Rosenthal's words, as "rather shameful" personal subjects; this characteristic alone became their trademark.

To best understand the confessional movement, one must first be aware of the historical and cultural context that gave rise to it. America had just suffered through its second world war. The devastation of Hiroshima and Nagasaki, coupled with the Cold War and the imminence of a nuclear attack, made the complete annihilation of mankind a conceivable notion that sank deep into communal consciousness. What resulted was best explained by the critic Walter Blair with a passage from John Steinbeck's *The Winter of Our Discontent* (1961): "When a condition or a problem becomes too great . . . it goes inward and . . . what comes out is . . . a compulsion to get something—anything—before it is all gone. Maybe the assembly-line psychoanalysts aren't dealing with complexes at all but with those warheads that may one day be mushroom clouds." So it stands to reason that, in the atomic age, poets would turn their focus inward to the *atomic* machinery of human emotion.

In the postwar years America as a whole was straining with growth. Deurbanization breathed life into the suburbs, and a renewed sense of conformity for some meant alienation to others, thereby begging contemplation for the mindful poet. Racial tensions were escalating, as were calls for equality. The confessional poets, however, did not address these issues as directly as their more socially conscious contemporaries. Instead, they turned inward to explore the "self" as it related to familial roles, commonly held beliefs, and the cultural norms of the day. This is not to say they cowered from the uncertainty of their times. To the contrary, they internalized their uncertainty only to re-envision the endemic alienation and procedural dehumanization in their writing, believing that the commonality of human privacy was their last, best hope. This was an age when all hope for salvation seemed to have vanished from public life. So confessional poets excavated their souls in hopes of finding something infinite in the finite.

As Mark Doty explains in his essay "The 'Forbidden Planet' of Character: The Revolutions of the 1950s," the confessional poets emerged on the literary scene not by opening the window but by breaking it down. Compared to the dogma of their Modernist predecessors, who aimed to write impersonal poetry, the confessional poets' more-candid style was revolutionary. In many ways, the confessionalists were the Modernists' natural heirs, due in no small part to their similar themes. Alienation is one of the more obvious thematic parallels. Take, for example, the utter hopelessness in the conclusion to Lowell's "Walking in the Blue" (1946): "We are all old-timers / each of us holds a locked razor." Another theme shared with the Modernists—and more specifically, T. S. Eliot—was the depiction of the world as a vast wasteland. In Eliot's *The Waste Land* (1922), the hallmark of Modernist poetry, he describes the world as a disjointed collection of random pieces that may or may not amount to a whole. The Modernists believed that only hollow men could people such a world. Yet another sensibility shared in Plath's poem "The Thin People" (1957): "They are always with us, the thin people / Meager of dimension as the gray people."

Although the confessionalists' penchant for lavishing their verses in exquisite language was also consistent with Modernist practices, it is in their technique that they differed most. Unlike their forbears, the confessional poets frequently offset their dense poetic language with autobiographical insight written in such a frank, colloquial tone that it felt like a confession between friends. A good example of this tendency is seen in Lowell's "Skunk Hour (1959)," in which the poet writes, "Lights turned down, / they lay together, hull to hull, / where the graveyard shelves on the town." He then stops in mid thought and admits, "My mind's not right." Sexton displays a similarly typical candor in "The Black Art" (1962): "A woman who writes feels too much . . . / She thinks she can warn the stars. / A writer is essentially a spy. / Dear love, I am that girl."

Another divergence was marked by the prominence of metaphor and personification rather than reliance on the solitary image or allusion that often characterized Modernist poetry. Whereas Ezra Pound describes the world in his "Canto XXX" (1948) with an obscure allusion to papal corruption, Plath uses the metaphor of an axle that "grinds round, bearing down" in her poem "Heavy Women" (1962). Where Modernist William Carlos Williams's "Death the Barber" (1922) makes a haircut an image of death, a spider "marching through the air" turns into a metaphor as Lowell's poem "Mr. Edwards and the Spider" (1946) concludes with the lines, "To die and know it. This is the Black Widow, death." "Little houses" become a metaphor for secrets in Sexton's "Barefoot" (1969), just as John Berryman's "Dream Song 29" (1964) depicts a recurring thought as "the little cough somewhere, an odour, a chime." Personification also dominates confessional poetry, mainly as an attempt to restore something missing to the world. For instance, by keeping the attributes of the moon and the woman ambiguous in "Barren Woman" (1961)—"The moon lays a hand on my forehead, / Blank-faced and mum as a nurse"—Plath allows nature to personify the woman and vice versa. Personification functions similarly in most confessional poetry. By making the poet's soul a surrogate for nature, humanity and the world are reconnected, one becoming an intrinsic part of the other.

Confessional poetry also introduced new personal subject matter, which challenged the New Critical approach, popular in the 1950s, that focused sharply on the work rather than the author. The confessional poets created poetry from everyday occurrences; from the monotony of routine they drew enlightenment. Plath's poem "Mirror" (1961) could stand as their credo: "I am silver and exact . . .

/ Whatever I see I swallow immediately / Just as it is, unmisted by love or dislike. / I am not cruel, only truthful." Plath called this the poetry of "real situations, behind which the great gods play the drama of blood, lust and death." Critics Kate Sontag and Donald Graham reiterate this idea: "First-person lyrics can embrace a larger social vision, achieving . . . universal resonance." For example, Sexton's "The Fury of Sunsets" (1974) captures universal doubt in a few short personal questions: "Why am I here? / why do I live in this house? / who's responsible?"

For any poem to render meaning, it must first coax its reader into becoming an accomplice, which confessional poetry achieves by relating to the reader, reducing the provocations of the larger society to a microcosm of everyday life. As such, Plath identifies not only the acceptable mores of motherhood but also those darker privations of being human. In "Words for a Nursery" (1957) she offsets a positive view of motherhood with one more sinister: "I learn, good circus / Dog that I am, how / To move, serve, steer food, / . . . My master's fetcher." Similarly, Berryman uses the persona of Henry in his poem "Dream Song 1" (1964) to explore the role of men in the world: "All the world like a woolen lover / once did seem on Henry's side. / . . . I don't see how Henry, pried / open for all the world to see, survived." Merely in the act of translating society's expectations into their own words, Plath and Berryman regain control and are, in a sense, emancipated by their understanding.

Confessional poetry was also interested in the psychology of marriage, parenting, love, work, and faith. This is especially true of Sexton, who is famous for saying, "Poetry led me by the hand out of madness." Notice her distinctively psychological overtures in "Despair" (1976): "Despair, / I don't like you very well. / You don't suit my clothes or my cigarettes. / Why do you locate here . . . ?" Lowell shows a similar inclination in "Waking in the Blue": "Absence! My heart grows tense / as though a harpoon were sparring for the kill. / (This is the house for the "mentally ill.")" What Berryman is saying with his use of capitalization in "Dream Song 14" (1964) is no accident either: "And moreover, my mother told me as a boy / (repeatedly) 'Ever to confess you're bored / means you have no / Inner Resources.' I conclude now I have no / inner resources, because I am heavy bored."

Many critics have argued that this intensely psychological style is to blame for the steep decline in the popularity of poetry over the latter half of the century, overlooking the fact that any substantive explanation of this trend must include a variety of other factors as well. There is little doubt, however, that the confessional poets' search for resolution in the latent power of the human psyche prompted movements such as Personalism, Language Poetry, and New Formalism. Poets Sharon Olds, Denise Levertov, Adrienne Rich, and Audre Lorde (to name a few) owe them an equally profound debt because, in the end, confessional poetry's groundbreaking techniques, themes, and subject matter ignited a revolution that changed the landscape of poetry in the second half of the twentieth century.

TOPICS FOR DISCUSSION AND RESEARCH

1. Ralph Waldo Emerson wrote in "The American Scholar": "Let us be Americans . . . As the source of truth is not books, but mental activity, we are to cultivate self-trust . . . in ourselves we find the law of all nature." With regard

to this statement, is it wise to single out any specific group of American poets as "confessional"? Use specific examples from other movements in American poetry to defend your argument. See Yezzi's article "Confessional Poetry & the Artifice of Honesty" in *The New Criterion* and Gregory's article "Confessing the Body: Plath, Sexton, Berryman, Lowell, Ginsberg and the Gendered Poetics of the 'Real'" in *Modern Confessional Writing: New Critical Essays*.

2. Poets Walt Whitman and Emily Dickinson were among the first American poets to explore the idea of the "self." What common themes, techniques, and subject matter associated with confessional poets also appear in the poetry of Whitman and Dickinson? In what ways are the confessional poets distinct from these American predecessors?

3. Confessional poetry was both a continuation of and a reaction to the Modernists' impersonal poetry. Choose any anthologized Modernist poem and one of a confessional poet and analyze the literary devices used. In what specific ways does the confessional poem modify the approach to poetry illustrated by the Modernist poem?

4. A common theme in the work of Plath and Sexton is the role of women as daughters, wives, and mothers. Take Plath's poem "Daddy" and Sexton's poem "All My Pretty Ones" and compare the poets' attitudes toward their fathers and their own role as women in society. For insight into their work see Bundtzen's *Plath's Incarnations: Woman and the Creative Process,* as well as Hall's chapter titled "Transformations: Fairy Tales Revisited" in *Anne Sexton*.

5. Confessional poetry internalizes cultural issues rather than addresses them directly. Analyze either "To Speak of Woe That Is in Marriage" or "Man and Wife," both written by Lowell, and explain how the poet approaches society's views of gender indirectly, then compare Lowell's approach to Berryman's in "Dream Song 29." For further insight into these two poets, see Cosgrave's *The Public Poetry of Robert Lowell,* Williamson's *Pity the Monsters: The Political Vision of Robert Lowell,* and Thomas' *Berryman's Understanding: Reflections on the Poetry of John Berryman*.

RESOURCES

Criticism

Lynda K. Bundtzen, *Plath's Incarnations: Woman and the Creative Process* (Ann Arbor: University of Michigan Press, 1983).
Critical essays with unusual perspectives on the feminine identity in Plath's work.

Patrick Cosgrave, *The Public Poetry of Robert Lowell* (New York: Littlehampton Book Services Ltd., 1970).
Review of Lowell's poetry that prompted him to dedicate a revised draft to Cosgrave.

Jo Gill, ed., *Modern Confessional Writing: New Critical Essays* (London: Routledge, 2005).
Multiple perspectives on the influence of the confessionalists on contemporary writers.

Caroline King Barnard Hall, *Anne Sexton* (Boston: Twayne, 1989).
An introduction to Sexton's life and works.

Hall, *Sylvia Plath* (New York: Twayne, 1998).
An introduction to Plath's life and works.

Jack Elliot Myers, David Wojahn, and Ed Folsom, eds., *A Profile of Twentieth-Century American Poetry* (Carbondale: Southern Illinois University Press, 1991).
Critical essays on the aesthetic and cultural influences on American poetry, including Mark Doty's "The 'Forbidden Planet' of Character: The Revolutions of the 1950s," much of which examines the role of Lowell and the Confessionalists in that decade.

Kate Sontag and David Graham, eds., *After Confession: Poetry as Autobiography* (St. Paul, Minn.: Graywolf Press, 2001).
Poets Billy Collins, Louise Gluck, and others discuss the poetry of the self.

Harry Thomas, *Berryman's Understanding: Reflections on the Poetry of John Berryman* (Boston: Northeastern University Press, 1988).
Critical essays, reviews, interviews, and memoirs regarding Berryman and his work.

Alan Williamson, *Pity the Monsters: The Political Vision of Robert Lowell* (New Haven, Conn.: Yale University Press, 1974).
A study of Lowell's poetry in light of his discontent with American society.

David Yezzi, "Confessional Poetry & the Artifice of Honesty," *New Criterion*, 16.10 (June 1998): 14.
A retrospective review of the confessional movement prompted by the publication of *Birthday Letters* (1998), a collection of poems by Plath's husband, the British poet Ted Hughes.

PEOPLE OF INTEREST

John Berryman (1914–1972)
Pioneered the confessional style. His works include *Poems* (1942); *The Dispossessed* (1948); *Seventy-seven Dream Songs* (1964), which won a Pulitzer Prize; *Berryman's Sonnets* (1967); *The Dream Songs* (1969); and *Love and Fame* (1970). His drinking problem and paralyzing despondency led him to leap to his death from a bridge.

Robert Lowell (1917–1977)
One of the most influential American post–World War II poets. His works include *Lord Weary's Castle* (1946), which won the Pulitzer Prize; *The Mills of the Kavanaughs* (1951); *Life Studies* (1959); and *For the Union Dead* (1964). Lowell was plagued by manic depression and drug addiction throughout his life. He died of a heart attack.

Sylvia Plath (1932–1963)

Among the most notorious poets of her period. Her collections include *The Colossus, and Other Poems* (1960), *Ariel* (1965), *Crossing the Water* (1971), *Winter Trees* (1971), her novel *The Bell Jar* (1963), and the Pulitzer Prize–winning *Collected Poems* (1982). Her lifelong battle with depression ended in suicide.

Theodore Roethke (1908–1963)

Won the Pulitzer Prize for *The Waking* (1954) and two National Book Awards, for *Words for the Wind* (1957) and for *The Far Field* (1964). He suffered from depression and died of a heart attack.

Anne Sexton (1928–1974)

Began writing to deal with depression. Her collections include *To Bedlam and Part Way Back* (1960), *All My Pretty Ones* (1962), *Love Poems* (1969), *Transformations* (1971), and *The Death Notebooks* (1974). Her third collection, *Live or Die* (1966), won the Pulitzer Prize. She committed suicide by poisoning.

W. D. Snodgrass (1926–2009)

Like Plath and Sexton, studied under Robert Lowell. His first collection, *Heart's Needle* (1959), won the Pulitzer Prize. He taught at Cornell, Syracuse, and Old Dominion University and also published criticism and translations before his death from lung cancer.

—*F. Rutledge Hammes*

The Counter Culture and Literature

For Theodore Roszak, who coined the term in his 1969 study *The Making of a Counter Culture*, the counter culture referred to the disaffected youth of the 1960s whose interests "in the psychology of alienation, oriental mysticism, psychedelic drugs, and communitarian experiments comprise a cultural constellation that radically diverges from values and assumptions that have been in the mainstream of our society at least since the Scientific Revolution of the seventeenth century." Over time, the counter culture has become associated with a very broad range of radical cultural and political movements of the time: civil-rights and gay-rights movements, feminism, the anti–Vietnam War movement, and the free-speech movement, to name a few. However, Roszak excludes most of these groups from his definition due to their tendency to use conventional political strategies to achieve their aims. He instead confines the term to a minority of young adults and adolescents—mostly from white, middle-class backgrounds—who used unconventional, frequently nonpolitical means to dissent against the social restrictions and repressions that emerged in the mainstream society of the 1950s. This group is best represented by the hippie culture and its figureheads, such as Allen Ginsberg, Abbie Hoffman, and Ken Kesey.

Ginsberg is especially notable, as he represents a crossover figure from the Beat movement from which the hippie counter culture evolved. While the influence of the Beat generation on the counter culture of the 1960s is universally acknowledged, there are important differences. Particularly, the counter culture replaced the Beats' darker, existentialist attitude with a sense of playfulness and a celebration of the possibility of social change. As Scott MacFarlane observed, "the hippie belief that 'we can change the world' most distinguished the counterculture from the Beat sentiment that preceded it."

At the same time, the influence of the Beat movement should not be understated. Ginsberg's *Howl* (1956) is considered a foundational text for the counter culture. And Jack Kerouac's *On the Road* (1957) provided a sort of guidebook for the nomadic life style often practiced by hippies. Like the Beat movement, the counter culture featured a return to spirituality as opposed to the secularism of prior social movements, which tended to view religion as an obstacle rather than an aid to social progress. Along with Ginsberg and Kerouac's poetic representations of Oriental mysticism, Alan Watts's dissemination of Zen thought had a significant impact on the counter culture. Zen philosophy's passive, Naturalistic approach to encountering the world especially appealed to counter-cultural concerns about ecology and communal lifestyles. Watts's Westernized and psychologized version of Zen Buddhism provided guidelines for engaging the world through direct, subjective experience rather than through the intellect.

Another form of counter-cultural spirituality emerged through the use of psychedelic drugs—particularly potent psychedelics such as LSD, psilocybin, mescaline, and peyote. These drugs were believed to induce a profound change in consciousness that was often thought to allow a direct personal experience of the divine. The most famous proponent of the use of psychedelics for spiritual pursuits was the psychologist Timothy Leary. Though his early research into psilocybin mushrooms and LSD focused on the applications of the drugs in psychotherapy, he soon began to emphasize the mystical and spiritual qualities of the psychedelic experience. He even founded a religion, the League for Spiritual Discovery, in which he attempted to declare LSD a holy sacrament. More-secularly-minded users saw the potential for initiating social change through the alteration in personal consciousness that psychedelics made possible. Kesey, for example, led a group called the Merry Pranksters, who staged large parties, called "acid tests," during which LSD-spiked punch was distributed to the attendees. The LSD, along with psychedelic music, films, and light shows, was meant to create a mass change in consciousness.

Politically, the counter culture was represented by groups such as Hoffman and Jerry Rubin's Yippies, or Youth International Party. Though they shared common causes with many other political groups—such as free-speech, antiwar, and social-reform movements—the Yippies distinguished themselves with the use of unconventional methods including pranksterism and guerilla theater. Their anarchistic use of humor to exploit mass media solidified their positions as counter-culture icons. On the West Coast, the Diggers used similar techniques to push for social reform, though they avoided media attention and public spectacle.

Though the counter culture of the 1960s is widely recognized to have been best represented by the rock music of the time, certain works of literature played important roles in its emergence and characterization as a cultural movement. Thomas Pynchon's *V.* (1962) features an early representation of the counter culture in its depiction of The Whole Sick Crew. The novel's schlemiel protagonist, Benny Profane, a human yo-yo, exemplifies the nomadic lifestyle of much of the hippie culture. Kesey's *One Flew Over the Cuckoo's Nest* (1962) offers a protagonist, Randle P. McMurphy, who exemplifies the rebellious aspect of the counter culture in his use of unconventional means to resist the inflexible and repressive agent of dehumanizing authoritarianism, Nurse Ratched. The novel's narrator, derived from a vision Kesey had under the influence of peyote, is eventually inspired by McMurphy to emerge from the alienation and dehumanization produced by technocratic society. And Richard Brautigan's *Trout Fishing in America* (1967, written in 1961) creates a narrative in which the zeitgeist of the counter culture is, itself, the protagonist. Appearing as a character, an action, and a specter that inhabits the whole novel, *Trout Fishing in America* expresses the spirit of transcendence and liberation for which the counter culture strived.

Other important works of counter-culture literature include Hunter S. Thompson's *Hell's Angels* (1966), an early example of New Journalism in which intersubjectivity and literary techniques are employed to report on events. This technique exemplified the counter culture's privileging of experience over objectivity. Diane di Prima's various works of poetry and prose, including *Earth Song* (1968), *Memoirs of A Beatnik* (1969), and *Revolutionary Letters* (1971), reflected the counter culture's concern with Buddhist spirituality and anarchistic thought. She was also active in several counter-culture projects such as the Diggers group and Leary's experiments with psychedelics. Herman Hesse's *Siddhartha* (1921) and *Steppenwolf* (1927), though originally published much earlier, had a profound impact on the counter culture of the 1960s because of their explorations of personal alienation and of transcendence through the use of Oriental spiritualism. Depictions of free love and drug use also contributed to *Steppenwolf*'s counter-cultural value.

TOPICS FOR DISCUSSION AND RESEARCH

1. The use of psychedelics was an important aspect of the counter culture and thus plays a significant role in its literature. Explore the ways in which literature addresses and/or incorporates the psychedelic experience. For example, examine how the New Journalism approach of Tom Wolfe's *The Electric Kool-Aid Acid Test* (1968) or the Gonzo technique of Thompson's *Fear and Loathing in Las Vegas* (1971) employs intersubjectivity and literary technique to represent psychedelic culture. Or discuss the use of experimental narrative techniques in Brautigan's *Trout Fishing in America* or William Burroughs's *Naked Lunch* (1959) to reflect the hallucinatory qualities of psychedelics. See Roszack's discussion of psychedelics in *The Making of a Counter Culture*.

2. Much like the Beats before them, the counter culture of the 1960s featured a strong spiritual element. Explore the ways in which spirituality—especially Oriental and shamanic traditions—influenced counter-culture literary works such as Ishmael Reed's *Mumbo Jumbo* (1972) or the poetry of Ginsberg. Alternately, examine how spiritually minded works like Hesse's *Siddhartha* or John Neihardt's *Black Elk Speaks* (1961) affected counter-culture thought. See MacFarlane's *The Hippie Narrative* for discussion on spiritual literature that influenced the counter-culture movement.

3. Though not strictly counter-cultural movements, the civil-rights, gay-rights, and feminist movements of the 1960s were often associated with the counter culture. Discuss the impact of the works as well as the activism of writers such as Ralph Ellison, Adrienne Rich, or di Prima on the counter culture. Or locate and analyze the influence of these movements on literary works such as Kesey's *One Flew Over the Cuckoo's Nest* or Rich's *Necessities of Life: poems, 1962–1965* (1966). See Terry H. Anderson's *The Movement and The Sixties* for a detailed study of social activism in the 1960s.

4. Several counter-culture works addressed the importance of alternative lifestyles, such as communal living and the transient or nomadic nature of the hippie culture. Analyze the significance of communal living in Brautigan's *In Watermelon Sugar* (1968). Or examine nomadic existences as represented in *The Electric Kool-Aid Acid Test* or Pynchon's *V.*

5. The counter-culture movement of the 1960s distinguished itself from the earlier Beat movement by the addition of humor and playfulness to its anti-authoritarian, antimainstream stance. Consider the use of humor and play in works such as Brautigan's *Trout Fishing in America*, Pynchon's *V.*, or Kurt Vonnegut's *Slaughterhouse-Five* (1969). How does the humor in these novels reflect the disaffection and alienation felt by the counter culture? See Roszak's *The Making of a Counter Culture*. Also see Ronald Sukenick's *Down and In: Life in the Underground* for an examination of counter culture's antimainstream sensibilities as they are manifested in 1950s and 1960s Greenwich Village.

RESOURCES

Criticism

Terry H. Anderson, *The Movement and The Sixties* (New York: Oxford University Press, 1996).
An extensive study of the various protest movements and social activist groups that emerged in the 1960s.

Peter Braunstein and Michael William Doyle, eds., *Imagine Nation: The American Counterculture of the 1960s and 70s* (New York: Routledge, 2002).
A collection of essays examining the multiple aspects of 1960s and 1970s counter culture, including discussions of communal living, recreational drug use, political activism, and race and gender issues.

Betty Friedan, *The Feminine Mystique* (New York: Norton, 1963).
A groundbreaking feminist text that challenged the social and especially the domestic roles of women in post–World War II America.

Christopher Gair, *The American Counterculture* (Edinburgh: Edinburgh University Press, 2007).
Explores the issues and ideologies of American counter culture from 1945 to 1972—divided into two periods, 1945–1960 and 1960–1972—by analyzing its fiction, music, painting, and film.

Abbie Hoffman, *The Autobiography of Abbie Hoffman* (New York: Four Walls Eight Windows, 2000).
Originally published in 1980 as *Soon to Be a Major Motion Picture,* Hoffman's autobiography, which he wrote while a fugitive living underground in the late 1970s, is an excellent firsthand chronicle of major counter-culture events, including the bizarre Chicago Seven trial and the attempt to levitate the Pentagon to end the Vietnam War.

Timothy Leary, *High Priest* (New York: World, 1968).
Leary's own chronicle of his League for Spiritual Discovery. An overly zealous but still interesting account of the kind of religiosity that emerged around the use of psychedelic drugs.

Scott MacFarlane, *The Hippie Narrative: A Literary Perspective on the Counterculture* (Jefferson, N.C.: MacFarland, 2007).
Explores the major aspects of the hippie counter culture as represented in the literature of the time. MacFarlane's critical study creates a sort of counter-cultural literary canon, including works such as *One Flew Over the Cuckoo's Nest, Trout Fishing in America, Siddhartha,* and *Slaughterhouse-Five.*

Timothy Miller, *The Hippies and American Values* (Knoxville: University of Tennessee Press, 1991).
Miller's study resists the temptation to trivialize or denigrate hippie culture and instead seriously considers the contributions of hippie ethics to subsequent American values. Some subjects covered include free presses, sexual liberation, and eco-consciousness.

James E. Perone, *Music of the Counterculture Era* (Westport, Conn.: Greenwood
    Press, 2004).
Examines various counter-culture issues—the antiwar movement, black power,
feminism, etc.—through the lens of the popular music of the time.

Theodore Roszak, *The Making of a Counter Culture: Reflections on the Technocratic
    Society and Its Youthful Opposition* (Garden City, N.Y.: Doubleday, 1969).
The first and probably still the most thorough sociological examination of the
counter-culture movement of the 1960s. Written in 1969, in the midst of the
counter-culture movement, it suffers from the absence of hindsight available to
authors of later books.

Ronald Sukenick, *Down and In: Life in the Underground* (New York: Beech Tree
    Books, 1987).
An account of the underground arts culture inhabiting Greenwich Village, predominantly in the 1950s and 1960s. Sukenick examines this culture and its figures
largely through the venues they inhabited.

PEOPLE OF INTEREST

Richard Brautigan (1935–1984)

Perhaps most accurately captured the zeitgeist of the hippie culture in novels such
as *A Confederate General from Big Sur* (1964), *Trout Fishing in America*, and *In
Watermelon Sugar* (1968). As a participant in the Haight-Ashbury scene in 1960s
San Francisco, he distributed his poetry for free on street corners and participated
in various events sponsored by the Diggers.

Diane di Prima (b. 1934)

Like Allen Ginsberg, a crossover figure between the Beats and the counter-culture
movement. In addition to writing several important works of poetry and prose,
she was also active in several counter-culture projects such as the Diggers group
and Leary's experiments with psychedelics. Along with Amiri Baraka (Leroi
Jones), she edited the important counter-culture literary magazine *The Floating
Bear*. She continues to be a major presence in post–World War II poetry.

Herman Hesse (1877–1962)

German-Swiss writer who died before the counter culture was fully formed.
However, his spiritually oriented novels, including *Siddhartha* (1922), *Steppenwolf*
(1927), and *Journey to the East* (1932), had profound influence on the new-age
spirituality of the counter culture. In 1946 Hesse was awarded the Nobel Prize
in literature.

Abbie Hoffman (1936–1989)

Political activist and founding member of the Yippies, or Youth International
Party. His counter-culture status was solidified after his arrest for conspiracy and
inciting riot at the 1968 Democratic National Convention and his subsequent
courtroom antics during the infamous Chicago Seven trial. His counter-culture
writings included *Revolution for the Hell of It* (1968) and *Steal This Book* (1971).

Ken Kesey (1935–2001)

Considered by many, including MacFarlane, "America's First Hippie." An early advocate of psychedelic drug use, he was perhaps most famous for the cross-country bus trips he made with his Merry Pranksters and for his LSD-driven "acid test" parties, all of which are chronicled in Tom Wolfe's 1968 book, *The Electric Kool-Aid Acid Test*. Kesey wrote two of the most important counter-culture texts: *One Flew Over the Cuckoo's Nest* (1962) and *Sometimes a Great Notion* (1964).

Thomas Pynchon (1937–   )

One of the most critically revered living novelists, known for the complexity of his narratives and the astounding diversity of subject matter that his novels contain. Little is known about Pynchon after his 1959 graduation from Cornell University. In fact, along with J. D. Salinger, he is one of literature's most famous recluses. He is frequently credited with being among the first writers of Postmodern literature. His early novels, *V.* and *The Crying of Lot 49*, feature counter-cultural themes and characters.

Hunter S. Thompson (1937–2005)

Early practitioner of New Journalism along with Tom Wolfe and Truman Capote. His first book, *Hell's Angels* (1966), features a brief section of what later became Thompson's "Gonzo" technique in which, rather than observing events objectively from outside, he instead actively participates and becomes a central figure in the story. Thompson fully developed the Gonzo style in his most famous work, *Fear and Loathing in Las Vegas* (1971). His role as a counter-culture icon may have had more to do with his outrageous, drug-induced personality than with his writing.

—Micheal Sean Bolton

Modern Primitive Poets

Carl Jung observed that the rise of Western civilization necessitated the progressive repression of human instinctual life. Over time this repression created an environment relatively free of disruptive instinctual aggression and facilitated more and more cooperation among the members of Western society. It also promoted a refinement of manners and moral behavior, which was reflected in the arts. A problem for the most sensitive members of society, and for artists in particular, was that the ascendancy of reason at the expense of instinct separated the individual from sources of psychic energy in the lower and more primitive regions of the brain. Cognitive studies today have explained the reasons for this problem scientifically, but in the late nineteenth century, when the problem was becoming acute, when many felt that the abstractions of modern culture had created barriers between themselves and experience of the physical world, artists addressed the problem intuitively. This reaction can best be seen in the visual arts, where painters like Paul Gauguin chose primitive subjects and reverted to forms that were intuitive rather than realistic and reasonable. In the early twentieth century Pablo Picasso's fascination with primitive African masks was the primary element that led to his 1907 masterpiece *Les demoiselles d'Avignon*, which broke radically with the rational and realistic traditions of Western art. In poetry T. S. Eliot felt this crisis most acutely, in his personal life and in his understanding of Western culture. Eliot, however, found no solution to the problem and could only vent his intellectual and spiritual frustrations in *The Waste Land* (1922). A poet who did find a means to address the crisis was Robinson Jeffers: he isolated himself on the wild coast of California and chose for subjects the people of the area (as in his poem *Roan Stallion* [1925]), who were not separated by modern culture from their instinctual life. He also chose to use poetical lines derived from Anglo-Saxon and early Icelandic poetry (qualitative and alliterative, rather than modern quantitative, syllabic verse) to evoke an unsophisticated world not yet separated from its instinctual roots. Although Jeffers began his career quite early in the twentieth century, he continued to write until his death in 1962, well after the Second World War.

The most important figure among these Modern Primitives was William Carlos Williams. Like Jeffers, he began his career writing in traditional poetic forms but, also like Jeffers, found these forms inadequate to deal with what he saw as a civilization separated from the sources of vitality by excessive refinement and cultural intervention between the world of objects and the individual's experience of them. Early in his career he attempted to subvert the rational world by plunging into the unconscious—both his own and that of his characters. This is most apparent in *Kora in Hell* (1920), where Kora (the feminine) represents the instincts which have been held in captivity by Hades (the masculine), representing the modern rational world. The book is an attempt to free the instincts and thus reestablish a more direct experience of the world. A poem that carries this process a step further is "The Rose" (1923), in which Williams attempts to strip the rose of its many traditional associations and symbolism so the flower can be experienced for its naked self. Although Williams also began his poetic career early in the century he continued to write after the Second World War, publishing some of his best work in the 1940s and 1950s. His long epic poem *Patterson* appeared in five parts between 1946 and 1958. A repeated motto of the epic is "no ideas but in things." In other words, meanings should not be assigned to objects, for the object is thus obscured: only those ideas provoked by the object are to be considered. As the critic Kenneth Burke once said of Williams: "There is the eye, and there is the thing upon which the eye alights; while the relationship existing between the two is the poem. . . . Williams thus becomes . . . one of our most distinguished Neanderthal men."

In his attempts to reestablish an unmediated experience of the objective world Williams rejected traditional forms and meters and purified his language by imitating the speech rhythms and vocabulary of common people, thus avoiding what he considered the deadening effects of high culture. In important ways Williams was the successor to Walt Whitman in his creation of an American populist poetry, but he was more acutely aware of the ways in which the language of refinement and respectability affected the individual's ability to respond to the physical world.

A poet strongly influenced by Williams was Theodore Roethke, whose major work appeared in the two decades following the Second World War. Roethke felt stultified by the cultural and poetic traditions that shaped his early work. In the years during the war and immediately after he attempted to slough off the cultural overlays which inhibited his poetic voice. In *The Lost Son* (1948) he does this by rejecting the human world and plunging into the slime of primordial existence. The underlying idea of these poems is that we contain within ourselves our evolutionary past: the residual history of our immense journey from the lowest life forms to our present status as humans. Thus, in these poems, Roethke descends into the abyss of slime, slugs, minnows, worms—which are essentially metaphors for his own instincts. Human culture is temporarily abandoned as the poet tries to understand himself in terms of his most rudimentary animal nature. Once he reaches this understanding, he can begin his physical and spiritual ascent to recover the human, which he does by reentering society through a feminine figure (anima), who first rises out of his unconscious but later assumes the form of a real woman. The ascent out of the primitive self is a slow one, but the human world, once recovered, is prized all the more. In his last book, *The Far Field* (1964), he can accept and is comfortable with his animal, instinctual self and his connections with the natural world.

Roethke's poetics in *The Lost Son* are a radical departure from the traditional poetic forms he had used in his early poetry. He uses primitive rhythms, suggesting the heartbeat, and, at times, his phrasing and vocabulary imitate the babbling of a young child. Indeed, in several poems the child is depicted in the womb, and the imagery attempts to capture what he might experience there. As the poet gradually returns to the adult human world in the volumes *The Waking* (1953) and *Words for the Wind* (1958), the verse forms become more traditional, indicating that he is now at home in the modern world, but this reconciliation has been achieved only after the ordeal of his descent into the primitive instinctual self. Now he understands the complex nature of human life: how the instincts are the foundation upon which the conscious rational self rests.

Robert Penn Warren was another poet of Roethke's generation who struggled with the same psychological and cultural problems. His solutions were somewhat different, however. Warren grasped how modern rationalism—the result largely of the implications of John Locke's philosophy, which denied the existence of instincts in humans—had isolated individuals from one another. Locke's idea that our minds are initially "blank tablets," and that we each create our own reality in the act of perception, implied that we all live in separate worlds: this effect is known philosophically as *solipsism*. Warren's solution to this problem was to suggest an undeniable connection between all humans in the unconscious instinctual self. In "Bearded Oaks" (1937) the poet describes himself and his lover as "twin atolls on a shelf of shade." The image implies that above the ocean's surface (the conscious rational world) the two appear to be separated from one another; but beneath the surface (the unconscious instinctual world) they are joined by the shelf of shade on which they rest. This shelf has been formed by our long evolutionary history: it consists of savagery, tribal aggression—all those aspects of the human psyche that we do not want to accept, and thus, we deny our instincts, which are the result of that evolutionary past.

Although Warren began publishing in the 1920s, his most important poetry appeared in the five decades following World War II; and although he formed his ideas about the importance of our instincts in the 1920s, these ideas inform his poetry throughout his career: only by accepting one's instinctual life and darker selves can he understand who he is and join in a common humanity. This is particularly evident in *Brother to Dragons* (1953; revised edition, 1979), about Thomas Jefferson's reaction to his nephew's murder of a slave, and *Audubon: A Vision* (1969), about the Naturalist-painter's difficulties in discovering his destiny. Warren's poetics remained largely traditional throughout his career, but he loosened meter and line length and took many liberties with traditional forms, such as the sonnet and ballad, to suggest that intuition and instinct took precedence over the rational orderly world of traditional prosody.

James Dickey was also aware of the problems modern culture created by preventing us from discovering our essential instinctual selves. The clearest manifestation of this idea is in his first novel, *Deliverance* (1970), where the four major characters experience the wildness of an untamed river and the savagery of two degenerate mountain men they encounter on their journey. The three men who survive the journey come away with a vivid understanding of primitive violence (the wild river and the mountain men) that lies under the placid surface (the lake that is slowly covering over the river) of modern life.

Similar themes are found in much of Dickey's poetry prior to *Deliverance:* his characters seek ways of entering the natural world through hunting and imaginative projection of themselves into the lives of animals. In "Springer Mountain" (1962) a hunter sheds his clothes and tries to enter the world of his prey: finally, he realizes the absurdity of his gesture and reclaims his clothing; but he understands that his attempt was a necessary one. In "Approaching Prayer" (1964) the poet looks through the mounted head of a boar he once killed with an arrow and tries to see himself from the boar's point of view—even devising a language for the boar to describe what he saw and felt. Dickey believed that humans should attempt to empathize with their fellow creatures, for through them we can begin to understand the instinctual parts of ourselves.

For Dickey the sacramental vision—the belief that all things are interrelated—was of utmost importance. His characters thus frequently attempt to enter and join with nature. The theme appears in poems and fiction throughout his career. It culminates at the end of his final novel, *To the White Sea* (1993), where the main character is literally absorbed into the landscape.

Like Williams, Dickey avoided traditional poetic forms because he found them inhibiting. In his early poetry he used most frequently a three-beat line like that in Roethke's "Lost Son" poems, to much the same effect: a primitive hammered rhythm, suggesting the heartbeat of someone intent on capturing his subject. In his later poetry he used what he called a "split line": wide spaces between groups of words suggested thought and speech units. Thus, like Jeffers, Williams, Warren, and Roethke (in his "Lost Son" poems), Dickey avoided the rational orderly pattern of traditional meters and verse forms.

Of course, no poet can entirely escape the rational world of modern culture and return to a primitive state of being, nor would he want to, but he can reduce the distance between himself and the concrete world in which he lives. He can also attempt to understand his own instinctual nature. That is what the five poets discussed above set out to do—each in his own way. They were not "primitive" in a literal sense, for all were among the most discerning artists of their era, but their ability to recover a more primitive mode of apprehending the world was a means of revalidating the physical realm and renewing life at its most vital levels.

TOPICS FOR DISCUSSION AND RESEARCH

1. All five poets treated here thought of their work as a reaction to modern culture, but William Carlos Williams was the most pointed in his disapproval of modern reductionism and abstraction. Analyze his 1923 volume *Spring and All* structurally and thematically to discover what he found objectionable in the complexities of modern life and what correctives he offered. James E. B. Breslin's *William Carlos Williams: An American Artist* offers important insights in this regard.

2. The anthropologist Claude Lévi-Strauss observed that myths are superstructures built upon important human instincts. How do Robert Penn Warren in "The Ballad of Billie Potts" and Robinson Jeffers in "Roan Stallion" use myth to emphasize the importance of instinct as a primary motivating force in human life?

3. All five of these poets could be considered nature poets, but Theodore Roethke was more consciously writing in the tradition of English and American nature poetry than the other four. One of his most important insights is that nature is internal as well as external. By analyzing "The Lost Son" and "Meditation at Oyster River" show how Roethke moved from despair to salvation, from helpless submersion in nature in the early poem to transcendence through nature in the later poem. Rosemary Sullivan's *Theodore Roethke: The Garden Master* offers excellent ideas about Roethke as a nature poet.

4. James Dickey's first book, *Into the Stone*, drew on and developed poetic techniques and rhythms he had discovered in Theodore Roethke's "Lost Son" poems. Compare the prosody of the two poets in those works and show how their rhythms, images, and themes attempted to recover a "primitive" and vital experience of the world.

5. Robert Penn Warren's *Brother to Dragons* is a criticism of the Enlightenment's explanations of human behavior. In that poem he uses Thomas Jefferson as an embodiment of Enlightenment values, which are undermined by the criminal behavior of his own nephew. Using the 1979 version of the poem, analyze Warren's characterization of Jefferson and explain how Warren's own understanding of human behavior is antirational and based on instinct as the most powerful motivating force. Victor Strandberg's *The Poetic Vision of Robert Penn Warren* is particularly helpful in offering a Jungian reading of Warren's psychology.

RESOURCES

James E. B. Breslin, *William Carlos Williams: An American Artist* (Chicago: University of Chicago Press, 1985).
An excellent, concise, and accurate study of the doctor-poet-novelist, which offers important insights into Williams's aesthetic and character.

Kenneth Burke, "The Vegetal Radicalism of Theodore Roethke," *Sewanee Review*, 58 (Winter 1950): 68–108.
An illuminating early article by one of the most important critics of the period.

Robert Kirschten, *James Dickey and the Gentle Ecstasy of Earth* (Baton Rouge: Louisiana State University Press, 1988).
A sensitive study of Dickey's ability to draw on nature for energy and renewal.

Victor H. Strandberg, *The Poetic Vision of Robert Penn Warren* (Lexington: University Press of Kentucky, 1977).
The best single study of the poet: it takes a Jungian approach to the work.

Rosemary Sullivan, *Theodore Roethke: The Garden Master* (Seattle: University of Washington Press, 1975).
Offers a careful study of the poet's use of natural imagery and themes.

PEOPLE OF INTEREST

James Dickey (1923–1997)
Born in Buckhead, Georgia, into a prominent family. He attended Clemson University for one semester before enlisting in the Army and becoming a navigator in a night-fighter squadron, an experience that furnished material for his poetry and fiction. After the war he earned his bachelor's and master's degrees from Vanderbilt University. He taught at Rice University and the University of Florida before becoming an advertising executive in Atlanta and New York. In 1968 he became

poet-in-residence at the University of South Carolina, where he remained until his death. *The Whole Motion: Collected Poems, 1945–1992* appeared in 1992.

Robinson Jeffers (1887–1962)

Born in Allegheny, Pennsylvania, the son of a Presbyterian minister and biblical scholar. He attended school in Switzerland and graduated from Occidental College in California at the age of eighteen. In 1913 he and his wife Una moved to Carmel, California, where they built, with stones gathered along the coast, Tor House and Hawk Tower, which figure in several of Jeffers's poems. Most of Jeffers's poems are set in the rugged coastal area of California around Carmel and Monterey. The last of five volumes of *The Collected Poetry of Robinson Jeffers* was published in 2001.

Theodore Roethke (1908–1963)

Born in Saginaw, Michigan, where his family owned and operated large greenhouses. His early experiences among flowers shaped his attitudes toward "growing things," which appear frequently as motifs in his poems. He was educated at the University of Michigan and, briefly, at Harvard. He became a dedicated and brilliant teacher—at Lafayette College, Pennsylvania State, Bennington, and the University of Washington. Roethke suffered several mental breakdowns: his bipolarity is a key to understanding his poetry, particularly his "Lost Son" sequence. *The Collected Poems of Theodore Roethke* appeared in 1970.

Robert Penn Warren (1905–1989)

Born in Guthrie, Kentucky. He attended Vanderbilt University, where he became a member of the Fugitive Group and won a Rhodes Scholarship. He is the only writer to receive the Pulitzer Prize in both fiction (*All the Kings Men* [1947]) and poetry (*Promises* [1958] and *Now and Then* [1979]). He became a respected critic as well: his *Understanding Fiction* (coauthored with Cleanth Brooks) was one of the most influential critical works published during the postwar period. *The Collected Poems of Robert Penn Warren* was published in 1998.

William Carlos Williams (1883–1963)

Born in Rutherford, New Jersey, where he practiced medicine until near the end of his life. In addition to his demanding medical practice, he found time to write nearly every day, and, on weekends, socialized with writers and painters of the avant-garde in New York City. Although ignored by critics during his early career, by the postwar period he had become recognized as one of the most influential writers of the twentieth century. *The Collected Poems of William Carlos Williams*, two volumes, was published in 1986.

—Keen Butterworth

Popular Music as Literature

In the preface to Beowulf *to Beatles: Approaches to Poetry* (1972) David R. Pichaske writes, "Laughter and unqualified ridicule are the usual reactions within the halls of academia to any mention of rock and roll lyrics as poetry." Pichaske's conviction that "such reactions are no longer entirely justified" led him to publish the first poetry textbook to balance the work of acknowledged literary titans such as the British Romantic William Wordsworth, whose poem "Ode: Intimations of Immortality" (1807) closes the anthology, with that of contemporary rock stars such as Jim Morrison of The Doors, whose song "Twentieth Century Fox" (1967) opens the volume. For many, "such reactions" persist, as evinced by controversy surrounding singer-songwriter Bob Dylan's ninth Nobel Prize nomination in 2004, the same year Christopher Ricks, professor of humanities at Boston University, published his critical study *Dylan's Visions of Sin*. Filmmaker Gordon Ball, who teaches literature and film at the Virginia Military Institute, explained his rationale for repeatedly nominating Dylan for the Nobel Prize in literature: "Poetry and music are linked, and Dylan has helped strengthen that relationship, like the troubadours of old." As Ball's comment implies, Dylan's merger of poetry and music is hardly new. Even before the medieval troubadours, the Anglo-Saxon scops, the Greek poets and the Old Testament prophets were singing lyrics that have long been collected and studied as literature. But in the 1960s contemporary songwriters, following the example of Dylan, whose own influences were plentiful, redefined popular songwriting, often composing lyrics that demonstrate the aesthetic sophistication and thematic relevance of the finest English-language poetry.

As with other major literary transformations that developed during the second half of the twentieth century, World War II was largely responsible for the emergence of what Pichaske labeled "the poetry of rock." Migration during the war years lifted two musical genres beyond their isolated audiences, which were primarily in the rural south. Jazz and blues songs performed primarily by and for African Americans, "race music" as it was called, was renamed "rhythm and blues" after the war, and, like its white counterpart, hillbilly music—redubbed country and western—the popularity of rhythm and blues spread to urban areas. Both genres were edgier than mainstream music, a result of their folk roots, tackling subjects such as infidelity, hard drinking, and poverty. Pioneers of these early genres such as the bluesman Robert Johnson and the country singer Jimmie Rodgers lived the dangerous lives they wrote and sang about. Their postwar musical heirs, such as Muddy Waters and Hank Williams, respectively, wrote lyrics about everyday hardship, conveying the genuine emotion of their words with ragged, passionate vocal styles, a contrast to the smooth delivery of mainstream crooners, whose generally sentimental or lighthearted love songs were still written by professional lyricists. While many of these lyricists, notably Cole Porter, were poets in their own right, crafting memorable lyrics marked by wit, irony, and a deft handling of rhyme and rhythm, their subject matter only occasionally and subtly tested the boundaries of propriety. Songs such as Muddy Waters's "Rollin' Stone" (1950), however, glorify the freedom of the open road as opposed to the stasis of middle class, domestic life portrayed by postwar radio and television shows such as "Father Knows Best" and "The Adventures of Ozzie and Harriet." "Rollin' Stone" was a precursor of the rock 'n' roll era. That song provided the name for perhaps the most definitive rock 'n' roll band, The Rolling Stones; it influenced the title for a definitive rock 'n' roll song written by Bob Dylan, "Like a Rolling Stone" (1965); and it ultimately inspired the title of the magazine that has chronicled the genre since 1971, *Rolling Stone*. Williams, sometimes called "the Hillbilly Shakespeare," who died at age twenty-nine after writing thirty-six top-ten country and western songs, also sang about the unsettled life and paved the way for rock 'n' roll music with songs such as "Move It on Over" (1947), which is rhythmically and melodically nearly identical to the song often credited with jump-starting the rock 'n' roll era, "Rock around the Clock" (recorded in 1952 by Sunny Dae and His Knights; rerecorded by Bill Haley and His Comets in 1954).

The merger of country and western with rhythm and blues, which found its voice in the early songs of Elvis Presley, helped create rock 'n' roll, a genre that liberated contemporary songwriting both lyrically and musically, offering expression to the restlessness of a generation of young people stifled by the expectations of an increasingly conservative postwar culture. The booming economy that closely followed the war affected young people's spending potential in unprecedented ways, and they increasingly became the target audience of record producers and songwriters. Artists such as Chuck Berry, for example, sang about cars, girls, and rock 'n' roll itself, writing catchy, witty lyrics delivered at driving speed to an electrified musical backing. Performers such as Berry, Little Richard, and Buddy Holly were among the first mainstream performers to write their own lyrics, rather than interpret the songs of others, as their popular contemporaries such as Frank Sinatra had been doing. Holly's death on 3 February 1959, commemorated in Don McLean's "American Pie" (1971), is called "the day the music died." Rock 'n' roll music mellowed in the early 1960s; the period was characterized by a string of popular ballads ("It's Now or Never," "Are You Lonesome Tonight") recorded in 1960 by Presley, freshly returned from Germany where he had spent the last years of the 1950s serving in the United States Army. This hiatus, which lasted until the so-called British Invasion of 1964, marked by The Beatles' first tour of the United States, made room for a pivotal new brand of music—urban folk, which spawned Bob Dylan.

Another effect of the economic boom that followed the war was the dramatic rise in the number of Americans attending college over the next two decades, both veterans and their baby-boomer offspring. Many baby boomers reached college age in the early and mid 1960s as urban folk music gained popularity. The genre defined itself against rock 'n' roll—then dominated by songs written with new dance styles in mind, such as "The Twist"—as music for a sophisticated audience, blending socially conscious lyrics with music that did not distract listeners with the temptation to dance. Pete Seeger was at the forefront of this movement, which evolved out of the work of another working-man's musician, Woody Guthrie. A champion of the oppressed, Guthrie wrote "This Land is Your Land" in 1940, as a rough-edged response to songwriter Irving Berlin's "God Bless America." Guthrie's song includes a verse that challenges Berlin's notion of "a land that's free":

In the squares of the city, In the shadow of a steeple;
By the relief office, I'd seen my people
As they stood there hungry, I stood there asking,
Is this land made for you and me?

The modern, more-refined folk movement had an unlikely literary ally in its crusade against consumerism, discrimination, and conformity in the Beat writers. The most prominent figurehead among this movement was the novelist Jack Kerouac, whose penchant for recreational drug use and jazz music distinguished him and his fellow Beats from Seeger and his folk followers. In 1963 Bob Dylan merged the influence of these two groups by uniting folk rhythms with the highly imagistic and symbolic lyrics characteristic of the Beats in the apocalyptic "A Hard Rain's A-Gonna Fall," which borrows its structure from the medieval ballad "Lord Randall." Dylan had enrolled in the University of Minnesota the year Buddy Holly, one of his musical heroes, died. Dylan dropped out shortly after discovering two books that prompted him to hitchhike to New York City and begin a career that revolutionized American music and culture: Guthrie's *Bound for Glory* (1943) and Kerouac's *On the Road* (1957).

In New York City Dylan began a disciplined routine of self-education, reading voraciously while churning out folk songs others began rerecording. His "Blowin' in the Wind," recorded by Peter, Paul, and Mary, reached number two on the *Billboard* pop chart and brought Dylan national recognition as a protest singer, rallying his listeners against discrimination, war, and poverty. His lyrics began to draw a clear distinction between the blind, constraining ways of the older generation and the lucid, liberating potential of the young, warning "mothers and fathers," "senators and congressmen," and "writers and critics" that "the old road is rapidly fading," in "The Times They Are A-Changing" (1964). Dylan attracted the attention of his Beat mentors, who welcomed his ability to infuse popular music with poetry. Lawrence Ferlinghetti, owner of City Lights Bookstore, a haven for Beat writers, welcomed Dylan when the singer performed at the University of California, Berkeley, in 1964, and Dylan formed an enduring friendship with several Beats, including Allen Ginsberg. The Beat influence became more prominent in Dylan's new songs, such as "Mr. Tambourine Man" (1965), with richly textured lyrics about transcending the banal that seemed to strain against the confines of the folk medium. In the summer of 1965 Dylan substituted an electric guitar for his acoustic model at the Newport Folk Festival and appalled folk purists such as Seeger with his new rock songs "Maggie's Farm" and "Like a Rolling Stone," acerbic diatribes that displaced Dylan's concern for broad social causes, with a more universal concern for individual freedom.

Rock music, as the variety became known in the 1960s, extended Dylan's reach, carrying his work not only to the jukebox but also onto college syllabi, to the resentment of such poet-scholars as John Ciardi, who complained about his nephew's considering Dylan a poet: "Like all Dylan fans I have met, he knows nothing about poetry. Neither does Bob Dylan." Other writers such as Paul Simon also found their way to mainstream listeners by writing increasingly complex folk songs that highlighted poetic lyrics. Dylan's first meeting with the

Beatles when they toured America in 1964 proved instrumental to heightening the literary level of popular songwriting. It was shortly after this meeting that Dylan moved beyond folk music and The Beatles began writing more mature lyrics. During the second half of the decade America welcomed a host of first-rate lyricists whose careers flourished on U.S. soil—some British, like John Lennon and Paul McCartney of The Beatles and Mick Jagger and Keith Richards of The Rolling Stones; some Canadian, like Leonard Cohen and Robbie Robertson; and many native, like Simon, Lou Reed of The Velvet Underground, Grateful Dead lyricist Robert Hunter, and Jim Morrison of The Doors. Some bands, such as Morrison's (who alluded to Aldous Huxley's *The Doors of Perception*, 1954) and the Canadian band Steppenwolf (after Herman Hesse's novel), took literary names. Others based songs on literary classics, such as "Richard Corey" (1966), Paul Simon's nod to Edwin Arlington Robinson, and "White Rabbit, (1967), Jefferson Airplane's homage to Lewis Carroll. Dylan's songs often echoed the titles of Kerouac's novels: "Desolation Row" (1965), "On the Road" (1965), "Subterranean Homesick Blues" (1965), and "Visions of Johanna" (1966). After his recovery from a 1966 motorcycle accident, Dylan seemed to mellow in much the same way as Elvis Presley after his military service. Dylan's *John Wesley Harding* (1968), while lyrically astute, was stripped of the psychedelic influence of his monumental 1966 record *Blonde on Blonde* and signaled the beginning of the country-rock movement that characterized the early part of the next decade. A new group of singer-songwriters, including James Taylor and Jackson Browne, blossomed in the 1970s. While the emphasis in popular music shifted back to dance in the mid seventies, the influence of Dylan and his fellow poets of rock carried on in their own work as well as in that of such American songwriters as Billy Joel and Bruce Springsteen.

The lyrics of many of these songwriters have been collected in individual volumes in recent years: *Hank Williams: The Complete Lyrics* (1993); Bob Dylan's *Lyrics: 1962–2001* (2004); Paul Simon's *Lyrics, 1964–2008;* and Lou Reed's *Pass through Fire: The Collected Lyrics* (2008). Pichaske's work on music and culture in the 1960s is still among the finest secondary resources. Michael Gray's *Song and Dance Man III: The Art of Bob Dylan* (2004) is the best of many critical analyses of Dylan's lyrics. Larry Starr and Christopher Waterman's *American Popular Music: From Minstrelsy to MTV* (2003) is an indispensable source of the historical and cultural context within which popular music has developed. Brian Ward's study is an incisive look at the role songwriters such as James Brown and Sam Cooke and others in the industry played in the Civil Rights and Black Power movements.

TOPICS FOR DISCUSSION AND RESEARCH

1. Many of the early protest songs of Bob Dylan confront the social issues that characterized the postwar years: "Let Me Die in My Footsteps" "Talkin' John Birch Society Blues," "Masters of War," "A Hard Rain's A-Gonna Fall," "Talking World War III Blues," and "With God on Our Side," for example, are all reactions to the Cold War. "The Death of Emmett Till," "Oxford Town,"

"Only a Pawn in Their Game," and "The Lonesome Death of Hattie Carroll" address racial inequality. Students might listen to the songs and read the lyrics to analyze how Dylan treats these subjects as both social critic and poet.

2. Students might compare both William Wordsworth's "The World is Too Much with Us" and Samuel Taylor Coleridge's "Kubla Khan" with Dylan's "Mr. Tambourine Man." In what ways might these pieces be thematically similar? What aspects of Romanticism can be found in Dylan's song?

3. In his 1965 song "It's Alright Ma, I'm Only Bleeding," Dylan wrote, "He not busy being born is busy dying." What other writers of the postwar years embrace this theme and in what ways? Students might also analyze Dylan's own evolution or rebirth in three songs that seem to reflect his, and perhaps his generation's, evolving views regarding authority: "Maggie's Farm," "Dear Landlord," and "Gotta Serve Somebody." Can the differing stances these songs convey be reconciled?

4. The lyrics of Paul Simon are frequently concerned with alienation, superficiality, and the often-empty promise of the American dream. Students might analyze the lyrics of "The Dangling Conversation," "I Am a Rock," "America," and "The Boxer" and discuss how Simon poetically renders the themes that writers such as J. D. Salinger treat in prose.

5. Allusions fill the work of American songwriters during the 1960s. Students might analyze the references to biblical, historical, and cultural figures in popular songs of this era and discuss why these figures might be important to the songwriters who allude to them. David Pichaske's chapter "A Poem is a Thing," in Beowulf *to Beatles and Beyond,* devotes a helpful section to this subject. Students might also analyze Don McLean's highly allusive song "American Pie" and discuss it as an allegory of popular music history in the postwar years.

6. Choose a song by one of the artists discussed here. Listen to it, then read the lyrics. How is the experience different? Is the meaning different? Defend your answer.

RESOURCES

Jim M. Curtis, *Rock Eras: Interpretations of Music and Society, 1954–1984* (Bowling Green, Ohio: Bowling Green State University Popular Press, 1987).
Provides several helpful chapters for students interested in popular music as literature, particularly "Chapter 12: Dylan's Words in Freedom," and "Chapter 13: High Culture as Popular Culture."

Michael Gray, *The Song & Dance Man III: The Art of Bob Dylan* (New York: Continuum, 2004).
A painstakingly researched and carefully detailed study of Dylan's work through 1997's *Time out of Mind.*

David R. Pichaske, Beowulf *to Beatles and Beyond: The Varieties of Poetry,* revised edition (New York: Macmillan, 1981).
This revised edition of Pichaske's 1972 anthology is an excellent text that teaches all the elements of poetry through the works of the traditionally acknowledged masters of poetry and contemporary songwriters.

Pichaske, *A Generation in Motion* (Granite Falls, Minn.: Ellis Press, 1989).
This slightly modified reprint of Pichaske's 1979 volume is an essential study of the development of the counter culture of the 1960s, particularly the music that grew out of it.

Pichaske, *The Poetry of Rock: The Golden Years* (Peoria, Ill.: Ellis Press, 1981).
Analyzes the genesis and development of the great lyricists of the 1960s, devoting chapters to Dylan, The Doors, The Jefferson Airplane, and others.

Christopher Ricks, *Dylan's Visions of Sin* (New York: Ecco, 2003).
Analysis of Bob Dylan's lyrics as they relate to the seven deadly sins, the four virtues, and the three graces.

Larry Starr and Christopher Waterman, *American Popular Music: From Minstrelsy to MTV* (New York: Oxford University Press, 2003).
An indispensable chronicle of the evolution of popular music in America, which includes two conpact discs so that many texts can be heard, not merely read.

Brian Ward, *Just My Soul Responding: Rhythm and Blues, Black Consciousness, and Race Relations* (Berkeley: University of California Press, 1998).
Traces the contribution of African American singers, songwriters, and record producers in the struggle for racial equality during the postwar years.

PEOPLE OF INTEREST

Bob Dylan (1941–)
Born in Duluth, Minnesota. After a semester at the University of Minnesota, Dylan hitchhiked to New York City where he regularly visited the ailing Woody Guthrie and began making his mark as a songwriter. Having released more than fifty recordings of original songs, Dylan continues to tour and pays homage to the songwriters who have inspired him on his "Theme Time Radio Hour." The first installment of his memoir *Chronicles I* (2004) provides an enthralling firsthand account of his early days in Greenwich Village and his attempt to escape the public attention he came to loathe.

Woody Guthrie (1912–1967)
Born in Okemah, Oklahoma, and began traveling the country, writing and performing folk songs during the Great Depression, many of which were recorded on *Dust Bowl Ballads* (1940). Guthrie died of Huntington's disease from which he suffered for nearly two decades. His son, singer-songwriter Arlo Guthrie, was a prominent counter-culture figure in the late 1960s and early 1970s.

Pete Seeger (1919–)
Born in New York City. His career as a folksinger led to his friendship with both the elder Guthrie and Dylan. In the early 1950s Seeger, part of the band The Weavers, was investigated for communist ties. In 2009, at age ninety, he performed Guthrie's "This Land Is Your Land" during the inauguration celebrations of President Barack Obama.

Paul Simon (1941–   )
Born in Newark, New Jersey, and began his career performing with Art Garfunkel with whom, as Tom and Jerry, he had a hit single at the age of fifteen. The 1967 movie *The Graduate,* for which Simon wrote the soundtrack, helped bolster the career of Simon and Garfunkel. Simon went on to a successful solo career in the 1970s and in 1986 recorded a landmark album, *Graceland,* merging his lyrics with South African musical styles.

Muddy Waters (1913–1983)
Born in Rolling Fork, Mississippi, and later took his Delta blues–influenced style to Chicago, where he became nationally known, inspiring generations of blues and rock musicians in America and England.

Hank Williams (1923–1953)
Born in Mount Olive, Alabama, and, like Dylan, wrote songs that were covered by mainstream performers before establishing himself as a national act. Williams was a prolific songwriter, penning such songs as "Your Cheatin' Heart" and "Hey Good Lookin.'" Plagued by drug and alcohol abuse, Williams died of a heart attack at age twenty-nine. The last hit song to be released before he died was titled "I'll Never Get out of This World Alive."

—John Cusatis

Postmodernist Fiction

American literary Postmodernism flourished in the period after World War II, though most critics place its inception in the late fifties and early sixties. It was a reaction to the times: the end of World War II, Hiroshima and the atomic bomb, the Civil Rights movement, the assassination of President John F. Kennedy, Vietnam, the global economy, and the technology boom. Owing to these culture-altering events, many American writers realized that the received forms of the past did not accommodate the concerns of the Postmodern condition of contemporary American life—the general cultural upheaval resulted in a literary upheaval, as well. Writers such as John Barth, Donald Barthelme, Robert Coover, William Gass, Vladimir Nabokov, Thomas Pynchon, and Kurt Vonnegut began to redefine the basic elements of literature; the notions of genre, narrative, character, plot, reader, and author were all being revised.

American Postmodernist writers focused on dismantling the grand narratives, or the grand truths, of modern literature. Vladimir Nabokov uses parody and a combination of revising and subverting popular literary genres in *Lolita* (1955); John Barth questions the ontological status of author, reader, and text in *Lost in the Funhouse* (1968) through the interjection of self-reflexive commentary and experimentation with the short-story form; Donald Barthelme interrogates master narratives, through parodying Realist and Modernist novels, by intertextuality, self-reflexive prose, and an explosion of form in *Come Back, Dr. Caligari* (1964) and *Snow White* (1967); and Thomas Pynchon disrupts narrative structure, through form and content, forestalls closure, and celebrates indeterminacy, chaos, and open-endedness in *The Crying of Lot 49* (1966).

"What is Postmodernism?" This question has plagued many a critic, student, reader, and author alike. Most theorists have their own working definition, but "Postmodernism" is not neatly definable. One can, however, trace a few key terms and qualities of Postmodernism to give a sense of what the term implies: metafiction, parody, pastiche, intertextuality, the simulacrum, the mistrust of totalizing grand narratives or metanarratives, the fragmentation of the self, multiplicity and heterogeneity, the impossibility of representation, and the instability of language. To an extent, critics conflated the advent of this literature with the explosion of the deconstructionist and poststructuralist theories of Jacques Derrida and Roland Barthes in their struggle to define the term Postmodern because of the shared notions of truth, self, and representation. There are shared concerns, but simply defining Postmodernism as the aesthetic realization of poststructuralist theory reduces it to a fixed definition, which goes against the very heart of Postmodernism. But Postmodernism's interrogative and demystifying impulse, its impact on the grand "truths" and dominant ideologies of American culture (historical and contemporary), and its questioning of the unified, cohesive self, or the static and culturally sanctioned identity commonly put forth in traditional narratives, can be traced in the literary production of American Postmodern writers.

Embedded in the swell of Postmodern theory was the realization that, at bottom, Postmodern literature is a reaction to and against conventional narratives and the values that inform those narratives. In *The Postmodern Condition:*

A Report on Knowledge (1979), the French theorist Jean-François Lyotard posits that Modernism embraces totalizing narratives that legitimize a unified, rational subject, coherent meaning, and totalizing knowledge or truth, while Postmodernism questions and subverts those grand narratives. Furthermore, the self is simply a *construction* of language and culture. Any system that reduces human subjectivity to neat, tight, static categories of being is unreliable. There is no longer any cohesive or totalizing narrative. Truth is not universal, but local.

In American Postmodern fiction, then, there is an explosion of the subject and of form to accommodate the Postmodern condition. Narrative is often nonlinear, nonrational, indeterminate, fragmentary, and open-ended. Furthermore, characters within these narratives cannot claim a unified and coherent subjectivity because the author cannot claim that for himself. The persona of the author self-consciously emerges as a character in the text who critiques the narrative, which is termed "metafiction." Characters themselves question their function in the world of the text and their position in the world at large. The presence of the author and the idea that narrative is simply a construction are emphasized in Postmodern fiction. Consequently, narrative truth is presented as questionable and unreliable.

Other key terms associated with Postmodernism are simulacra, intertextuality, and pastiche. Jean Baudrillard, in *Simulation and Simulacra* (1995), argues that in Postmodern times, there is no longer a "real" that we can embrace; even though we model our own subjectivities and narratives on the real, it is only an imagined real. In fact, we find that the real has never existed, but only its image; this is the simulacrum. Another central idea in Postmodern theory is intertextuality, which is achieved through pastiche and parody. Frederic Jameson, in *Postmodernism, or The Cultural Logic of Late Capitalism* (1984), insists that in the Postmodern condition we can no longer embrace the ideological and unified narratives of the past, for these narratives have lost all meaning and power. According to Jameson, Postmodernists replaced this ideological foundation and deeply personal style with *pastiche,* the superficial imitation of dead styles. Postmodern art is simply a piecemeal regurgitation of past forms, empty and signifying nothing. Linda Hutcheon, in *The Politics of Postmodernism* (1989), replaces the term pastiche with *parody*. In many Postmodern novels, genre and narrative are reminiscent of the past and yet critiqued and revised to adjust to Postmodern concerns. Therefore, intertextuality, through parody or pastiche, is a highly effective Postmodern strategy commonly found in American Postmodern literature.

In sum, Postmodern American literature is generally concerned with questioning and problematizing the ways in which a Modernist's notion of the self or a Realist's faith in representation lays claim to authenticity, unity, and universality. Selected literary texts of certain male writers have evolved into what is understood as the canon of Postmodern American literature. These writers have also been at the center of Postmodern literary criticism. More recently, however, women and minorities have entered the literary landscape of Postmodernism, have taken up Postmodernism as a viable alternative to conventional forms, and are pushing their way into critical consideration.

TOPICS FOR DISCUSSION AND RESEARCH

1. Postmodern writers regularly subvert literary conventions. Examine John Barth's collection of short stories *Lost in the Funhouse* (1968) and discuss how Barth experiments with various elements of fiction: plot, setting, author, reader, and typography. See Barth's discussion of Postmodern literature in *The Friday Book* (1997), particularly "The Literature of Exhaustion," for greater insight into his aesthetic motivations.

2. Several Postmodern writers draw attention to the process of writing fiction or the constructed nature of works of literature. Read Donald Barthelme's *Snow White* and analyze the ways in which Barthelme updates and revises the popular fairy tale. See Linda Hutcheon's discussion of parody and pastiche in *The Politics of Postmodernism* (1989) to analyze this typically Postmodern strategy.

3. Readers' expectations are often frustrated in the Postmodern novel. Read Thomas Pynchon's *The Crying of Lot 49* (1966) and discuss the ways in which the ending denies closure for the reader and what impact that has on the text as a whole. See Brian McHale's *Postmodernist Fiction* (1989) for reasons why this lack of closure is a characteristic of Postmodern fiction and for more authors, like Pynchon, whose works are similarly open-ended.

4. Although Postmodern fiction signals a shift from Modernist fiction, there are still ties that bind the two types of literature. For example, fragmentation and literary experimentation are central concerns for both the Postmodernist and Modernist writer. Look at any Postmodern text and compare it to any experimental Modernist text (for example, the later works of William Faulkner, James Joyce, or Virginia Woolf) and trace the similarities and differences. See Ihab Habib Hassan's *The Postmodern Turn* (1987) to discover the ways in which Postmodernism is simultaneously an extension *and* a rejection of Modernism.

5. The American literary Postmodern canon seems inundated with male writers. Look through *Postmodern American Fiction: A Norton Anthology* (1998) to locate women's Postmodern American fiction. Analyze how women writers employ Postmodern strategies in their fiction. See Linda Nicholson's *Feminism/Postmodernism* (1990) and Magali Cornier Michael's *Feminism and the Postmodern Impulse: Post–World War II Fiction* (1996) to research the overlapping concerns of feminism and Postmodernism.

RESOURCES

Bibliography

Larry McCaffery, ed., *Postmodern Fiction: A Bio-Bibliographical Guide* (New York: Greenwood Press, 1986).
Serves students of American Postmodernism from 1945 to 1970 as a useful roadmap to locating the works of the chief practitioners of that time period.

Criticism

John Barth, *The Friday Book* (Baltimore: Johns Hopkins University Press, 1997).

A collection of his nonfiction essays about the nature of writing in a Postmodern era. In "Literature of Exhaustion" Barth argues that Postmodernism is a consequence of the "used-upness" of literature.

Jean Baudrillard, *Simulation and Simulacra,* translated by Sheila Faria Glaser (Ann Arbor: University of Michigan Press, 1995).
A groundbreaking investigation of Postmodernism that introduces the concept of the simulacrum and its relationship to Postmodern culture.

Paula Geyh, Fred Leebron, and Andrew Levy, eds., *Postmodern American Fiction: A Norton Anthology* (New York: Norton, 1998).
Offers a wide collection of Postmodern works, including fiction, criticism, and other forms.

Ihab Habib Hassan, *The Postmodern Turn: Essays in Postmodern Theory and Culture* (Columbus: Ohio State University Press, 1987).
Explains the relationship between Modernism and Postmodernism and includes an oft-quoted list of features of both that serves to visually represent the differences between the two in a concise and very readable format.

Linda Hutcheon, *The Politics of Postmodernism* (London: Routledge, 1989).
Defends Postmodernism's political impulse, particularly in the characteristic use of parody and historiographic metafiction, by using examples from literature, visual art, and architecture.

Fredric Jameson, "Postmodernism, or the Cultural Logic of Late Capitalism," *New Left Review,* 146 (July–August 1984): 53–92.
One of the most famous critiques of Postmodernism. Jameson's article discusses the "depthlessness" of Postmodernism and its consequent reliance on pastiche, or the imitation of dead styles.

Jean-François Lyotard, *The Postmodern Condition: A Report on Knowledge,* translated by Geoff Bennington and Brian Massumi (Minneapolis: University of Minnesota Press, 1984).
A groundbreaking volume that introduces students of Postmodernism to the concept of the grand narrative and the petite narrative, and the institutional practice of legitimating knowledge through the use of metanarratives. Lyotard questions the credibility of any system of knowledge that claims to hold universal truth.

Brian McHale, *Postmodernist Fiction* (London: Routledge, 1989).
An indispensable study that focuses on Postmodernism as a literary practice rather than a time period, a cultural condition, or a religious era. McHale offers one of the first studies and the only comprehensive one devoted to the analysis of Postmodernist fiction, tracing its roots and development.

Magali Cornier Michael, *Feminism and the Postmodern Impulse: Post–World War II Fiction* (Albany: State University of New York Press, 1996).
Offers a historical view of the intersection of feminism and Postmodernism in literature. Tracing women's experimental fiction after World War II, Cornier offers

a glimpse of how women writers were adopting characteristically Postmodern practices in their fiction.

Joseph P. Natoli and Linda Hutcheon, eds., *A Postmodern Reader* (Albany: State University of New York Press, 1993).
A collection of many of the seminal critical and theoretical texts in Postmodern study. This hefty volume serves as an accessible and comprehensive primer on Postmodern intellectual theory and philosophy.

Linda J. Nicholson, ed., *Feminism/Postmodernism* (New York: Routledge, 1990).
A broad and illuminating discussion of both feminism and Postmodernism as philosophies to highlight the similarities and differences between the two.

PEOPLE OF INTEREST

John Barth (1930–   )
The most famous of the early Postmodern American writers. With the publication of *Lost in the Funhouse* (1968), Barth solidified his position as one of the key practitioners of American Postmodern fiction. While all of his novels and short stories have a metafictional element, they are reader-friendly, despite the experimentation. His novel *Chimera* (1972) won the National Book Award.

Donald Barthelme (1931–1989)
Revolutionized the short-story form through his experimentation with conventional narrative, which is evidenced in his earliest works, *Come Back, Dr. Caligari* (1964) and *Unspeakable Practices, Unnatural Acts* (1968). Many of his most famous short stories are collected in *Sixty Stories* (1981), and a collection of previously unpublished works, *Flying to America: 45 More Stories* (2007), has recently been published.

Robert Coover (1932–   )
Published over twenty books, notably *The Universal Baseball Association, Inc., J. Henry Waugh, Prop.* (1968), *Pricksongs and Descants* (1969), and *The Babysitter* (1969). His body of work includes typically Postmodern uses of metafictional techniques. His most famous use of historiographic metafiction is in *The Public Burning* (1977), which deals with the trials of Julius and Ethel Rosenberg.

William Gass (1924–   )
A fiction writer, essayist, and literary critic. His short-story collection *In the Heart of the Heart of the Country* (1968) and his novel *Willie Masters' Lonesome Wife* (1968) helped secure his place in the Postmodern American literary canon because of his experiments with linear narrative and typography. He won the American Book Award for his novel *The Tunnel* (1997) and a National Book Critics Circle award for his book of criticism, *Tests of Time* (2003).

Vladimir Nabokov (1899–1977)
Defied categorization since he served as a bridge between the High Modernists and the Postmodern era of American literature. However, several of his novels are

Postmodern in form and content. A trio of novels, *Lolita* (1955), *Pale Fire* (1962), and *Ada of Ardor: A Family Chronicle* (1969), place Nabokov in the Postmodern camp. Nabokov's experimentations with language, metafictional techniques, and narrative time influenced later writers.

Thomas Pynchon (1937–   )

Holds a place in Postmodern American letters that rivals that of John Barth. His novels have generated a mountain of critical investigation, and he has created a persona that rivals the mystery and intrigue of his novels. With the publication of *The Crying of Lot 49* (1966), Pynchon cemented his place in the American Postmodern literary canon. His unique blending of the sciences, philosophy, mathematics, popular culture, and philosophy in his novels has challenged readers for over forty years. Pynchon wrote *Inherent Vice* (2009).

Kurt Vonnegut (1922–2007)

Associated with American Postmodernism because of the experimentation with linear time and the metafictional quality of much of his work. Vonnegut's novels *Cat's Cradle* (1963) and *Slaughterhouse-Five* (1969) both included unconventional and fabulous narrative elements. His masterful use of parody and satire was also appreciated as a deeply Postmodern impulse. Vonnegut published more than twenty books, a mix of fiction and nonfiction, during his long career.

—Seema Kurup

Science Fiction

Though writers and scholars disagree on the precise boundaries of the Golden Age of science fiction and the New Wave, both are associated with the years after World War II. In his anthology *Before the Golden Age,* Isaac Asimov dates science fiction's Golden Age as beginning in 1938, when John Campbell became editor of *Astounding Stories,* to 1950, when magazines such as *Galaxy* and *The Magazine of Fantasy and Science Fiction* entered the field. In his anthology *Modern Science Fiction,* Norman Spinrad dates the Golden Age from 1966 to 1970, with the rise of the New Wave.

Until 1950 fans could read every science-fiction magazine and book and still have time to publish their reactions in fanzines. Authors could keep up with one another's work. This was a period not only of flowering but of consensus. Readers and writers knew what science fiction was: it was what appeared in the pulp magazine *Astounding Stories.* Through the 1940s, *Astounding Stories* dominated the genre, and John W. Campbell dominated *Astounding Stories.* As editor from 1938 to 1971, Campbell made the magazine in his own image and captured readers' imaginations and beliefs. Many other magazines were published, some of them claiming circulations considerably larger than that of *Astounding Stories*—Ziff Davis's *Amazing Stories,* for example—but the stories that defined science fiction appeared in Campbell's magazine.

Through the 1940s magazines were the major—and sometimes only—publishing medium for science fiction. Even when anthologies began to be published in book form, they were largely made up of stories from the magazines, and science-fiction novels were reprinted serials. But even beyond the centralizing fact of the magazines, 1940s science fiction displayed a unification of diverse influences, a developing consensus. Campbell shaped that consensus and talked about it in his controversial editorials. Writers got large doses of theory in conversation, in long letters, and in rejection slips. ("Amusing," he might write, "but it ain't science fiction.") In 1952 he defined science fiction in an article for *Modern Science Fiction:* "Fiction is only dreams written out; science fiction consists of the hopes and dreams and fears (for some dreams are nightmares) of a technically based society." Campbell's authors included Asimov, Arthur C. Clarke, L. Sprague de Camp, Robert A. Heinlein, L. Ron Hubbard, Henry Kuttner and C. L. Moore (individually and as a team writing under pseudonyms), Lester del Rey, Eric Frank Russell, Clifford Simak, Theodore Sturgeon, A. E. van Vogt, Jack Williamson, and many others.

Campbell and his writers satisfied, almost as a by-product of their activities, the third criterion for the existence of science fiction: they freed themselves from old concepts about the nature of the universe—cultural and religious—and began an extended debate about the beginning and the end of things, and the fate of humanity, which resulted in a kind of consensus within science fiction. Heinlein expressed this by revealing that what had attracted him to science fiction was a quality called "time-binding," a term invented by Alfred Korzybski to describe how the human animal lives not only in the present but in the past and in the future. Most people, Heinlein said, live from day to day or plan ahead for a year or two. He went on to say that science fiction readers "differ from most of the rest of the race by thinking in terms of racial magnitudes—not even centuries but thousands of years."

The fictional debate resulted in a consensus future history that Donald Wollheim summed up in *The Universe Makers*. Although Heinlein was the first to base his stories and novels on a consistent future history, the consensus drew on Asimov's *Foundation* stories and works from earlier authors such as E. E. "Doc" Smith, Edmond Hamilton, and Olaf Stapledon. Later additions and refinements were made by such authors as Poul Anderson, James Blish, Larry Niven, and Ursula K. Le Guin.

Other directions emerged around 1950 with the appearance of *The Magazine of Fantasy & Science Fiction (F&SF)* edited by Anthony Boucher and J. Francis McComas, and of *Galaxy Science Fiction,* edited by H. L. Gold. They looked at science fiction from other viewpoints, and the consensus, though it still had influence, began to fragment. *F&SF* reunited the streams of fantasy and science fiction in a turbulent bed. It produced a tolerance for anything written well, encouraging established writers to attempt stories that previously would have been unpublishable within the genre, and attracted into the field new writers, such as Ray Bradbury, who found Campbell's requirements incompatible or uninspiring. *Galaxy* specialized in social satire, and a generation of writers who had been working on the fringes of Campbell's world found a home for their darker visions. Much of what *F&SF* published was difficult to categorize. *Galaxy,* on the other hand, established its own rigor. Gold wanted science fiction written to his tastes. His view of life was ironic. He wanted fiction not about scientists and engineers but entertaining works about average citizens caught up in worlds not of their making who find ways not to cure but to endure.

The 1950s also brought a boom for new magazines. Between three and fourteen new science-fiction magazines a year started publication between 1949 and 1953; many died quickly, and in 1953 more magazines were killed than born. Publishers overestimated the influence of the atom bomb and rocketry on the magazine-buying public; although people lived in a science-fiction world, they had not yet recognized it. Nevertheless, dozens of science-fiction magazines were available, encouraging new writers.

Prior to World War II, book publishers had virtually ignored science fiction, but soon afer the war anthologies and novels began to appear. Magazine readers read them avidly, but rather than alter tastes, book publication reinforced them, for they mined twenty years of magazines for treasure: short stories for anthologies and serials for novels. As Ace Books began to publish original science fiction, the opportunity to publish without regard for the magazines and their requirements became a significant alternative. In 1951 this freedom was applied to short stories as well with the publication of Raymond J. Healy's anthology of original fiction, *New Tales of Space and Time*. In 1952 Frederik Pohl began editing *Star Science Fiction,* a series of original anthologies for Ballantine. These provided new markets, less restricted by editorial requirements than magazines and often better paying. These original anthologies and novels encouraged individual expression over conformity, diffusing the genre.

Between 1940 and 1965, world events shaped science: World War II illustrated the increasing impact of technology on civilization. Atom bombs and a hundred other laboratory products for war demonstrated the need for scientists and engineers, as well as educated citizens who could understand what was going on and control the direction of society. Money poured into research and education, inevitably accelerating technological change. With the launch of Sputnik in 1957, the shock of Soviet primacy in space reinforced the notion that the world had changed. Technologies such as the nuclear fission reactor and the hydrogen bomb were perfected.

All this seemed to affirm what Campbellian science fiction said: atom bombs and rockets symbolized science fiction's prophetic power and authenticated its concern for the future. What the prewar authors wrote was coming to pass; the issues they raised pressed upon humanity. We lived, as Asimov put it, in a science-fiction world, but not everybody liked it. The horrors of total war brought disillusionment with the science and technology that had put power into the hands of madmen; for many people the world moved too fast, and they felt powerless to affect their fates. And the future held the prospect of World War III, the nuclear war that could eliminate humanity.

During the same time revelations came to light about atrocities committed under the Third Reich in Germany and Joseph Stalin in the USSR. The Korean War broke out. The Cold War heated up. Joseph McCarthy symbolized an era of hysteria, blacklists, investigations, and purges. Space exploration began, and President John F. Kennedy launched a competition to be first on the moon. France exited Indochina, and the Vietnam War escalated to massive American involvement. Increasing power over nature, traumatizing world events, and accelerating change meant, for many, increasing frustration. How should power be used? How should change be directed? Should both be rejected? Students questioned how to organize society and rank its values. Led by veterans of civil-rights battles, fueled by sentiment against the Vietnam War, these questions escalated into a near-revolution over fundamental issues that discouraged one president from running for a second term and embittered the tenure of another, while undermining confidence in higher education. The most vocal young people questioned the value of knowledge and learning, and elevated feeling into a philosophic position.

In this period a new group of writers emerged. Michael Moorcock began his tenure over *New Worlds* in 1964, and Damon Knight launched his influential series of original anthologies, *Orbit*, in 1966. These forces led to what later would be called the "New Wave," and these new editors attracted young writers more interested in literature than in science and disposed to disregard, resent, or react against earlier science fiction. But this revolutionary period neither began as abruptly as it seemed nor was as unified as it appeared.

Moorcock encouraged the most extreme expressions of morality and writing style. His model was J. G. Ballard. In Ballard's wake came Brian Aldiss,

John Brunner, Charles Platt, Thomas Disch, John Sladek, Pamela Zoline, Norman Spinrad, and James Sallis. *New Worlds* lost distribution and perhaps some readers, but it managed to thrive with the help of grants from the British Arts Council. Roger Zelazny and Gene Wolfe began to appear in its pages.

A veteran from the Campbell era, writer-editor Judith Merril had been editing the most influential and, for a time, the only best-of-the-year anthology. Captivated by *New Worlds,* she began a personal campaign to spread it from the United Kingdom to the United States, first naming the movement the "New Wave," then including examples of it in her anthologies, culminating in *England Swings Science Fiction* (1968). Her campaign inspired Harlan Ellison to announce that he would publish *Dangerous Visions* (1967), an anthology of taboo-breaking stories that could not be published in the magazines.

The New Wave writers reinterpreted science fiction in personal terms. They moved from an objective universe to a subjective one; their writing resembled fantasy in its abandonment of the world of shared experience for the world of subjective interpretation. Their intensely personal viewpoints tended to challenge the established order and even the traditional way of perceiving reality. Their stylistically experimental methods emphasized the personal over the general.

Over time, the revolution ended. Much of what the rebels wanted is now accepted, and the urge to shock and break taboos has diminished to occasional youthful exuberance. Even traditional science-fiction writers enjoy the new freedom and broader audience that the New Wave attracted.

TOPICS FOR DISCUSSION AND RESEARCH

1. Science fiction is the literature of evolution and change, both technological and biological. It is about transcendence. The best science fiction dismantles comfortable familiarity and asks us to consider alternatives. Science fiction does not concern itself with restoring order but with understanding and planning for change. This central theme suggests many directions for research. Students might compare the perspective on social and cultural change apparent in science fiction with that of mainstream literature, citing relevant works from both camps that exhibit contrasting attitudes. They might compare a work of science fiction with a work of fantasy or a pastoral work. Students could discuss how science fiction inoculates its readers against the stresses of change and prepares them for a future that not only is different from what is expected but from what we *can* expect. Use Alexei Panshin and Cory Panshin's *The World beyond the Hill* (1989) as a guide to help frame your questions.

2. Science fiction is also the literature of other perspectives and alienation, exploring what it means to be human through stories about aliens as well as alien perspectives on our species. It explores alien worlds, times, and ideas, suggesting that our ways of thinking are not the only ways, our structures of morals and values and culture are arbitrary or environmental. It reinforces the notion

that we also change, and that resisting alienation leads to stagnation. Find a few short science-fiction stories that exemplify this theme and discuss how the authors use alienation and to what effect. James E. Gunn's *Inside Science Fiction* (2006) offers insights and direction, and his definitive four-volume anthology *The Road to Science Fiction* (1977–1982) includes appropriate stories in chronological context.

3. Combining elements of space opera, metaphysics, religion, politics, and ecology, Frank Herbert's *Dune* (1965) transcended the boundaries between early science fiction, the Golden Age, and the New Wave, and had a profound effect on the genre. Some argue that it is more a work of fantasy than science fiction. Many other works similarly defy categorization and altered the course of the field. Students might discuss how definitions affect readings of a particular work. Several works listed below will guide your research, including Kingsley Amis's *New Maps of Hell* (1960).

4. Very early, science-fiction readers and authors built a community that grew out of letters to the magazines and evolved into "fandom," with its unique subcultures and multitude of conventions. In 1934 Hugo Gernsback (editor of *Amazing Stories*, the first science-fiction magazine, established in 1926), founded the Science Fiction League, which later spun off other fan groups, notably the Futurians, which counted as members some of the most-influential personalities of the Golden Age. Research the evolution of fandom in relation to science fiction and discuss how it has affected the field. Of particular interest is David Hartwell's *Age of Wonders: Exploring the World of Science Fiction* (1996).

5. Because most science fiction from the Golden Age was published in magazines, the genre was characterized by the literary tastes of only a few editors, including Anthony Boucher, John Campbell, Harlan Ellison, H. L. Gold, Judith Merril, Michael Moorcock, and Frederik Pohl. Using a variety of the suggested sources, analyze how the genre evolved with the advent of original anthologies and novels.

RESOURCES

Primary Work

John Clute and Peter Nicholls, eds., *The Encyclopedia of Science Fiction* (New York: St. Martin's Griffin, 1999).
A vast and comprehensive work covering 4,300 entries, including 2,900 authors.

Criticism

Brian Aldiss and David Hargrove, *Trillion Year Spree: The History of Science Fiction* (New York: Atheneum, 1986).
An essential work that traces the history of science fiction from Mary Shelley through the movements discussed here.

Kingsley Amis, *New Maps of Hell* (New York: Harcourt, Brace, 1960).
British mainstream literary writer's history and examination of the field that helped the literary world accept the serious study of science fiction.

Colin Greenland, *The Entropy Exhibition: Michael Moorcock and the British "New Wave" in Science Fiction* (London & Boston: Routledge & Kegan Paul, 1983).
Examines the New Wave through the lens of Moorcock's tenure at *New Worlds*.

James E. Gunn, *Inside Science Fiction*, second edition (Lanham, Md.: Scarecrow Press, 2006).
Through two dozen short essays, shares what it was like growing up with science fiction from its roots through modern work; what it is and how it evolved; and how to read, write, and teach science fiction.

David G. Hartwell, *Age of Wonders: Exploring the World of Science Fiction* (New York: Tor, 1996).
By one of the field's most prominent editors, reveals the inner workings of science-fiction subculture ("fandom"), spawned during this period.

Damon Knight, *In Search of Wonder: Essays on Modern Science Fiction*, third edition (Chicago: Advent, 1996).
Incisive essays about the genre by one of the first science-fiction scholars and critics.

Sam Moskowitz, *Explorers of the Infinite: Shapers of Science Fiction* (Westport, Conn.: Hyperion Press, 1974).
Excellent collection of early author profiles by one of the genre's leading editors and critics who specialized in science fiction's pulp origins.

Moskowitz, *Seekers of Tomorrow* (Westport, Conn.: Hyperion Press, 1974).
Complements Moskowitz's collection of early author profiles with those of modern writers.

Alexei Panshin and Cory Panshin, *The World beyond the Hill: Science Fiction and the Quest for Transcendence* (Los Angeles: J. P. Tarcher, 1989).
A comprehensive history of science fiction that discusses how the genre reaches into the mythic imagination and shapes society.

Robert Scholes and Eric S. Rabkin, *Science Fiction: History, Science, Vision* (New York: Oxford University Press, 1977).
An influential work that examines the history of science fiction and science.

Darko Suvin, *Metamorphoses of Science Fiction: On the Poetics and History of a Literary Genre* (New Haven, Conn.: Yale University Press, 1979).
Explores cognitive estrangement, utopia in science fiction, alternative history, and much more. Suvin is an important scholar of Russian science fiction.

Donald A. Wollheim, *The Universe Makers: Science Fiction Today* (New York: Harper & Row, 1971).
Traces the history of science fiction from Jules Verne and H. G. Wells through the Golden Age, examining themes and outlining the consensus future-history as envisioned.

PEOPLE OF INTEREST

Isaac Asimov (1920–1992)
Born to a Jewish family in Russia, started selling stories at the age of nineteen and soon became a major influence on the genre. *I, Robot* (1950) established his "Three Laws of Robotics" that have served science-fiction writers ever since. His *Foundation Trilogy* (1951–1953) is central to science fiction's consensus future about humans in space and introduced the term "psychohistory." His work is characterized by a rational humanist perspective. Much of Asimov's vast literary output was nonfiction about science. In 1987 he was named Grand Master by the Science Fiction and Fantasy Writers of America.

John Campbell (1910–1971)
As editor of *Astounding Science Fiction* (later named *Analog Science Fiction and Fact*) from 1937 until his death, almost single-handedly directed the course of science fiction through most of the Golden Age. He began as a writer of space opera, then turned to more subtle and philosophical stories (as Don A. Stuart), before realizing that many more of his ideas could see print by sharing them with his stable of writers.

Robert A. Heinlein (1907–1988)
Often called "the dean of science fiction." He wrote and spoke often about science fiction, and he was the one of the first science-fiction authors to reach best-seller status. His early writing included young-adult works still popular today, such as his first novel, *Rocket Ship Galileo* (1947), and his "future-history" collection, *The Past through Tomorrow* (1967). Much of his later fiction is concerned with political philosophy, as in *Starship Troopers* (1959), and alternative lifestyles, as in *Stranger in a Strange Land* (1961).

Judith Merril (1923–1997)
Called "the mother of science fiction" by many, succeeded in a field dominated by men and helped launch the New Wave. The majority of her efforts came as editor of year's best science-fiction collections. Her fiction is also influential and well-regarded, and of her three novels, two are coauthored with Cyril M. Kornbluth. She was also a political activist in the United States and Canada. One of her three marriages was to fellow Futurian Frederik Pohl.

Michael Moorcock (1939–   )
Incubated the New Wave when he took the helm of *New Worlds* in 1964, where many of his stories had appeared. Moorcock's science fiction, fantasy, and mainstream literary work has earned many awards, and in 2008 he was given the Damon Knight Memorial Grand Master Award. His opinionated views on writing and the genre, particularly his criticism of Heinlein, have earned him many followers as well as detractors.

Frederik Pohl (1919–   )
Has served science fiction as author, agent, and editor for more than seventy years. He edited both *Galaxy Science Fiction* (founded by Horace Gold in 1950) and *if: Worlds of Science Fiction* magazines from 1959 to 1969, offering non-Campbellian

authors an outlet where they could explore ideas arising from sociology rather than engineering and write satire rather than pulp adventure. When the magazines were sold, Pohl left to pursue his writing career, frequently coauthoring with fellow Futurian Cyril M. Kornbluth (notably *The Space Merchants*, 1953) and Jack Williamson. His novel *Gateway* (1977) won several major awards. In 1993 he was named Grand Master by the Science Fiction Writers of America.

—James Gunn and Christopher McKitterick

Part III
Study Guides
on Works and Writers

Edward Albee, *Who's Afraid of Virginia Woolf?*

(New York: Atheneum, 1962)

With the 1962 Broadway premiere of *Who's Afraid of Virginia Woolf?* Edward Albee (1928–) cemented his reputation as the preeminent American playwright of his generation. The play opened to mixed reviews—some of them actually hostile—but became an immediate commercial success and media sensation, largely owing to its adult language and subject matter. Although Albee wrote many other critically and commercially successful plays, *Who's Afraid of Virginia Woolf?* remains the work for which he is best known and most celebrated.

The adopted son of wealthy and emotionally distant parents, Albee was expelled from or dropped out of a succession of boarding schools and universities. As a young man he broke ties with his family and moved to New York's Greenwich Village to write poetry but, on the advice of the dramatist Thornton Wilder, turned to writing plays. He achieved early critical success with experimental one-act plays such as *The Zoo Story* (1959) and *The American Dream* (1961). Controversy over the selection of *Who's Afraid of Virginia Woolf?* for the Pulitzer Prize resulted in no award being granted that year, but it did win a Tony and a New York Drama Critics' Circle Award. His next play, *Tiny Alice* (1964), baffled audiences and critics, but Albee went on to receive Pulitzer Prizes for *A Delicate Balance* (1966) and *Seascape* (1975). While the plays he wrote through the 1970s and 1980s did not match his earlier successes, in 1991 he secured his position as America's leading playwright with his third Pulitzer Prize for *Three Tall Women*. Albee won his second Tony in 2002 for *The Goat; or, Who Is Sylvia?* Throughout his career Albee has also adapted the work of other authors for the theater, including Carson McCullers's *Ballad of the Sad Café* (1963) and Vladimir Nabokov's *Lolita* (1981), and the libretto for a musical version of Truman Capote's *Breakfast at Tiffany's* (1966).

Who's Afraid of Virginia Woolf? establishes Albee's frequent dramatic situation of battling spouses. The play is set in the home of a middle-aged couple, George and Martha, on the campus of a small New England college. George is a member of the history department, and Martha is the daughter of the college president. Albee claimed that the naming of the lead characters after the first American president and his wife was a "small irony, not a large truth." The action begins in the wake of an evening faculty party; the inciting incident is the arrival of Nick, a new hire in the biology department, and his wife, Honey. In the course of the night George and Martha viciously attack each other and bait their young guests into sadistic games and humiliating confessions. The crisis occurs when Nick and Honey realize that George and Martha's idealized son is only a fictional creation of the older couple. As punishment for Martha's revealing the existence of the invented child to their guests—a taboo subject with outsiders—George "kills" the boy by inventing a telegram bearing the bad news of his accidental death. The play ends at dawn with George comforting Martha, who confides that she is afraid of Virginia Woolf—that is, of living without self-delusion.

Study of *Who's Afraid of Virginia Woolf?* benefits from an understanding of Albee's other plays. The early one-act *The Zoo Story* advances the idea that to be truly alive and aware of reality one must break ordinary, infantile illusions of conformist society. *The American Dream* similarly deconstructs the stereotypical family unit as banal and stifling. Albee dissects the dynamics of a marriage in *A Delicate Balance* when a middle-aged couple whose home is invaded by their "best friends" reassess their lives and come to a new understanding as the play, like *Who's Afraid of Virginia Woolf?*, ends at dawn. A scandalous—almost absurd—discovery about her husband's sexual proclivities is made by the wife in *The Goat; or, Who Is Sylvia?*

The best source for information on Albee's career and for evaluations and explanations of his plays is Mel Gussow's detailed and authoritative biography, *Edward Albee: A Singular Journey* (1999), which exploits Gussow's long acquaintance with his subject and quotes from many of their conversations. Also of value are the playwright's comments in *Conversations with Edward Albee* (1988) and *Stretching My Mind: The Collected Essays of Edward Albee* (2005). *The Cambridge Companion to Edward Albee* (2005) is an excellent resource both for criticism and for facts about Albee's life and career. Stephen J. Bottoms's *Albee: Who's Afraid of Virginia Woolf? (Plays in Production)* (2000) is a book-length study of production problems and challenges regarding the play. Finally, Barbara Lee Horn's *Edward Albee: A Research and Production Sourcebook* (2003) provides a good bibliography and production history of Albee's plays.

TOPICS FOR DISCUSSION AND RESEARCH

1. The title of the play, a parody of the song "Who's Afraid of the Big Bad Wolf?" from Walt Disney's *Three Little Pigs* (1933), comes from a joke the partygoers had shared earlier in the evening. (For copyright reasons the actors in the original production sang the line to the tune of "Here We Go Round the Mulberry Bush.") The title introduces the image of fear into the play's nightmarish atmosphere. Albee described his play as being "about people of more than average intelligence getting to the point where they can no longer exist with a whole series of games, tricks, and false illusions, and then knocking down the entire untenable superstructure. The end result: something may or may not be built in its place." Albee leaves the final tableau of *Who's Afraid of Virginia Woolf?* ambiguous. Students might discuss the direction the characters' lives may take after the end of the play. Will Martha overcome her fear of reality and live a fulfilled life or lapse back into illusion?

2. Students might consider how Albee uses the tension between reality and illusion to provide the thematic conflict of the play. Although critics often associate Albee with the theater of the absurd, as practiced, for example, by Eugene Ionesco, *Who's Afraid of Virginia Woolf?* conforms to traditional Realism. This fact poses many questions as to what is "real." Whether George really killed his father in a car accident and whether Martha's perfect son really exists are ambiguities, but they are not the violations of logic or of physical laws characteristic of absurdist drama. Albee uses party games as a metaphor for

competition in a marriage (the title of act 1 is "Fun and Games"). Although George and Martha appear to despise each other, they ultimately reveal their relationship to be a symbiotic love-hate one in which they emotionally feed on each other's insults and vitriol. The manufactured child underlines the emptiness and sterility of their union. Near the end of the play Martha confesses her dichotomous reliance on her husband, whom she has belittled throughout the evening: "George who is good to me, and whom I revile; . . . who can hold me at night, so that it's warm, and whom I will bite so there's blood; who keeps learning the games we play as quickly as I can change the rules; who can make me happy and I do not wish to be happy, and yes I do wish to be happy." Albee also comments on marriage through the relationship of Nick and Honey. Their marriage, like George and Martha's, is haunted by a ghost child, as Honey's premarital pregnancy was either hysterical or ended in an abortion. Students might compare the two marriages in the play. Is there evidence to suggest that Nick and Honey represent George and Martha in their younger days?

3. Albee frequently uses religious imagery in the play, as illustrated by both couples' "ghost" children. Albee titled act 2 "Walpurgisnacht" (the witches' Sabbath). The title suggests a sense of supernatural foreboding, in which evil forces formulate charms or spells in preparation for future destructive acts. Act 3, "The Exorcism," fulfills this expectation as George performs like Torquemada, the Spanish Inquisitor, torturing Martha with the murder of their fictitious child. Martha's suffering is necessary if she is to make the transition from fantasy to reality; George thus exorcises the demon of self-delusion. He explains his method to an uncomprehending and horrified Honey: "When people can't abide things as they are . . . they do one of two things . . . either they turn to a contemplation of the past as I have done, or they set about to alter the future. And when you want to change something . . . you BANG! BANG! BANG! BANG!" Students will benefit by analyzing other supernatural references and images in the play and discussing their significance to the work.

4. Students may also examine the play's philosophical conflict between art and science in the arguments between George, a failed novelist, and Nick, an ambitious, amoral biologist. George accuses Nick of planning a fascist-like future of biological conformity and perfection. Ironically, George and Martha describe their fictional son as the stereotypical ideal: athletic, blonde, and blue-eyed. What does the play suggest about scientific progress? About art? Does it suggest that a future society of confident Nicks would be better than one of failed and bitter Georges?

5. Students will benefit from comparing *Who's Afraid of Virginia Woolf?* to the works of other playwrights. Like many Postmodernist works, Albee's play draws from multiple sources. The famous opening line, "What a dump," is taken from the 1949 Bette Davis movie, *Beyond the Forest*. The play also quotes from Tennessee Williams's *A Streetcar Named Desire* (1948) and Samuel Beckett's *Waiting for Godot* (1952). Albee regards both playwrights as inspirational to his work. The dramatic situation of *Who's Afraid of Virginia Woolf?* bears a strong resemblance to August Strindberg's *Dance of Death* (1900), which depicts a marriage as a battleground. Albee has described *Who's Afraid*

of Virginia Woolf? as a "grotesque comedy," and several critics have characterized the vicious barbs of George and Martha as an adult Punch and Judy show. Albee lists as one of his major influences for the play the work of the American humorist James Thurber—specifically, the stories "The Breaking up of the Winships" and "One Is a Wanderer" and the play *The Male Animal* (1939), coauthored by Elliott Nugent. Albee also acknowledges a strong thematic connection between his play and Eugene O'Neill's *The Iceman Cometh* (1940). In O'Neill's tragedy a ragtag group of bums, alcoholics, and other social outcasts commiserate in Harry Hope's bar, dreaming of never-to-be achieved salvation; Albee reverses O'Neill's thesis: he has commented that "O'Neill says you have to have false illusions. *Virginia Woolf* says get rid of them." Can Albee's play be considered hopeful in any way? Students might also analyze the illusions of Albee's characters in conjunction with those of the Tyrone family in O'Neill's autobiographical tragedy *Long Day's Journey into Night* (1928). Students will benefit from exploring other thematic and stylistic similarities between Albee's plays and any of the influential works mentioned.

RESOURCES

Primary Works

The Collected Plays of Edward Albee, 3 volumes (Woodstock, N.Y.: Overlook Press, 2004–2005).
Collects Albee's dramatic works, including his groundbreaking early one-act plays, his less famous works of the 1970s and 1980s, and his late critical successes, such as *Three Tall Women* and *The Goat; or, Who Is Sylvia?*

Conversations with Edward Albee, edited by Philip C. Kolin (Jackson: University Press of Mississippi, 1988).
Newspaper and journal interviews from throughout Albee's career.

Stretching My Mind: The Collected Essays of Edward Albee (New York: Carroll & Graf, 2005).
Albee's nondramatic prose, including commentary on his own plays and those of his contemporaries and on American culture.

Bibliography

Richard E. Amacher and Margaret Rule, *Edward Albee at Home and Abroad* (New York: AMS Press, 1973).
Primary and secondary bibliography, with many non-American citations.

Charles Lee Green, *Edward Albee: An Annotated Bibliography, 1968–1977* (New York: AMS Press, 1980).
Supplement to the Amacher and Rule bibliography.

Barbara Lee Horn, *Edward Albee: A Research and Production Sourcebook* (Westport, Conn.: Praeger, 2003).
Bibliography and production history of Albee's plays.

Richard Tyce, *Edward Albee: A Bibliography* (Metuchen, N.J.: Scarecrow Press, 1986).
Earlier bibliography and production history of the plays.

Robert A. Wilson, *Edward Albee: A Bibliographical Checklist* (New York: Moretus Press, 1983).
Bibliography of primary works.

Biography

Mel Gussow, *Edward Albee: A Singular Journey* (New York: Simon & Schuster, 1999).
The only thorough and useful biography, enhanced by the author's long relationship and many recorded interviews with the playwright.

Criticism

C. W. E. Bigsby, ed., *Edward Albee: A Collection of Critical Essays* (Englewood Cliffs, N.J.: Prentice-Hall, 1975).
Twenty-one essays, including three by the editor, a leading English scholar of American drama.

Stephen J. Bottoms, *Albee: Who's Afraid of Virginia Woolf? (Plays in Production)* (Cambridge & New York: Cambridge University Press, 2000).
Examines the play in critical detail with a particular emphasis on Albee's stagecraft and the production problems and challenges posed by the play.

Bottoms, *The Cambridge Companion to Edward Albee* (Cambridge, England & New York: Cambridge University Press, 2005).
Essays by Bottoms and others examining Albee's plays from a variety of perspectives. The book includes a detailed chronology of the author's life and career.

Martin Esslin, *The Theatre of the Absurd,* revised edition (Woodstock, N.Y.: Overlook Press, 1973).
Seminal work explicating the genre often associated with Albee.

Bruce J. Mann, ed., *Edward Albee: A Casebook* (New York: Rutledge, 2003).
Essays examine not only Albee's influences but also his own dramatic innovations.

Bob Mayberry, *Theatre of Discord: Dissonance in Beckett, Albee, and Pinter* (Rutherford, N.J.: Fairleigh Dickinson University Press, 1989).
Examines Albee in the context of two of his most significant contemporaries.

Matthew C. Roudané, *Understanding Edward Albee* (Columbia: University of South Carolina Press, 1987).
Introductory overview of Albee's themes.

—Park Bucker

James Baldwin, *Go Tell It on the Mountain*
(New York: Knopf, 1953)

James Baldwin (1924–1987) was not only one of America's finest and most socially perceptive essayists of the twentieth century but is also highly regarded as a short-story writer, playwright, poet, and novelist. His first novel, *Go Tell It on the Mountain* (1953), was also his first major publication and introduced topics that became quintessentially Baldwinian, such as family conflict, the African American experience, religion, and homosexuality.

James Arthur Jones was born in Harlem to Emma Berdis Jones; he took the last name of his stepfather, David Baldwin, a preacher, who married his mother and adopted her son in 1927. By the age of fourteen James Baldwin was an ordained preacher and was delivering sermons in a Pentecostal Holiness church. He and his stepfather had a strained relationship that later informed some of Baldwin's most lasting works—including the semiautobiographical *Go Tell It on the Mountain*, in which the protagonist, John Grimes, is often at odds with his stepfather, Gabriel. After David Baldwin's death in 1943, James Baldwin moved to Greenwich Village in Manhattan. There he was introduced to the novelist Richard Wright, who helped him to secure a writing fellowship in 1945. In 1948 Baldwin left the United States for Paris, in part because of the hostile climate in America for blacks and homosexuals. His later novels include *Giovanni's Room* (1956), *Another Country* (1962), *Tell Me How Long the Train's Been Gone* (1968), *If Beale Street Could Talk* (1974), and *Just above My Head* (1979).

Go Tell It on the Mountain, Baldwin's most critically acclaimed novel, explores the life of young John Grimes and his family in Harlem in 1935. The novel commences on a Saturday, John's fourteenth birthday, and chronicles events that lead to John's spiritual awakening and conversion that evening. John's stepfather, Gabriel, is an authoritarian preacher at the Temple of the Fire Baptized. The three-part novel also follows John's aunt Florence; his mother, Elizabeth; and other family members, but the tension and alienation between John and Gabriel, as well as John's bouts with issues of individuality, identity, and spiritual certainty, give the novel its narrative force. Baldwin incorporates flashbacks that allow him to place the Grimes family in a broader historical context, especially with respect to African American migration patterns and social conditions in the early twentieth century.

While the characters are African American, and the setting is primarily Harlem, the extent to which Baldwin emphasizes race and the African American community produced substantive dialogue among literary critics and scholars at the time of the publication of the book. Students should keep in mind that works produced by African Americans in the 1950s were often compared to each other, even if the thematic similarities between them were not readily apparent. The reason for this comparative analysis was to gain greater insight into the "black experience." Baldwin's novel was published one year before the 1954 U.S. Supreme Court's *Brown v. Board of Education* decision made segregated educational facilities unconstitutional and, therefore, reached American readers during a period of intense national discourse about the future of race relations in the United States. Perhaps this context explains why some reviewers and critics argued that race was not really at the core of *Go Tell It on the Mountain*. For example, Richard K. Barksdale's 1953 essay, "Temple of the Fire Baptized," began: "James Baldwin has written a very fine first novel. It is a story by a Negro, about Negroes, set in a predominantly Negro environment; and yet it is not essentially a 'Negro' novel." In 1958, on the other hand, Robert Bone claimed that race is the most important element of the novel because the book reflects how Baldwin had been a victim of white society during childhood. Students should keep these opposing perspectives in mind while reading the novel.

Likewise, students would be well advised to read Baldwin's other novels, particularly *Giovanni's Room* and *Just above My Head*, for a richer understanding of his recurring themes. His *The Price of the Ticket: Collected Nonfiction, 1948–1985* (1985) should also be consulted for his direct reflections on race. In addition, one would be wise to consult Michael Fabre's essay "Fathers and Sons in James Baldwin's *Go Tell It on the Mountain*" (1974), especially for his insights on the relationship between John and Gabriel. Biographers Herb Boyd, David Leeming, and William J. Weatherby have examined Baldwin's life and works from multiple perspectives, but James Campbell's *Talking at the Gates: A Life of James Baldwin* (1991) is the most useful to readers of *Go Tell It on the Mountain*. Critical studies of Baldwin, such as Carol E. Henderson's *James Baldwin's* Go Tell It on the Mountain: *Historical and Critical Essays* (2006) and Trudier Harris's *New Essays on* Go Tell It on the Mountain (1996), should prove useful, as well.

TOPICS FOR DISCUSSION AND RESEARCH

1. While *Go Tell It on the Mountain* is based in part on Baldwin's life, the novel is not a strict autobiography; a reader interested in unearthing biographical information about the author should become familiar with his essays, which are almost always grounded in his personal experiences. The two essays that make up *The Fire Next Time* (1963) and are collected in *The Price of the Ticket* are a good starting point. Discovering how much or how little Baldwin alters his actual experiences in his literary work can be fascinating. Students should explore what these suggest about Baldwin as a man and artist. Does he make matters better or worse for his characters through these alterations? What impact do the alterations have on readers and on the dramatic arc of the novel? On the other hand, students should ask whether Baldwin's novel relies too heavily on autobiographical components or whether it benefits aesthetically from them. Do the distractions produced by the biographical information make the reader less able to appreciate the imaginative aspects of the work?

2. Geography plays an important role in the novel. During flashbacks a few characters relive their experiences as part of the Great Migration of African Americans from the South to the North and other parts of the country in the early 1900s, when more than a million individuals sought better lives after generations of slavery and oppression. How does Baldwin present the South and the North in his novel? Is the North portrayed as a land of opportunity,

or is it depicted as a slightly less sinister version of the South? Do the characters find the quality of life they were seeking? How typical or atypical are the characters' experiences within the scope of the Great Migration? For comparative purposes students might read Baldwin's short play, *Blues for Mister Charlie* (1964), in which many of the characters, especially Richard, discuss the differences between the North and the South around the middle of the twentieth century. How much does *Go Tell It on the Mountain* resemble *Blues for Mister Charlie* with respect to the expectations and realities of life in the North?

3. The title of Baldwin's novel is taken from a traditional Christian spiritual and immediately communicates that the novel will contain spiritual elements. The song is about the birth of Christ; the following lines constitute the opening lyrics and refrain:

> Go tell it on the mountain,
> Over the hills and everywhere,
> Go tell it on the mountain,
> Our Jesus Christ is born.

Clearly, Christianity and the Bible inform the novel. A few characters, such as John, Gabriel, and Esther, have particularly biblical names. The plot, too, revolves around religion and salvation. John, for example, struggles mightily with the profane and the sacred. References to Ham and Noah can also be found in the novel. Students should explore the relevance and significance of these allusions. For example, what role does the angel Gabriel play in the Bible, and does that role have relevance to the novel? For all its religious trappings, however, *Go Tell It on the Mountain* should not automatically be assumed to be a religious novel. Students might discuss which characters show a devotion to Christ; which characters express sincere faith in religion; and which characters, if any, consistently exhibit Christian values.

4. Race is a constant theme in the novel, and students should engage the issue from both historical and contemporary perspectives. One might attempt to ascertain how Baldwin establishes the characters' identities as Negroes. Is such an identity essential to understanding the plight of the characters, or does race serve as an additional layer of complexity in the novel? Do characters suffer solely because they are black, or might their conditions be the result of universal challenges? Is Baldwin attempting to make statements about the state of race relations, or is he simply writing about a black family struggling to find common ground? Harris's *New Essays on* Go Tell It on the Mountain offers engaging perspectives on the issue of race in the novel.

5. Bryan R. Washington addresses the subject of homosexuality in the novel in "Wrestling with 'The Love That Dare Not Speak Its Name': John, Elisha, and the 'Master,'" included in *New Essays on* Go Tell It on the Mountain. Washington discusses the homoerotic tensions between John and Elisha, a seventeen-year-old Sunday-school teacher and the nephew of Father James. John clearly admires Elisha and behaves at times as if he is infatuated with the older teen. At one point Baldwin writes, "John stared at Elisha all during the lesson, admiring the timbre of Elisha's voice, much deeper and manlier than

his own, admiring the leanness, and grace, and darkness of Elisha in his Sunday suit, and wondering if he would ever be holy as Elisha was holy." Although no sexual contact occurs, the two boys often wrestle playfully. Students might explore how the undercurrent of same-sex desire contributes to the emphases on identity and religion in the novel. How does Baldwin's depiction of homosexual desire impact the characters and plot in *Go Tell it on Mountain?* Students might also compare Baldwin's treatment of homosexuality in this novel with the way he deals with it in *Giovanni's Room, Another Country,* or *Tell Me How Long the Train's Been Gone?*

RESOURCES

Primary Works

Another Country (New York: Dial, 1962).
Baldwin's third novel, about a black jazz musician. Like *Go Tell It on the Mountain,* it treats the issue of homosexuality.

Blues for Mister Charlie: A Play (New York: Dial, 1964).
Dedicated to the assassinated civil-rights leader Medgar Evers and loosely based on the 1955 lynching of fourteen-year-old Emmett Till. Depictions of the North in the play are useful to readers of *Go Tell It on the Mountain.*

Conversations with James Baldwin, edited by Fred L. Standley and Louis Pratt (Jackson: University Press of Mississippi, 1989).
Comprises twenty-seven interviews from 1961 to 1987.

Giovanni's Room (New York: Dial, 1956).
Baldwin's second novel, set in post–World War II Paris. Like *Go Tell It on the Mountain,* it concerns internal conflicts and issues of sexuality.

The Price of the Ticket: Collected Nonfiction, 1948–1985 (New York: St. Martin's Press, 1985).
Collects Baldwin's essays, including "The Fire Next Time," "No Name in the Street," and "The Devil Finds Work."

A Rap on Race, by Baldwin and Margaret Mead (Philadelphia: Lippincott, 1971).
Conversations between the writer and the anthropologist on race and other social issues of the time.

Tell Me How Long the Train's Been Gone (New York: Dial, 1968).
Novel about a black actor who struggles with racial and sexual identity.

Bibliography

Fred L. Standley and Nancy V. Standley, eds., *James Baldwin: A Reference Guide* (Boston: G. K. Hall, 1979).
Includes an annotated secondary bibliography. The work is a bit dated but still useful for locating print sources.

Literary History.com <http://www.literaryhistory.com/20thC/Baldwin.htm> [accessed 11 November 2009].
Includes criticism, reviews, and teaching resources, with links to texts.

Biography
James Campbell, *Talking at the Gates: A Life of James Baldwin* (New York: Viking, 1991).
A careful study of the author's life and work.

Criticism
Harold Bloom, ed., *James Baldwin* (Philadelphia: Chelsea House, 2006).
Collects a range of critical essays on Baldwin's works, including *Go Tell It on the Mountain.*

Robert Bone, "The Novels of James Baldwin," *Tri-Quarterly,* 2 (Winter 1965): 3–20.
A critical examination of Baldwin's fiction.

Jane Campbell, "Retreat into the Self: Ralph Ellison's *Invisible Man* and James Baldwin's *Go Tell It on the Mountain,*" in her *Mythic Black Fiction: The Transformation of History* (Knoxville: University of Tennessee Press, 1986), pp. 87–110.
Compares confessional aesthetics in the novels.

Michael Fabre, "Fathers and Sons in James Baldwin's *Go Tell It on the Mountain,*" in *James Baldwin: A Collection of Critical Essays,* edited by Keneth Kinnamon (Englewood Cliffs, N.J.: Prentice-Hall, 1974), pp. 120–138.
Explores the religious and psychological symbolism of the novel.

James R. Giles, "Religious Alienation and 'Homosexual Consciousness' in *City of the Night* and *Go Tell It on the Mountain,*" *CLA Journal,* 7 (March 1964): 369–380.
Discusses religion and homosexuality in the novels by John Rechy and Baldwin.

Trudier Harris, ed., *New Essays on* Go Tell It on the Mountain (Cambridge, England: Cambridge University Press, 1996).
Collection in which five academics examine Baldwin's novel from various perspectives.

Carol E. Henderson, ed., *James Baldwin's* Go Tell It on the Mountain: *Historical and Critical Essays* (New York: Peter Lang, 2006).
Essays by seven scholars, including the editor, with a selected bibliography of secondary sources.

Louis H. Pratt, *James Baldwin* (Boston: Twayne, 1978).
Examines Baldwin's early works.

—*Jeffrey Coleman*

⌐◦⟨⟨◯⟩⟩◦⟩

Saul Bellow, *Seize the Day*

(New York: Viking, 1956)

Generally recognized as the preeminent American novelist of the third quarter of the twentieth century, Saul Bellow (1915–2005) was born Solomon Bellows in Lachine, Canada, the fourth child of émigrés from Russia. In 1924 the family moved to Chicago. Bellow entered the University of Chicago in 1933 but transferred to Northwestern University in 1935; he pursued a dual major in anthropology and English and graduated with honors in 1937. "I read Marx and Bertrand Russell and Morris R. Cohen; I read the logical positivists. I read Freud and Adler and the Gestalt psychologists and the rest. And I know how a modern man is supposed to think. . . . The fact is there are other deeper motives in a human being." The budding novelist was preparing to explore those motives.

According to Bellow, his first two novels, *Dangling Man* (1944) and *The Victim* (1947), "are well made. . . . I accepted a Flaubertian standard . . . one which, in the end, I found repressive." These early examples of "victim literature" had only modest sales. In *The Adventures of Augie March* (1953) Bellow opened up the scope and language of American fiction. He claimed that the novel "represented a rebellion against small public art and the inhibitions it imposed." The work was a Book-of-the-Month Club selection and was on *The New York Times* best-seller list for ten consecutive weeks; it also won the National Book Award, the Friends to Literature Award, and the Certificate of Distinguished Service to Literature. Bellow said that in the novella *Seize the Day* (1956) "I was again under good control. But . . . the liberating effects of *Augie* are apparent to me," especially in the figure of Dr. Tamkin. Although *Seize the Day* seems to be a return to the first two tightly organized "victim" novels, this compact masterpiece also suggests a movement to a new and unexpected transcendence. *Henderson the Rain King* (1959) returns to the wide scope and open style of *The Adventures of Augie March* and enhanced Bellow's reputation among intellectuals. It was followed by the novel *Herzog* (1964), which was made a full selection of the Literary Guild and won the National Book Award; in addition, it became a number-one best seller, remaining on *The New York Times* list for nine months. *Herzog* may be the supreme example in modern American publishing of the best literature—and difficult, introspective literature, at that—being also the most popular.

In 1965 a *Book Week* poll of two hundred writers, critics, and editors declared Bellow to have written "the most distinguished fiction of the 1945–1965 period." Only two novelists had more than one title on the list of twenty "best" novels: Vladimir Nabokov had two, and Bellow four. *Henderson the Rain King* was ranked fifteenth, *The Adventures of Augie March* sixth, *Seize the Day* fifth, and *Herzog* fourth.

Mr. Sammler's Planet (1970) evoked a mixed response. Because it could be interpreted as a conservative attack on the rebelliousness and lawlessness of the late 1960s, it was often judged along partisan political lines. But few could deny its artistic merits, and it won another National Book Award. Bellow said that he put the best of himself into *Humboldt's Gift* (1975), which combines the sprawling plot, huge cast of characters, and humor of *The Adventures of Augie March* with the intellectual protagonist, subjectivity, and philosophical seriousness of *Herzog*, and confronts most directly the final issues: death and the survival of the spirit. *Humboldt's Gift* won the Pulitzer Prize. The following year, Bellow was awarded the Nobel Prize in literature.

As a novella, *Seize the Day* is pared down to the essentials. Bellow maintained that in modern literature "drama has passed from external action to internal movement." In a span of approximately six hours the character and fate of the salesman Tommy Wilhelm—known as Wilhelm Adler before he changed his name in a youthful attempt to become an actor—are revealed. His encounters with others, especially his father and his wife, expose his desperation, his need for help, and his loneliness. Bellow indicated that Tommy's struggle with his father, Dr. Adler, is the main theme: "I examined a man who *insisted* on having a father, who demanded that his father *be* a father to him." But Bellow also described the theme as "the city dweller's attempt to fulfill his needs through strangers." The two statements are complementary. Because his father rejects him, Tommy turns to Dr. Tamkin. Although Tommy suspects, correctly, that Tamkin is little better than a confidence man, he is the only one who offers help and talks about important things—human matters. Tamkin's lecture on "seizing the day" may be a parody of Gestalt therapy; but it is not inappropriate for Tommy, who continually regrets the past and is anxious about the future. As Bellow says, Tamkin "is always somewhere near the truth."

So Tommy Wilhelm is another victim—or is he? At the end Tommy seizes the instant or is seized by it. His elderly father and his own recurrent failures have forced him to confront the question of death. At the funeral of a stranger, Tommy's congested heart finally bursts forth in a flood of emotion: he "sank deeper than sorrow, through torn sobs and cries toward the consummation of his heart's ultimate need." He has found a kind of release, but is it a triumph or a defeat?

To gain a better understanding of *Seize the Day* the student might read *Herzog* and *Humboldt's Gift*, whose protagonists have Tommy's problems with family, women, and money but whose characters are developed at greater length. Another primary source, *Conversations with Saul Bellow* (1994), is an invaluable collection of Bellow's views on literature and life. Daniel Fuchs and Allan Chavkin have studied the manuscript material, which throws considerable light on *Seize the Day* and the workings of the creative mind. In two articles Mark Weinstein examines the two most problematic aspects of *Seize the Day*—Dr. Tamkin and the ending—by placing them in the context of Bellow's other work.

TOPICS FOR DISCUSSION AND RESEARCH

1. During the conservative, gray-flannel-suit 1950s, American fiction was dominated by the theme of alienation. Many of the most memorable protagonists—including Holden Caulfield in J. D. Salinger's *The Catcher in the Rye* (1951),

Hazel Motes in Flannery O'Connor's *Wise Blood* (1952), the nameless narrator of Ralph Ellison's *Invisible Man* (1952), Neil Klugman in Philip Roth's *Goodbye, Columbus* (1959), and Rabbit Angstrom in John Updike's *Rabbit, Run* (1960)—are alienated young men. Is Tommy Wilhelm alienated? Does it make a difference that all of the other protagonists mentioned are younger than Tommy, who is in his mid forties?

2. Bellow frequently complained that too much criticism is content with convenient labels, while the creative artist seeks the density of actual experience: "People who stick labels on you are in the gumming business. . . . What good are these categories?" Is Bellow right, or do literary categories serve a useful purpose? If they do, to what category does *Seize the Day* belong? Is it a tragedy? Even though it observes the Aristotelian unities so important to medieval and French conceptions of tragedy—unity of action, time, and place—it is certainly not a tragedy by any traditional definition. But if Arthur Miller's play *Death of a Salesman* (1949), about the bewildered, well-intentioned, unsuccessful traveling salesman Willy Loman, can be referred to as a modern, middle-class tragedy, why not the story of the salesman Tommy Wilhelm?

3. Popular American fiction, as perhaps best exemplified by the Horatio Alger novels, has often stressed the pursuit and attainment of the American dream. But that tradition has called into existence its negative reverse image. In Theodore Dreiser's *An American Tragedy* (1925) and F. Scott Fitzgerald's *The Great Gatsby* (1925), for example, Clyde Griffiths and Jay Gatsby are destroyed by their pursuit of the American dream; in *Seize the Day* Tommy Wilhelm left his family, college, and medical career to pursue fame and fortune in Hollywood—and failed. Does placing *Seize the Day* into the same category as *An American Tragedy* and *The Great Gatsby* help to illuminate it? Is some other category more helpful? Or are these categories simply critical games, as Bellow believed?

4. It may be rewarding to study how Bellow achieves his effects. Consider, for example, his handling of point of view. Much of the action takes place within Tommy's mind; the reader shares his deepest thoughts and feelings, and this understanding leads to sympathy for him. (Bellow once said, "I can sympathize with Wilhelm but I can't respect him.") But the narrator often rises above Tommy's thoughts to become impersonal, objective, and ironic, revealing truths about Tommy that Tommy does not suspect. Significantly, this ironic, complex point of view was absent from the earliest version of the story. Finally, the narrative occasionally switches to Dr. Adler's point of view to present a completely condemnatory perspective on Tommy. By thus sliding subtly from the subjective to the ironic-objective to the condemnatory point of view and back again, the narrative presents a well-rounded picture of the protagonist and complicates the reader's response. The student might take one aspect of Tommy—for example, his appearance, as described in the opening sentence of the novella—and compare how it is seen from the subjective, objective-ironic, and condemnatory points of view.

5. Carefully developed image patterns also contribute to the meaning and emotional impact of the book. Largely absent in the earliest version, water imagery

runs throughout *Seize the Day*. It is introduced subtly in the opening paragraph—"sank and sank," "billowed," "like sails." It soon becomes more explicit. Tommy loves the beautiful line from John Milton's "Lycidas" (1638): "Sunk though he be beneath the wat'ry floor." Tommy is a drowning man emotionally, which is why it is funny when Dr. Adler prescribes hydrotherapy as a cure. The water imagery culminates in the final paragraph: "the heavy sea-like music came up to his ears. . . . He heard it and sank deeper than sorrow, through torn sobs and cries toward the consummation of his heart's ultimate need." What other image patterns run through the novella? How do they help to unify the book and deepen its meaning? How does it complicate matters to consider that Milton's line in "Lycidas" occurs in the concluding context of resurrection?

6. A comparison of the book with the 1986 movie version of *Seize the Day* offers fascinating study opportunities. As Bellow said, in *Seize the Day* drama has turned away from external action to internal movement. Does the movie capture this internal movement? Does Robin Williams become Tommy Wilhelm? Or are the two media largely independent of each other, with different resources and different aims? A careful comparison should highlight the virtues of the novella and, perhaps, its limitations.

RESOURCES

Primary Works

Conversations with Saul Bellow, edited by Gloria L. Cronin and Ben Siegel (Jackson: University Press of Mississippi, 1994).
A collection of Bellow's interviews that is helpful in understanding his views on literature and life.

Herzog (New York: Viking, 1964).
Bellow's sixth and most popular novel, whose mature protagonist deals with many of the same problems as Tommy Wilhelm.

Humboldt's Gift (New York: Viking, 1975).
Bellow's eighth novel, which deals with the plight of the artist in America, the question of death, and the spirit's survival.

Bibliography

Gloria L. Cronin and Blaine H. Hall, *Saul Bellow: An Annotated Bibliography,* second edition (New York: Garland, 1987).
A comprehensive collection of primary materials from 1941 to 1985, and the most comprehensive compilation of secondary materials from 1944 to 1986.

Biography

James Atlas, *Bellow* (New York: Random House, 2000).
An indispensable work. The most thorough biography, it illuminates the author's life with new material, relates the life to the art, and is beautifully written.

Criticism

Allan Chavkin, "'The Hollywood Thread' and the First Draft of Saul Bellow's *Seize the Day*," *Studies in the Novel,* 14, 1 (1982): 82–93.
A detailed description of the relationship between the earliest stages of *Seize the Day* and the final novella.

John J. Clayton, *Saul Bellow: In Defense of Man* (Bloomington: Indiana University Press, 1968; revised, 1979).
Studies the psychological patterns of Bellow's fiction.

Daniel Fuchs, *Saul Bellow: Vision and Revision* (Durham, N.C.: Duke University Press, 1984).
Demonstrates that a careful study of the manuscripts illuminates a reading of the novels.

Michael P. Kramer, ed., *New Essays on* Seize the Day (Cambridge, England: Cambridge University Press, 1998).
Six essays that reveal recent thinking about the novella.

Keith Opdahl, *The Novels of Saul Bellow: An Introduction* (University Park: Pennsylvania State University Press, 1967).
Defines the spiritual quest for transcendence as the goal of Bellow's heroes.

Mark Weinstein, "Bellow's Endings," in *Saul Bellow: A Mosaic,* edited by L. H. Goldman, Gloria L. Cronin, and Ada Aharoni (New York: Peter Lang, 1992), pp. 87–95.
Places the ending of *Seize the Day* in the context of Bellow's recurrent pattern of endings, suggesting that it is more of a triumph than a defeat.

Weinstein, "Bellow's Imagination-Instructors," *Saul Bellow Journal,* 2, no. 1 (1982): 19–22.
Places Tamkin in the context of a recurrent figure in Bellow's fiction.

—Mark Weinstein

Ray Bradbury, *Fahrenheit 451*

(New York: Ballantine, 1953)

In 2004 the National Endowment for the Arts awarded the Medal of Arts to Ray Bradbury (1920–), citing him as "the greatest living American writer of science fiction." Bradbury, however, has characterized his writing as fantasy, which he calls "the art of the impossible." Science fiction, "the art of the possible," he claims to have written only once, in *Fahrenheit 451* (1953).

Born in Waukegan, Illinois, Bradbury had a lifelong love affair with libraries. He recalls "smelling the books like imported spices, drunk on them before I even read them." Libraries, he believes, could be the solution to many of the world's social problems: "if we insure that by the end of its sixth year every child in every country can live in libraries to learn almost by osmosis, then our drug, street-gang, rape, and murder scores will suffer themselves near zero."

Periodic waves of hysteria throughout history horrified Bradbury. He "wept" when he learned at the age of nine that the ancient library of Alexandria had been burned. He suffered when Adolf Hitler burned books: "I felt it as keenly, please forgive me, as his killing a human, for in the long sum of history they are one and the same flesh." Then, during the Second Red Scare, Senator Joseph McCarthy ruined lives with his interrogations of writers and other artists. In 1952 Arthur Miller responded to this assault with his play *The Crucible,* changing the setting to 1692 Salem, Massachusetts, and suspected Communists to suspected witches. Bradbury, who traces his ancestry to a Salem woman accused of witchcraft, was also destined to protest this sort of loss of reason stemming from a fear of ideas.

Five Bradbury stories eventually merged into *Fahrenheit 451.* In "Bright Phoenix" book burners arrive at a library to find that readers have memorized the books. In "The Exiles" famous characters are sent to Mars to avoid being burned on Earth. "Usher II" describes book burners in an Edgar Allan Poe–inspired hell. Bradbury based "The Pedestrian" on a personal experience: questioned by the police when he was out for a stroll one night, Bradbury imagined a future in which walking was outlawed. Finally, in "The Fireman," which is set in the future, the title character does not put out fires—he starts them: he burns books for a living. One day, when he encounters the rebellious teen Clarisse, he realizes that he is not only wasting his own life but also ruining everyone else's lives. Driven to turn these stories into a novel, Bradbury rented a typewriter in the basement of the UCLA library and wrote *Fahrenheit 451* in nine days.

After the fireman Montag's vacuous wife, Mildred, attempts suicide, two handymen come to detoxify her; they treat her as if she were a carpet to be cleaned. The "family" to which she returns is not Montag but strangers on wall-sized television screens with whom she converses all day about nothing. Mildred's opposite is Clarisse, an oddly forthright girl who asks Montag if he is happy. Later, Montag witnesses a woman choosing to be burned alive with her books, and his metamorphosis begins. He says to his wife as he opens his first stolen book, "Let's see what this is." He soon realizes what he has missed, but he knows that what he has in his hands cannot last. Finally, he discovers a way to save books: memorize them, burn them, then pass them on orally until the world regains its sanity.

Students researching *Fahrenheit 451* should begin with Bradbury's own explanations of his life and influences. The interviews in Steven L. Angelis's *Conversations with Ray Bradbury* (2004) are an excellent resource, as are his two forewords and 1967 introduction to *Fahrenheit 451* that are included in the fiftieth-anniversary edition (2003). Sam Weller's authorized biography contains detailed accounts of Bradbury's life, his beliefs, and the genesis of each major book. Bradbury has published only two other novels, *Dandelion Wine* (1957) and *Something Wicked This Way Comes* (1962); but he wrote more than four hundred short stories. One of the most anthologized stories, and a good comparison piece to *Fahrenheit 451,* is "There Will Come Soft Rains," in which the world has just been destroyed by atomic war. Although in this society literature was revered—poetry is programmed into the space-age house—there is no one left to hear it.

TOPICS FOR DISCUSSION AND RESEARCH

1. When Bradbury was fifteen, Hitler ordered "un-German" books to be burned; in 1953 McCarthy was accusing innocent Americans of being Communists; and the Soviet Union was a totalitarian society under the dictatorship of Joseph Stalin. In this context, the future Bradbury created in *Fahrenheit 451* was not unthinkable; the novel is a cautionary tale designed to prevent such a future. Students might research the political climate of the 1950s to gain a better understanding of Bradbury's fears. Were they justified? Are they justified today?

2. Bradbury's dystopia more closely resembles that in Aldous Huxley's *Brave New World* (1932) than the one in George Orwell's *Nineteen Eighty-Four* (1949) because of its mindless, pleasure-seeking culture: the government takes pains to ensure that everyone is happy. Montag's boss, Beatty, points out that there is almost no need for firemen to burn books any more, because no one wants to take the time and mental energy required to read them; and Mildred overdoses on a drug similar to Huxley's Soma. In *"Fahrenheit 451* as Social Criticism" (2007) David Mogen describes Montag's world as one in which "the American Dream has turned nightmare." Bradbury, who had been asked over the years to comment on his 1950s prophecy, said in 1995 that his imagined world "is fast approaching ground zero . . . like . . . a brain-meltdown rocket." Weller's biography includes a detailed exploration of Bradbury's realized predictions, particularly of television's effects. Students might make their own assessments by comparing contemporary culture and society to those of *Fahrenheit 451*.

3. Bradbury's epigraph to *Fahrenheit 451*, taken from the Nobel Prize–winning Spanish poet Juan Ramón Jiménez, asks readers to be brave and to think for themselves, no matter the cost: "If they give you ruled paper, write the other way." America of the 1950s was the very picture of conformity. Those who went against the mainstream—women choosing careers over marriage and motherhood, employees questioning labor practices, anyone challenging authority—tended to be outcasts. Society offered wealth, convenience, and comfort, but those who did not follow the social rules, it seemed, were not in the club. Jonathan R. Eller and William F. Touponce assert that the even more comfortable and convenient world of *Fahrenheit 451* "produced not liberation, but further alienation." Those who accept the society, like Mildred, are suicidal without even knowing it, and those who question it, like Montag, are made outcasts at the first glimmer of deviation. Resembling a Franz Kafka protagonist, Montag is turned in by his wife and arrested by his boss. At the end Montag and his outcast friends envision a world where the memory of ideas will lead to "the healing of the nations." What other twentieth-century protagonists feel alienated by their society? In what way does their alienation mirror Montag's? How are their conflicts resolved?

EL CAMINO COLLEGE LIBRARY

4. Bradbury described coming up from the basement of the UCLA library after a nine-day marathon of writing *Fahrenheit 451* "dripping with hyperbole, metaphors and similes." The primary metaphor, fire, is a force of both good and evil: useful for heat and fuel, and dangerous as an agent of death and destruction. At the end, after the city is destroyed by fire, the group of book memorizers are the phoenix who will rise out of the ashes and carry the words. Students might identify and trace these and other metaphors throughout the story and determine how they illuminate the themes.

5. Ultimately, *Fahrenheit 451* is a plea for the value of the written word. Literary allusions, direct and indirect, abound. Montag reads Matthew Arnold's poems "Dover Beach" (1867) aloud to a group of women: "And we are here on a darkling plain . . . Where ignorant armies clash by night." He wants them to wake up and see what has been taken from them; instead, one woman breaks down, reaffirming to the others that literature brings grief and should be left in its assigned hell. Montag suggests to Mildred, "Maybe the books can get us half out of the cave"—one of many allusions to Plato's "Allegory of the Cave." George E. Conner analyses these references to Plato, while Peter Sisario considers the many biblical allusions in the novel. Students will benefit from identifying such allusions and discussing their bearing on the overall meaning of the work.

RESOURCES

Primary Works

Steven L. Angelis, ed., *Conversations with Ray Bradbury* (Jackson: University Press of Mississippi, 2004).
A collection of interviews spanning the years 1948 to 2002 that includes a brief biography.

Bradbury Stories: One Hundred of His Most Celebrated Tales (New York: Morrow, 2003).
Selected from Bradbury's nearly five hundred stories. This collection includes several of the stories that led to *Fahrenheit 451*, such as "Usher II" and "The Pedestrian."

Fahrenheit 451: 50th Anniversary Edition (New York: Simon & Schuster, 2003).
Includes indispensable forewords written by the author in 1967, 1993, and 2003.

Bibliography

The Center for Ray Bradbury Studies, Indiana University and Purdue University, Indianapolis <http://www.iupui.edu/~crbs/> [accessed 28 September 2009].
Includes many writings—even poetry—by and about Bradbury, as well as links and lists.

Lance Hawvermale, *Ray Bradbury: To the Canon by Rocketship: A Survey of the Critical Scholarship* <http://www.erinorourke.com/bradbury.html> [accessed 30 November 2009].
An excellent article with a link to a bibliography of fifty-two sources.

Eric Walker, "Other Ray Bradbury Resources," in *Great Science Fiction and Fantasy Works. Science-Fiction & Fantasy Literature: A Critical List with Discussions. Science-Fiction and Fantasy Books by Ray Bradbury,* The Owlcroft Company (15 August 2008) <http://greatsfandf.com/AUTHORS/RayBradbury.php> [accessed 30 November 2009].
A small but excellent list of resources, including a link to the Hawvermale essay.

Biography

Jonathan R. Eller and William F. Toupounce, *Ray Bradbury: The Life of Fiction* (Kent, Ohio & London: Kent State University Press, 2004).
Merges biography and criticism, including much about author's writing process; stresses "the crucial role of metaphor in his thematics."

Sam Weller, *The Bradbury Chronicles: The Life of Ray Bradbury* (New York: HarperCollins, 2005).
The authorized and best biography.

Criticism

Harold Bloom, ed., *Ray Bradbury's* Fahrenheit 451 (New York: Chelsea House, 2008).
Includes Bloom's favorite essay, Susan Spenser's comparison to Walter Miller's 1960 postapocalyptic novel *A Canticle for Leibowitz.* Bloom forgives what he sees as Bradbury's occasional imperfections because of the solution of memorization in the novel: "If you cannot read Shakespeare and his peers, then you will forfeit memory, and if you cannot remember, then you will not be able to think."

Bloom, ed., *Ray Bradbury's* Fahrenheit 451 (New York: Chelsea House, 2007).
Eight essays, including those by Sisario and Mogen. Bloom's annotated bibliography provides a good source for further study of these topics.

Katie de Koster, ed., *Readings of* Fahrenheit 451 (San Diego: Greenhaven, 2000).
Divided into three sections: "Symbol and Metaphor," "Dystopia and Utopia," and "A Reflection of the Real World."

Orville Prescott, *"Fahrenheit 451," New York Times,* 21 October 1953.
A review of the novel. Prescott wrote that Bradbury's "world . . . bears many alarming resemblances to our own."

—Susanne B. Drennan

⌐◦≫◦

Richard Brautigan, *Trout Fishing in America*

(San Francisco: Four Seasons Foundation, 1967)

Richard Brautigan (1935–1984) is considered both a Beat writer, because of his association with the San Francisco Beat movement of the late 1950s and early 1960s, and a hippie writer, because of his association with the San Francisco counter culture of the late 1960s and early 1970s. Born and raised in the Pacific Northwest, Brautigan moved to San Francisco in 1956 to realize his dream of becoming a writer. The Beat movement, although waning, was then still in evidence throughout the city's North Beach district; Brautigan, who always maintained he was not a Beat, was good friends with many of them and was often featured at their poetry readings. He is included in the historic photograph *The Last Gathering of the Beats,* by Larry Keenan, taken in 1965 in front of the City Lights Bookstore. Brautigan was not actively involved in the counter-culture movement, either, although he was often seen at its edges—observing, talking, or handing out broadside printings of his early poetry to tourists stepping down from the Gray Line "Hippie Hop" tour buses in the Haight-Ashbury district. Edward Halsey Foster suggests that Brautigan might best be seen as a bridge between the ebbing Beat Generation and the emerging counter-culture movement.

Brautigan wrote *Trout Fishing in America* in 1961, most of it during a camping trip with his first wife, Virginia Alder, and their daughter, Ianthe, in Idaho's Stanley Basin. He actually fished the streams he mentions in the novel, such as Silver Creek, Big Smokey Creek, Big Pine Creek, and Yellow Belly Lake Creek. Published in 1967, the novel quickly captured the attention of readers and critics looking for some sense of the counter-culture climate in San Francisco. More than one hundred thousand copies were sold initially; today, sales approach three million. Although it includes descriptions and discussions of fishing for trout, the book is not really about fishing. Instead, it is an examination of the American pastoral and its demise in the face of commercialism, environmental degradation, and social decay.

Trout Fishing in America typifies Brautigan's quirky, idiosyncratic, yet easy-to-read prose style: an offbeat combination of imagination; strange and detailed observation; a detached, anonymous first-person point of view; and episodic narrative structure filled with vivid, unconventional images powered by whimsy and metaphor. Critics have compared Brautigan to earlier American writers such as Henry David Thoreau, Mark Twain, and Ernest Hemingway while also referring to *Trout Fishing in America* as one of the first Postmodernist novels.

The late 1960s and early 1970s were Brautigan's heyday; his other best-known works—the poetry collection *The Pill versus the Springhill Mine Disaster* (1968) and his only short-story collection, *Revenge of the Lawn: Stories, 1962–1970* (1971)—also come from this period. Brautigan's later books combine and experiment with established literary genres. For example, *The Hawkline Monster*

(1974) is subtitled *A Gothic Western; Willard and His Bowling Trophies* (1975) is designated *A Perverse Mystery;* and *Sombrero Fallout* (1976) carries the subtitle *A Japanese Novel.* Critics met these books with diminished enthusiasm, put off by Brautigan's apparent preoccupation with sadness and death and refusal to continue writing in his earlier, more-humorous vein. Additionally, the political climate changed in the 1970s; conservative academics dismissed Brautigan's work as "literature for kids," while, as Carl Brucker and Farhat M. Iftekharuddin note, critics from the political Left decried his "lack of militancy." At the time of his death on 14 September 1984 Brautigan was largely ignored—or, worse, denigrated by critics and readers who considered his work trivial or naive.

Brautigan published ten novels, ten poetry collections, a short-story collection, and a spoken-word record album; a collection of previously unpublished poetry and short fiction and another novel appeared posthumously. While most literary careers continue on their trajectories after the authors' deaths, a steadily increasing cadre of scholars, researchers, publishers, readers, and fans have been attracted to Brautigan's writing or see him as central to study of the 1960s. This interest is international, as his works have been translated into more than twenty languages. There is also a large collector and rare-book market for Brautigan's long out-of-print books, and many have been reprinted by specialty presses. *Trout Fishing in America* remains his best-known, and is often acknowledged as his most inspired, work.

Students may wish to begin their study of *Trout Fishing in America* by getting a deeper sense of Brautigan's style. *Revenge of the Lawn,* which includes "The Lost Chapters of *Trout Fishing in America:* Rembrandt Creek and Carthage Sink," is a good starting place; *The Pill versus the Springhill Mine Disaster* traces the development of Brautigan's unique use of simile and metaphor, which he also employs in his fiction. Among secondary sources, Jay Boyer, Marc Chénetier, Edward Halsey Foster, and Terence Malley provide helpful overviews, analyses, and critiques, offering extended attention to *Trout Fishing in America.* A definitive Brautigan biography is forthcoming from William Hjortsberg; in the meantime, Ianthe Brautigan's insightful memoir of her father is a useful source of biographical information, and Keith Abbott's memoir has served as a de facto biography. John F. Barber's *Richard Brautigan: Essays on the Writings and Life* (2006) collects reflections on the memory and literary legacy of Brautigan. The *Brautigan Bibliography and Archive* website provides the most complete collection of bibliographical and biographical information available.

TOPICS FOR DISCUSSION AND RESEARCH

1. *Trout Fishing in America* marks Brautigan's first use of his seemingly impersonal and uninvolved narrator reporting a variety of observations and experiences regarding nature, the play between reality and imagination, and characters' mixed feelings. The result is a web of qualifying and contradictory impressions, an ambivalence on which Brautigan calls for both the creation of an art form—his novel, with its distinctive style and voice—and a simultaneous celebration and critique of the so-called American myth as both an ideal

and an evolving culture. For example, Brautigan's narrator describes fishing in pristine trout streams simply as "nice" and immediately moves on to discuss fishing in polluted waters where the only fish to be seen are dead ones floating on the surface. An ideal pastoral, fishing the streams of America, becomes an unemotional commentary on the effects wrought on the American wilderness by an ever-expanding civilization. Students might examine other ways in which this unspoken tension, ambivalence, and subtle balancing of opposing ideas plays out throughout the novel; Kent Bales's article will be helpful in this endeavor.

2. It is easy to read *Trout Fishing in America* as a novel that looks at society through its relationship with the natural environment. The narrator spends a good portion of his time in or alongside trout streams and rivers, searching for the perfect example of pastoral nature but finding instead a sense of what has been forgotten or lost. The real is often juxtaposed and contrasted with the ideal. Students might analyze scenes that illustrate human beings having distanced themselves from a wholesome connection with their natural environment.

3. A central notion of the English Romantic poets, especially William Wordsworth, is the power of imagination to provide an immersive memory of past experiences and thus to enable one to escape an undesirable reality. Brautigan makes imaginative escape a major theme of *Trout Fishing in America*. The escape is mostly triggered by language, which Brautigan uses in an almost formulaic fashion. For example, he often creates a simile, likening two objects; but in the course of a few sentences the first object becomes the second. For example, an overcrowded campground becomes a cheap hotel; a white staircase on a hillside becomes a trout stream. Students might analyze other examples of linguistically forged escape in *Trout Fishing in America*. In what ways does Brautigan create an alternative world? How does this world operate? What might Brautigan be suggesting about art itself with his novel? What elements of Romanticism are evident in the book and to what effect?

4. *Trout Fishing in America* challenges the definition of a novel; students might discuss whether or not it should be classified as such. Does it have a central character? If it is not a novel, into what genre does it best fall and why? Also, what aspects of the work make it Postmodern? Students might locate the metafictional devices in it and discuss their purposes.

5. Brautigan's poetry and fiction are filled with allusions. Students might research the historical and literary allusions in *Trout Fishing in America* and analyze their importance to its central concerns. William L. Stull's article will help with this topic.

6. One author to whose work Brautigan alludes in the novel is the Depression-era novelist Nathanael West, who is famous for his use of the grotesque. *Trout Fishing in America* is full of cripples—physical, emotional, creative, and psychopathic—whose worlds are trampled down, depleted, and garbage filled. Students might analyze such characters as "Trout Fishing in America Shorty" or the "Kool-Aid Wino." What are their functions in the novel?

RESOURCES

Primary Works

Revenge of the Lawn: Stories, 1962–1970 (New York: Simon & Schuster, 1971).
The only collection of Brautigan's stories and perhaps the best example of the author at the top of his craft, especially with regard to his unique use of imagination. The book includes "The Lost Chapters of *Trout Fishing in America:* Rembrandt Creek and Carthage Sink."

The Pill versus the Springhill Mine Disaster (San Francisco: Four Seasons Foundation, 1968).
Collection that illustrates Brautigan's often-repeated comment that he wrote poetry to learn to write a sentence so that he could then write novels. Many potential novels appear here in the space of only a few words.

Bibliography

John F. Barber, *Brautigan Bibliography and Archive* <http://www.brautigan.net> [accessed 24 September 2009].
A definitive, comprehensive online resource dealing with Brautigan's life and writings.

Biography

Keith Abbott, *Downstream from* Trout Fishing in America: *A Memoir of Richard Brautigan* (Santa Barbara, Cal.: Capra Press, 1989).
Recollections of experiences Abbott shared with Brautigan in San Francisco and Montana from 1966 to 1984. The book includes anecdotes and insights into Brautigan's life and works and concludes with comments on his writing and place in American literature.

Ianthe Brautigan, *You Can't Catch Death: A Daughter's Memoir* (New York: St. Martin's Press, 2000).
Book in which Brautigan's only child comes to grips with her father's death and provides anecdotes and information regarding his life and work.

Criticism

Kent Bales, "Fishing the Ambivalence; or, A Reading of 'Trout Fishing in America,'" *Western Humanities Review,* 29 (Winter 1975): 29–42.
Concludes that Brautigan skillfully handles the deliberate ambivalences that help to develop the theme of the novel.

John F. Barber, ed., *Richard Brautigan: Essays on the Writings and Life* (Jefferson, N.C.: McFarland, 2007).
Thirty-two essays that provide important reflections about the memory and contributions of Brautigan. The work includes previously unpublished photographs by Erik Weber and paintings and sketches by Kenn Davis.

Jay Boyer, *Richard Brautigan* (Boise, Idaho: Boise State University Press, 1987).
Provides an overview of Brautigan as a Western writer and interpretations of his novels.

Carl Brucker and Farhat M. Iftekharuddin, "Richard Brautigan 1935–1984," in
   Beacham's Encyclopedia of Popular Fiction, volume 1, edited by Kirk H. Beetz
   (Osprey, Fla.: Beacham, 1996), pp. 222–227.
Discusses Brautigan's life, publishing history, and critical reception. The authors
contend that being linked to the hippies limited Brautigan's appeal and that he
steadily lost readers as fashions changed in the 1970s.

Marc Chénetier, *Richard Brautigan* (London: Methuen, 1983).
Argues that Brautigan's dismissal by American critics has less to do with the quality of his writing than with the nature of the scholarship applied to it. Chénetier
says that Brautigan's work falls outside the scope of traditional American scholarship and that it seeks to liberate fiction from the premises on which traditional
mythology is based. He also attempts to provide a formula for a unified reading
of Brautigan's works.

John Clayton, "Richard Brautigan: The Politics of Woodstock," in *New American*
   Review, no. 11, edited by Theodore Solotaroff (New York: Simon & Schus-
   ter, 1971), pp. 56–68.
Equates Brautigan's work with the politics of the American counterculture.

John Cusatis, "Richard Brautigan," in *Greenwood Encyclopedia of American Poets*
   and Poetry, edited by Jeffrey Gray, James McCorkle, and Mary McAleer
   Balkun (Westport, Conn.: Greenwood Press, 2005), pp. 187–188.
Discusses Brautigan's stylistic and thematic devices, such as his preoccupation
with time, that figure into *Trout Fishing in America*.

Edward Halsey Foster, *Richard Brautigan* (Boston: Twayne, 1983).
Reconstructs the social and cultural circumstances surrounding Brautigan's rise
to popularity and analyzes his work through 1980. Foster notes that Brautigan's
writing offers a bridge between the Beats and the next generation of American
writers.

Thomas Hearron, "Escape through Imagination in 'Trout Fishing in America,'"
   Critique: Studies in Modern Fiction, 16, 1 (1974): 25–31.
Sees the novel as "firmly rooted in the American tradition" and claims that its
central point is the notion of "imaginative escape."

Terence Malley, *Richard Brautigan* (New York: Warner, 1972).
The first critical survey of Brautigan's work through 1971. Chapter 6, "Toward a
Vision of America," deals with *Trout Fishing in America*.

James M. Mellard, "Brautigan's 'Trout Fishing in America,'" in his *The Exploded*
   Form: The Modernist Novel in America (Urbana: University of Illinois Press,
   1980).
Discusses *Trout Fishing in America* as an exemplar of the sophisticated phase of
the Modernist novel and as the center of late Modernist fiction.

Joseph Mills, *Reading Richard Brautigan's* Trout Fishing in America (Boise, Idaho: Boise State University Press, 1998).
The lengthiest critical assessment to date of Brautigan's novel.

Kenneth Seib, "*Trout Fishing in America:* Brautigan's Funky Fishing Yarn," *Critique: Studies in Modern Fiction,* 13, 2 (1971): 63–71.
Comments on Brautigan's style, noting his apparent intent to project disillusionment with the American dream.

William L. Stull, "Richard Brautigan's *Trout Fishing in America:* Notes of a Native Son," *American Literature,* 56 (March 1984): 68–80.
Argues that the novel is far deeper and darker than early critics imagined and that it offers a rich network of references to classic and contemporary literary works and their authors and traces of the cultural context in which it was written.

David L. Vanderwerken, "*Trout Fishing in America* and the American Tradition," *Critique: Studies in Modern Fiction,* 16, no. 1 (1974): 32–40.
Argues that the novel pursues a traditional theme: "the gap between ideal America and real America."

—*John F. Barber*

⟳⟳⟳

James Dickey, *Deliverance*
(New York: Houghton Mifflin, 1970)

James Dickey (1923–1997) was born in Atlanta, Georgia, and educated in the public schools there. He played football during his first semester at Clemson University in South Carolina, but in December 1942 he left college to enlist in the United States Army Air Corps. After mixed success in flight-training school, he was deployed to the Pacific Theater in World War II. In poems and conversations he often recorded the slim odds for survival and regretted the loss of life in the war zone. One strategy for Dickey's individual psychological survival was his voracious reading of books of poetry and other literary works during the time he was not involved in combat missions.

When Dickey returned to the United States after World War II, he completed his B.A. and M.A. degrees in English at Vanderbilt University. After spending several years working for various advertising agencies (while writing poetry on weekends and at night), he was awarded a Guggenheim Fellowship to pursue independent study. He eventually settled into a distinguished twenty-eight-year teaching career at the University of South Carolina.

Dickey always believed that his foremost commitment was to the art of poetry. In 1966 he won the National Book Award for his poetry volume *Buckdancer's Choice* (1965), and his *Poems 1957–1967* (1967) received highly favorable reviews. A few of Dickey's poems set in nature, including "Fog Envelops the

Animals," "In the Mountain Tent," and "On the Coosawattee," foreshadow events and scenes in his first novel, *Deliverance* (1970).

Dickey wrote *Deliverance* during the late 1960s, and it became a national best seller. Two years after its publication, Warner Brothers released the film version. Sales of Dickey's second and third novels—which, like *Deliverance,* involve a journey, a rite of passage, and a struggle to survive—were not as impressive as those of *Deliverance. Alnilam* (1987) takes place early in World War II: Frank Cahill learns that his son, Joel, has crashed in a training accident at a North Carolina military base. Though he is blind, Cahill travels to the site to try to unravel the various mysteries of Joel's activities and presumed death. He learns that among the cadets Joel was the heroic leader of a secret cult that focused on the mysticism of flying. Dickey considered *Alnilam* his best novel, but for many readers and critics it was confusing and too long. *To the White Sea* (1993) is much shorter and easier to read, even though the main character becomes more and more unappealing as the story progresses. Air Corps Sergeant Muldrow is shot down over Tokyo during the final months of World War II and survives through courage, cunning, and increasingly brutal deeds.

Deliverance remains an engaging, suspenseful story, full of fast-paced mystery and beautiful prose describing the natural environment that will soon be destroyed by a power company's dam. It frequently appears on lists of the top one hundred novels of the twentieth century. Ronald Baughman's *Understanding James Dickey* (1985), Richard J. Calhoun and Robert W. Hill's *James Dickey* (1983), and William B. Thesing's *Reading, Learning, Teaching James Dickey* (2009) each devote a chapter of analysis to *Deliverance.* Five lively and perceptive essays in William B. Thesing and Theda Wrede's collection, *The Way We Read James Dickey: Critical Approaches for the Twenty-First Century* (2009), employ anecdotal, ecofeminist, and gender criticism to analyze the novel and the film. The most recent and thoroughly researched biography to date is Henry Hart's *James Dickey: The World as a Lie* (2000). *The Society for the Study of Southern Literature Bibliography* website and issues of the *James Dickey Newsletter* provide the most up-to-date secondary bibliographies.

TOPICS FOR DISCUSSION AND RESEARCH

1. Survival in nature against overwhelming odds is the main theme of *Deliverance.* The narrative thus fits into a long American literary tradition of adventure or journeys-into-the-wilderness stories. Students might consider the extent to which the forces of nature work against the struggle of the four men to survive in the remote Georgia wilderness and what changes these forces effect in the characters.

2. Critics have argued that the four major characters can be viewed either as foils to one another or as different aspects of Dickey's own complex and multifaceted personality. By focusing on the growth in strength, courage, and awareness of the narrator, Ed Gentry, the novel fits into the bildungsroman tradition, in which a young hero is educated about the starker realities of human experience and develops in the process. At the outset, Ed embodies the theme of the post–World War II American man's discontent, alienation, ennui, and unfulfillment

in his urban job. He works at an advertising agency that exploits women as sex objects in a sales campaign, and he worships the masculine physical strength and daring leadership of his friend, Lewis Medlock, who suggests and plans the canoe trip into the wilderness. Two other buddies, Drew Ballinger and Bobby Trippe, set out on the weekend outing. Drew is a sensitive soul who shows an aesthetic side with his love of music and guitar-playing skill; Bobby is cynical, overweight, and unhappy with the physical discomforts of the river trip. Students might discuss how particular characters serve as foils for each other and analyze the reasons why Ed's will and wisdom surpass those of his friends. Keen Butterworth's "The Savage Mind: James Dickey's *Deliverance*" (1996) sheds light on this inquiry.

3. Early scenes in the book depict the irreparable misunderstandings and preju- dices that exist in interactions of city and country—specifically, between the four Atlanta suburbanites and the mountain folk. On the first day the canoe- ists argue with the locals over directions and payment for shuttle services. The situation really turns ugly when Ed and Bobby step off the river to rest on the second day of the journey and are confronted by two menacing strangers in the deep woods. In one of the most shocking descriptions of homosexual rape in twentieth-century literature, the "rednecks," armed with guns and knives, strip, humiliate, and sexually assault Bobby; tied to a tree, Ed is forced to witness the event in terror and helplessness. Students might consider the economic, social, and psychological conditions that so often contribute to such intimidation and violence in Southern literature. Also, is the wilderness setting entirely horrific for the city dwellers, or does it serve as a beneficent force, as well? Is one or the other aspect more significant?

4. Lewis and Drew quietly arrive on the rape scene in their canoe, and Lewis kills one of the mountain men with his bow and arrow; the other escapes. Debate, mystery, pursuit, and resolution unfold through the second half of the novel. Issues of law come to the reader's attention as the four men debate what to do with the attacker's body. Believing that a fair trial will be impossible in a local courtroom, Lewis forcefully argues for immediate burial and silence. Only Drew dissents: he has a conscience and believes in the rule of law. Ed assumes leadership of the group after Lewis is seriously injured in the rapids and Drew is shot in the head and killed by an unknown assailant. Ed demon- strates remarkable courage in climbing a cliff and killing the presumed second criminal with an arrow. Students should consider how quickly conventional moral values can deteriorate to the "law of the jungle" in war or other unfa- miliar, chaotic situations. What other novels or short stories depict such moral deterioration, and in what ways do these stories resemble *Deliverance?*

5. By the end of the river journey, there are no clear winners. Ed has grown in his knowledge of the darker sides of human existence, but he is haunted by guilt and discontented with his lifestyle; Drew's wife views her husband's death as senseless; Lewis loses his male bravado and confidence; and Bobby feels degraded and suffers various business failures. Given the four characters' final outcomes, students might address the question: where is the *deliverance* mentioned in the title and epigraph of the book?

6. Dickey also emphasizes the theme of the continual threat to the natural environment. On the first day of the canoe trip the men observe with disgust the pollution that a chicken-processing plant has poured into the pure river; at the end of the journey they see the preparations for the power company's dam project that will ruin the river's vitality and force the relocation even of the coffins buried in country churchyards. Apparently, only greedy real-estate developers will gain any advantages from the rape and desecration of the land. Readers might consider to what degree Dickey, an avid hunter, seriously sought to promote environmental values in his life and writings, particularly *Deliverance*.

7. The personal and public consequences of the movie version of *Deliverance* should not be underestimated. Biographers agree that the fame and wealth that the film brought Dickey had lasting ill effects on both his personal and creative life. Furthermore, to this day the tune "Dueling Banjos" that is performed in the movie suggests images of the dangers lurking in remote wilderness settings and of hill people who are ignorant, perverted, and vicious. Students might want to compare differences in the dialogue and presentation of incidents in the novel and the film.

RESOURCES

Primary Works

Crux: The Letters of James Dickey, edited by Matthew J. Bruccoli and Judith S. Baughman (New York: Knopf, 1999).
Includes approximately forty letters that discuss the novel and film versions of *Deliverance*.

The One Voice of James Dickey: His Letters and Life 1970–1997, volume 2, edited by Gordon Van Ness (Columbia: University of Missouri Press, 2005).
Includes more than one hundred references to *Deliverance* as both novel and film.

The Voiced Connections of James Dickey: Interviews and Conversations, edited by Ronald Baughman (Columbia: University of South Carolina Press, 1989).
Includes several lively interviews in which Dickey reacts to the success of *Deliverance*.

The Whole Motion: Collected Poems 1945–1992 (Hanover, N.H.: Wesleyan University Press, 1992).
An expansive volume that includes several nature poems that could be compared to scenes in *Deliverance*.

Bibliography

James Dickey: A Descriptive Bibliography, edited by Matthew J. Bruccoli and Judith S. Baughman (Pittsburgh: University of Pittsburgh Press, 1990).
Lists the appearance of Dickey's works in various publication venues and includes a list of major works about him. The volume also describes a variety of hardbound and paperback versions of *Deliverance*.

The Society for the Study of Southern Literature Bibliography <http://www.missq.msstate.edu/sssl> [accessed 12 October 2009].
Includes more than 75 entries on *Deliverance* and nearly 170 on Dickey.

Biography

Christopher Dickey, *Summer of Deliverance: A Memoir of Father and Son* (New York: Simon & Schuster, 1998).
Candid revelations by Dickey's oldest son of his childhood and behind-the-scenes dramas of the filming of *Deliverance*.

Henry Hart, *James Dickey: The World as a Lie* (New York: Picador, 2000).
The most recent and thorough biography to date, meticulously researched and ultimately negative in its overall assessment of Dickey's life and accomplishments. Hart stresses that the fame of *Deliverance* exacted a high cost in Dickey's personal life.

Criticism

Ronald Baughman, *Understanding James Dickey* (Columbia: University of South Carolina Press, 1985).
Includes a chapter on *Deliverance* that offers a useful introductory guide but is a highly optimistic reading of Ed Gentry's transformation and transcendence.

Keen Butterworth, "The Savage Mind: James Dickey's *Deliverance,*" *Southern Literary Journal,* 28 (Spring 1996): 69–78.
Suggests that the four main characters can be understood to represent various aspects of the psyche.

Richard J. Calhoun and Robert W. Hill, *James Dickey* (Boston: Twayne, 1983).
Includes a chapter on *Deliverance* that stresses neo-Romantic tendencies and the search for transcendence in Dickey's poetry and fiction.

Casey Clabough, *Elements: The Novels of James Dickey* (Macon, Ga.: Mercer University Press, 2002).
Perceptive analyses of the interplay between three Dickey fictional protagonists—Ed Gentry, Joel Cahill, and Sergeant Muldrow—and their natural environments.

James Dickey Newsletter.
Biannual publication of the James Dickey Society, which includes essays, reviews, and updated bibliographic information regarding Dickey and his work. The organization's website is <http://www.jamesdickey.org>.

Robert Kirschten, ed., *Critical Essays on James Dickey* (New York: G. K. Hall, 1994).
Features four critics' views on *Deliverance,* including Carolyn Heilbrun's controversial remarks on Dickey's version of the masculine wilderness in the American novel.

William B. Thesing, *Reading, Learning, Teaching James Dickey* (New York: Peter Lang, 2009).
Includes a chapter on *Deliverance* that offers practical guidelines for confronting the issues in the novel and film and presents Dickey's last public remarks on his adventure tale.

Thesing and Theda Wrede, eds., *The Way We Read James Dickey: Critical Approaches for the Twenty-First Century* (Columbia: University of South Carolina Press, 2009).
Original critical essays on Dickey's works and reputation. Pat Conroy recalls his personal experiences on the Chattooga River; Wrede offers an ecofeminist reading of *Deliverance;* and Ed Madden, Jennifer Schell, and Jennie Lightweis-Goff treat controversial gender issues in the novel and film.

—*William B. Thesing*

Ralph Ellison, *Invisible Man*

(New York: Random House, 1952)

Invisible Man (1952), by Ralph Ellison (1914–1994), which won the National Book Award in 1953, remains one of the most important and influential American novels of the twentieth century and, perhaps, the most influential racially themed American novel of the twentieth century. To say that *Invisible Man* is about race in America is like saying that Herman Melville's *Moby-Dick* (1851) is about whaling—while the statement is not incorrect, it fails to capture the complexity, artistry, and breadth of the work. Even though race is a fine starting point for discussing and analyzing the novel, it should not also be the finish line—if such a place even exists for this novel. As Ellison's unnamed narrator might say, life is about becoming "more human"; and *Invisible Man* attempts to articulate just what that means, in terms much broader and deeper than simply those of black and white.

Named for the writer and philosopher Ralph Waldo Emerson, Ralph Waldo Ellison was born in Oklahoma City, Oklahoma. His grandparents had all been slaves; this connection to slavery is the first of many he shares with the narrator of *Invisible Man*. Ellison's parents grew up in the American Southeast—his mother in Georgia and his father in South Carolina—and they moved their family west to escape the racism and oppression in the early-twentieth-century South. Ellison's earliest artistic love was music; he particularly liked jazz, and the genre heavily influenced his writing both in style and content. Ellison acknowledged T. S. Eliot's use of symbolism and allusion in *The Waste Land* (1922) as instrumental in shifting his artistic focus toward literature.

Initially, Ellison intended to write a novel about an African American pilot in a German prisoner-of-war camp during World War II; though he dispensed with that plot, many of his original themes survive in the published novel. *Invis-*

ible Man began taking shape when Ellison hit on the idea of a nameless narrator who would spend the book describing his invisibility to the rest of the world. As did Ellison, his narrator journeys from humble roots in the South to New York City. He studies at an African American college that Ellison based on Tuskegee University in Alabama, which he himself attended. Along the way the narrator falls into dangerous, sometimes humorous, eye-opening situations that lead him to his conclusion (and beginning); the narrator's physical journey and travails parallel his mental journey toward self-realization. Ellison spent seven years writing the novel—a brief period compared to the forty-two years during which he worked on his next novel, which he did not live to see published.

Ellison published two collections of essays during his lifetime, *Going to the Territory* (1986) and *Shadow and Act* (1964); both are helpful, though not essential, to the study of *Invisible Man*. The two thousand manuscript pages of his unfinished novel were edited and posthumously published by Ellison's friend and editor, John F. Callahan, as *Juneteenth: A Novel* (1999). While the words in *Juneteenth* are Ellison's, the book's final form was not his doing; perhaps the novel is better viewed as an epitaph for the life and career of a great writer than as his final work. *Invisible Man* stands alone as a work that needs little support from other primary sources. A wealth of scholarship on both Ellison and *Invisible Man* should be readily available at most public and academic libraries. Particularly useful works are listed and annotated below under "RESOURCES."

TOPICS FOR DISCUSSION AND RESEARCH

1. Ellison establishes many of the main themes in *Invisible Man* through stark dichotomies such as black and white, right and wrong, and good and bad. In every case, however, he clouds the issue by bringing facts into question, confounding tradition, or contradicting expectations. Seemingly, nothing is absolute; everything and everyone appears to be a compilation of contradictions. For instance, the members of the Brotherhood peddle a constant rhetoric of equality and fairness; yet, they all react with hostility and pettiness when the narrator contradicts their recruitment efforts in Harlem. The narrator himself is especially composed of contradictions. At the beginning of the novel he desperately wants to be successful and accepted by the white community leaders and does anything he thinks they want him to do—even participating in a brutal, senseless brawl with other African American youths—but to the old white men he can never be truly acceptable because of his race. Students might try to locate various dichotomies and determine what themes they help to convey. They might also discuss the importance of this organizational style for its own sake. What effect does the constant creation of oppositions have on the tone and temperament of the novel? How does the novel make the reader feel?

2. The most significant opposition in the novel is seeing versus blindness. It is, figuratively speaking, blindness that renders the narrator invisible to the rest of the world and often to himself. Ellison deftly weaves issues of literal vision

problems throughout the text alongside metaphorical and symbolic issues of sight. Often the things that are most readily visible in the physical world of the novel are the things that the characters have the least ability to see. Also, the language of the novel is full of puns and double meanings concerning this theme. Students can begin to approach the theme by studying and discussing two early sections of the novel: the "Prologue" and the speech of Reverend Barbee in chapter 5. How does sight or the lack thereof play an important role in these sections? In what ways does Ellison invoke the idea of sight? What are some factors that influence how one sees or is seen?

3. Also significant is Ellison's use of color imagery and symbolism. In a novel explicitly about race in America, the colors black and white have obvious symbolic importance, and Ellison gets a great deal of mileage out of them. For instance, it is no accident that the color for which Liberty Paints is known is "Optic White," nor is it an accident that the narrator dilutes this color with black "dope" in his first job assignment. Ellison does not stop with black and white, however; for example, he continually reminds us that Brother Jack's hair is bright red, indicating Jack's uniqueness and symbolic connection to communism. Students should choose an incident that is particularly significant in terms of color imagery and discuss how Ellison uses color symbolically. To what extent does Ellison allow the reader to interpret the meanings of the colors? To what extent are such meanings already determined?

4. Another important opposition Ellison poses is that of reason versus emotion. The Brotherhood believes that it has the answer to injustice, inequality, and human suffering: science. By reasoning and theorizing, the Brotherhood seeks to impose its political agenda on the world. Seemingly, it stands against unreason and wild emotion—though it will use them to accomplish its ends, as the narrator finds out at the climax of the novel. The narrator is torn by his allegiance to the Brotherhood's theories and his persistent emotional responses to injustice. Students should be able to use the examples established in the novel to debate the positives and negatives of the Brotherhood's ideas and tactics. Do they achieve their aims? To what extent are these aims ethical and moral? Does Ellison completely condemn the scientific approach to achieving equality?

5. Finally, *Invisible Man* explores the Modernist idea of "man" as in *mankind* versus "man" as an individual. The title can be read in both ways: the narrator is an individual "invisible man," but African Americans as a group also seem to be largely invisible to "white" America. The narrator struggles between the responsibility he feels as an individual who suffers for and because of his race and as a representative of a larger group. Part of the Brotherhood's theory is that the individual is meaningless—everything is decided by "the committee," which the narrator never sees. Students should consider the ideas of the individual and of the group as Ellison presents them. Based on Ellison's narrator's experience, what does it mean to be an individual, and what does it mean to be part of a group—especially a racially defined one? And perhaps most important, how is an individual responsible to the group and the group to the individual?

RESOURCES

Primary Works

Conversations with Ralph Ellison, edited by Maryemma Graham and Amritjit Singh (Jackson: University Press of Mississippi, 1995).
An exhaustive collection of interviews in which Ellison candidly discusses his creative process, particularly in reference to *Invisible Man.*

Flying Home and Other Stories, edited by John F. Callahan (New York: Random House, 1996).
Thirteen short stories that span Ellison's career, several of which were published for the first time in this collection.

Going to the Territory: Essays (New York: Random House, 1986).
Ellison's second collection of nonfiction. Many of the pieces discuss topics similar to those with which he deals in his fiction.

Juneteenth: A Novel, edited by Callahan (New York: Random House, 1999).
Ellison's second novel, constructed from the two thousand manuscript pages he left behind at his death. Like *Invisible Man,* the work focuses on issues of race in America.

Shadow and Act: Essays (New York: Random House, 1964).
Ellison's first collection of nonfiction.

Bibliography

John F. Callahan, "Selected Bibliography," in *Ralph Ellison's* Invisible Man: *A Casebook,* edited by Callahan (New York: Oxford University Press, 2004), pp. 345–352.
Though certainly not an exhaustive catalogue of scholarly work on Ellison, offers an excellent foundation for the study of *Invisible Man.*

Biography

Arnold Rampersad, *Ralph Ellison: A Biography* (New York: Knopf, 2007).
A thorough study of Ellison's life. Roughly half of the book leads up to the publication of *Invisible Man,* while the second part details Ellison's life after writing the novel.

Criticism

Harold Bloom, ed., *Ralph Ellison's* Invisible Man (Philadelphia: Chelsea House, 1999).
An excellent collection of diverse scholarly work on the novel, including essays on gender, jazz, and the literary forebears of the book.

Mark Busby, *Ralph Ellison* (Boston: Twayne, 1991).
Provides extensive analysis of *Invisible Man.*

John F. Callahan, ed., *Ralph Ellison's* Invisible Man: *A Casebook* (New York: Oxford University Press, 2004).
A helpful selection of essays, equally divided between the literary aspects and the cultural and political aspects of the novel.

Lucas E. Morel, ed., *Ralph Ellison and the Raft of Hope: A Political Companion to* Invisible Man (Lexington: University Press of Kentucky, 2004).
A collection of scholarly essays on the political inspirations and consequences of *Invisible Man.* The issues treated range from citizenship and education to chaos and Communism.

Ross Posnock, ed., *The Cambridge Companion to Ralph Ellison* (New York: Cambridge University Press, 2005).
Considers much of Ellison's other work in addition to *Invisible Man* in relation to such topics as technology, law, photography, and religion.

—*David Wright*

c◯◯◯ɔ

Lorraine Hansberry, *A Raisin in the Sun*
(New York: Random House, 1959)

Since its critically acclaimed premiere on 11 March 1959 at the Ethel Barrymore Theater in New York, where it won the New York Drama Critics' Circle Award for the best American play of the season, *A Raisin in the Sun* by Lorraine Hansberry (1930–1965) has established a firm place in the American canon of classic plays. It was made into a successful movie in 1961 and adapted as the Tony Award–winning musical *Raisin* in 1973, but the original play is continually revived and continues to draw audiences five decades after its original performance. Hansberry, an African American, was born and raised in Chicago as the youngest of Carl Augustus and Nannie Perry Hansberry's four children. Her parents, prosperous real-estate brokers, attempted in 1938 to move into a neighborhood where a restrictive covenant did not allow minorities to own homes. Hansberry's father sued, and in 1940 the Illinois Supreme Court ruled in his favor. This event shaped Hansberry's life and her activities in the civil-rights movement, as well as significantly influencing the writing of *A Raisin in the Sun.*

In 1950 Hansberry left the University of Wisconsin without completing a degree and moved to New York City, where she went to work for *Freedom* magazine. She met her future husband, Robert Nemiroff, on a picket line; they were married in 1953. After the success of *A Raisin in the Sun,* NBC commissioned Hansberry to write *The Drinking Gourd* in 1960; it was never produced. In 1962 she completed *What Use Are Flowers?;* it, too, was not produced. In 1963 Hansberry was diagnosed with duodenal cancer. In 1964 she published *The Movement: Documentary of a Struggle for Equality.* That same year she and

Nemiroff were divorced, but she named him her literary executor. On 15 October 1964 *The Sign in Sidney Brustein's Window* opened on Broadway. Hansberry died on 12 January 1965. In 1969 *To Be Young, Gifted and Black,* adapted by Nemiroff from Hansberry's writings, opened at the Cherry Theater in New York; the published edition includes an introduction, "Sweet Lorraine," by James Baldwin. Hansberry's final work, *Les Blancs,* was completed by Nemiroff and opened on Broadway in 1970. It is included, along with *The Drinking Gourd* and *What Use Are Flowers?,* in *Les Blancs: The Collected Last Plays of Lorraine Hansberry,* edited by Nemiroff (New York: Random House, 1972). Although her career was brief, Hansberry's influence is still evident; she was a pioneer of contemporary American drama who affected the work of African American artists as diverse as the singer Nina Simone and the playwright August Wilson.

In *A Raisin in the Sun* the members of the Younger family individually and collectively come to grips with the "legacy" of their late husband and father, who has left them $10,000 from an insurance policy. Each of the characters views the money differently and has a "dream" of how to spend it. The major conflict in the play pits Walter Lee, who works as a chauffeur and wants to buy a liquor store to provide for the future of his wife, Ruth, and son, Travis, against his mother, Lena, who wants to send her youngest child, Benetha, to college and purchase a house in the suburbs so that the family can escape the stultifying atmosphere of Chicago's South Side. As happened with Hansberry's family, the residents of all-white Clybourne Park attempt to keep the Youngers from moving into their neighborhood after Lena makes a down payment on a house there. The family loses most of the insurance money, and they are faced with the decision whether to move into the all-white neighborhood or to take the money offered them by the Clybourne Park Improvement Association to remain where they are. They are faced with the same questions Langston Hughes asks in his poem "Harlem," from which the drama gets its title: "What happens to a dream deferred? // Does it dry up / like a raisin in the sun?" While viewers and readers of the play are often drawn to Lena, who is one of the strongest characters in the drama and was modeled after Nannie Perry Hansberry and Rosa Parks, Hansberry insisted that the real protagonist is Walter Lee: he is the central figure who must come to a decision that is both morally right and will also benefit his family.

TOPICS FOR DISCUSSION AND RESEARCH

1. While the play revolves around Walter Lee and Lena, other characters will also repay close analysis. For example, Benetha is caught between the values of the white middle class represented by George Murchison and the growing awareness of the new postcolonial Africa represented by Joseph Asagai. Students may wish to examine the value systems and outlooks that Murchison and Asagai represent and why Benetha has a difficult time deciding between them. She criticizes Murchison for being an "assimilationist," but she nevertheless is perfectly willing to go out to the theater and be seen socially with him. Hans-

berry often said that Benetha was herself "eight years ago," that is, eight years before the play opened. An interesting line of inquiry is to see how Benetha's dilemma within the play mirrors the dilemma Hansberry encountered eight years previously.

2. At the beginning of act 3 Asagai and Benetha have their final scene together, in which he asks her to marry him. Once again, she wavers, telling him that she has just had her "future taken out of my hands." Asagai responds with the play's most existential speech, regarding the conditions of the nations in the emerging postcolonial Africa. Students may want to explore whether or not, given the more than fifty years of African development since the speech was written, what Asagai says is irrelevant or prophetic.

3. Another productive avenue of exploration is the shifting ideological attitudes toward the relationships depicted in the play: family, racial, community, economic, and generational. The play was first presented amid the growing civil-rights movement of the late 1950s; even today it generates debate among historians, literary critics, and ideologues of all political persuasions. Usually, the debate centers on the "realism" of the situation and characters in the play—especially whether or not it presents a "realistic" portrait of working-class African American life. A study of this criticism should focus on two elements. First, the student should take an overview of the ebb and flow of ideas about the play and how these views have shifted over the past five decades—in other words, how do the shifts reflect the time periods in which they were generated? Second, the student should consider whether or not these ideological interpretations truly represent the "core" message of the play, and, indeed, whether they are of any value, given the student's perception of what the play is "about."

4. The film (1961) and television (1989) versions of *A Raisin in the Sun* successfully communicate the contrast between the open, carefully manicured white world of Clybourne Park and the closed, cramped apartment in which the Youngers live. Students might discuss how the apartment is the symbol of "crampedness" and how it affects the lives of those who live there. With the possible exception of Travis, each character feels that his or her dream or dreams have "shriveled up" within the confines of the apartment. How does the apartment act as a symbol for the lives and visions of the characters in the play? Will the characters be able to overcome their former surroundings even after they move to Clybourne Park? This argument might lead to a discussion of whether or not the play is "Realistic" or perhaps "Naturalistic."

5. An obvious generational conflict occurs in the play between Lena and Walter Lee. But a generational conflict also exists among Ruth, Lena, Walter Lee, and Benetha. Such conflicts are nothing new to drama, but how does the one in this play emerge in the hands of an African American playwright? An interesting and rewarding comparison might be made with another African American play in which generational issues are the major source of conflict. Wilson's *Fences* (1985), for example, involves a black working-class family caught in the shifting racial attitudes of the 1950s.

RESOURCES

Primary Works

The Collected Last Plays, edited by Robert Nemiroff (New York: New American Library, 1983).
Includes an excellent introduction by Nemiroff that sets the plays in their historical and cultural context.

"Lorraine Hansberry 1959," in *The Spectator: Talk about Movies and Plays with Those Who Make Them,* edited by Studs Terkel (New York: New Press, 1999).
A brief but perceptive interview conducted with Hansberry by Terkel in Chicago shortly after the success of *A Raisin in the Sun.*

A Raisin in the Sun: The Unfilmed Original Screenplay (New York: New American Library, 1992).
Hansberry's original screen adaptation of the play.

To Be Young, Gifted and Black: Lorraine Hansberry in Her Own Words, adapted by Nemiroff (Englewood Cliffs, N.J.: Prentice-Hall, 1969).
Uses excerpts from Hansberry's writings and speeches to craft an autobiographical portrait. The work includes an opening tribute by Hansberry's close friend James Baldwin.

Bibliography

Richard M. Leeson, *Lorraine Hansberry: A Research and Production Handbook* (Westport, Conn.: Greenwood Press, 1997).
An excellent source of bibliographical material about all of Hansberry's works. The book includes a "critical overview" of *A Raisin in the Sun* (pp. 27–33) and a bibliography of reviews of the 1959 production and the many mutations—including the musical—and revivals of the play.

Criticism

Steven R. Carter, *Hansberry's Drama: Commitment and Complexity* (Urbana: University of Illinois Press, 1991).
One of the most rewarding analyses of *A Raisin in the Sun.* Chapter 2 deals with all aspects of the play, including its initial critical reception, its structure, its characterizations, and its themes. Chapter 3 treats the film and musical versions.

Anne Cheney, *Lorraine Hansberry* (New York: Twayne, 1994).
An excellent starting point. Cheney's analysis of *A Raisin in the Sun* in chapter 4 is solid.

Lynn Domina, *Understanding* A Raisin in the Sun: *A Student Casebook to Issues, Sources, Historical Documents* (Westport, Conn.: Greenwood Press, 1998).
Analyzes the play, but the main strength of the book is its pointing to historical contexts and its comparison and contrast of contemporary readings in gender and race relations to Hansberry's original issues and themes.

Martha Gilman-Bower, *"Color Struck": Under the Gaze* (Westport, Conn.: Praeger, 2003).
Devotes chapter 4, "'Her World Divided in Half': The Aborted Search for Self in the Life and Plays of Lorraine Hansberry" (pp. 87–112), to a psychological study of how Hansberry's life, including her place in the structure of her family, influenced the writing of *A Raisin in the Sun*.

Ben Keppel, *The Work of Democracy: Ralph Bunche, Kenneth B. Clark, Lorraine Hansberry and the Cultural Politics of Race* (Cambridge, Mass.: Harvard University Press, 1995).
Includes two chapters devoted to Hansberry and *A Raisin in the Sun:* chapter 6, "The Political Education of Lorraine Hansberry" (pp. 177–202); and chapter 7, "The Dialectical Imagination of Lorraine Hansberry (pp. 203–229). Chapter 6 is especially helpful in defining themes—especially those surrounding Walter Lee—and, as Keppel puts it, in "negotiating the terms of a classic."

Loretta G. Woodard, "Lorraine Hansberry," in *African American Dramatists: An A–Z Guide*, edited by Emmanuel S. Nelson (Westport, Conn.: Greenwood Press, 2004), pp. 208–216.
Explores the themes of oppression, the search for dignity, the changing roles of women, the nature of marriage, the true worth of money, and African roots found in the play.

—*Bob Bell*

⌒⦷⌒

Joseph Heller, *Catch-22*

(New York: Simon & Schuster, 1961)

Until his entrance into the United States Army Air Corps in 1942, Joseph Heller (1923–1999) lived in a world that was largely confined to Coney Island, where he was born. Although he grew up happily, as befits a childhood spent in a neighborhood known for its beaches and amusement parks, he discovered while undergoing psychoanalysis in 1979 that the death of his father when he was five had informed his fiction. The event that was the more immediate inspiration for *Catch-22* (1961), however, and was more crucial to Heller's authorial career occurred on 15 August 1944 over Avignon, France, during Heller's thirty-seventh bombing mission. In notes about the mission, Heller recorded, "Man wounded in the leg. Wohlstein and Moon killed." Heller later disclosed that the details of the Avignon mission on which Snowden dies—Yossarian's thirty-seventh mission—correspond "perhaps ninety percent to what I did experience." In general, Heller viewed his wartime experiences as youthful adventures, and his service enabled him to take advantage of the GI Bill to earn his B.A. from New York University in 1948 and his M.A. from Columbia University in 1949, which led to a Fulbright Scholarship to Oxford University in 1949–1950. After a two-year stint teaching at Pennsylvania State University, Heller returned to New York and took a series of advertising and marketing jobs. In 1953 he began writing *Catch-22*, which was published when he was thirty-eight. Although the novel initially sold slowly and received comparatively little critical attention, its publication changed Heller's life forever, prompting the question that he would hear for the rest of his career: when was he going to write another novel as great or as funny? Over his remaining thirty-eight years he wrote six more novels, the antiwar play *We Bombed in New Haven* (1968), and two memoirs.

According to Heller, *Catch-22* had its genesis in the line: "It was love at first sight. The first time he saw the chaplain, Someone fell in love with him." Initially, he did not have a plot, characters, or a theme in mind. Over the course of a few hours, the book quickly evolved in his mind as he pursued his inspiration. As he wrote, Heller sketched his ideas about characters, events, and themes of the novel on note cards and eventually created a schematic outline for the novel on a desk blotter. These artifacts and the draft manuscript document the counterimpulses of the novel. On the one hand, Heller's comic sequences seemingly grow as improvisationally and anarchically as those of a stand-up comedian. On the other hand, Catch-22, as thematic imperative and bureaucratic structure, constrains the characters' choices and desires and, along with them, the plot of the novel. As critics have long noted, Yossarian, the great comic protagonist of the work, embodies life and possibility—his fears and appetites supply the counterforce to death and mortality. For Yossarian, "each day [constitutes] another dangerous mission against mortality," with threats to his life coming with equal frequency from enemy fire and from his own commanders and colleagues, who sacrifice others' lives to secure their own advancement. Milo Minderbinder, Heller's thematic counterpart to Yossarian, embodies the evils of the military-industrial complex and the moral self-deceptions of American capitalism. In one of the darkest episodes Milo bombs his own base to save his conglomerate, M & M Enterprises. Caught in this deadly world, Yossarian, a latter-day Huckleberry Finn, lights out for the Territories, with Sweden serving as refuge from Milo, capitalism, and the war.

The stories that preceded or were excerpted from *Catch-22;* Heller's many published interviews; and later works such as "'Catch-22' Revisited" (1967), the antiwar play *We Bombed in New Haven,* and the sequel to *Catch-22,* titled *Closing Time* (1994), illuminate Heller's creative process and his evolving understanding of the issues in the novel. Although the stories—many of which are collected in *Catch as Catch Can* (2003)—are imitative, they announce Heller's values and provide the opportunity to peer backward at the genesis of a novelist and observe his characteristic way with words. Students who want to understand how Heller thought about *Catch-22* at various stages in his career should turn to the interviews in *Conversations with Joseph Heller* (1993). The sequel, *Closing Time,* looks back pessimistically on the issues of *Catch-22;* as Heller describes its thesis: "things are coming to an end." In a self-reflective commentary on his own career, Heller includes an episode in which one of the characters says about Snowden's death, "It sounds immoral. But it gave me an episode, something dramatic to talk about." Although much darker in vision than *Catch-22, Clos-*

ing Time still ends with an affirmation of the comic spirit as Yossarian walks out into a nuclear apocalypse firmly convinced that he will "survive, flourish, and live happily—forever after." Among the wealth of secondary sources, Robert Merrill's *Joseph Heller* (1987), Sanford Pinsker's *Understanding Joseph Heller* (2009), Judith Ruderman's *Joseph Heller* (1991), David Seed's *The Fiction of Joseph Heller: Against the Grain* (1989), and David M. Craig's *Tilting at Mortality: Narrative Strategies in Joseph Heller's Fiction* (1997) provide illuminating analyses of the novel and collectively cover the main lines of the voluminous criticism. Although no biography of Heller is as yet available, his memoir, *Now and Then: From Coney Island to Here* (1998), can help readers who want to understand his life.

TOPICS FOR DISCUSSION AND RESEARCH

1. Although *Catch-22* is often thought of as a World War II novel, its principal themes have much more to do with America of the 1950s: the bureaucratic absurdities, the sometimes life-denying logic of capitalism, and the pressures to conform. Many of the novel's most famous comic sequences—the Major Major episodes, for example—mock bureaucratic structures and procedures. Major Major is promoted because of an IBM machine with a sense of humor, and ex-PFC Wintergreen becomes Milo's business partner and one of the most powerful characters in the novel because he controls the mimeograph machine. Heller uses Milo Minderbinder to make a scathing attack on American capitalism. Echoing General Motors president Charles E. Wilson's claim about his company, Milo asserts that "what is good for M & M Enterprises is good for the country" and proceeds to act on the principle regardless of the damage done and havoc wreaked. In pursuit of profit he removes morphine from the bombers' first-aid kits, contracts with the Germans to bomb American bases, and tries to feed the soldiers chocolate-covered cotton to recoup his losses on a deal gone bad. In such a world individuals are interchangeable parts, and the characters who recognize this fact are the most successful. Lieutenant Scheisskopf becomes General Scheisskopf as a result of his mania for parades and for schemes such as attaching hinged beams to his soldiers' backs to ensure that they make their parade turns in perfect alignment. Colonel Cathcart uses form condolence letters that begin: "Dear Mrs., Mr., Miss, or Mr. and Mrs." By exploring these and other instances of depersonalization students can examine Heller's critique of American capitalism and bureaucracy and arrive at their own conclusions about its validity.
2. Heller equally attends to individual ethics and motivations. He does so critically in characters such as Milo, Scheisskopf, and Cathcart and sympathetically in characters such as Chaplain Tappman and Nately. In the latter cases, however, goodness and a belief in American values lead to weakness and vulnerability: these characters are the victims in the novel. Portrayed by some critics as an antihero and by others as a hero for the modern age, Yossarian is Heller's vehicle for exploring the ethical values of an age that proclaims but, Heller believes, does not uphold them. Also, as *Closing Time*

shows even more dramatically and insistently, Heller depicts in Yossarian the tension in his own nature between ambition and its cost. Students can profitably analyze Yossarian's actions and decisions for the lens they provide on Heller's ethical vision.

3. In representing Cold War America, Heller satirically targets some of the most famous events of the mid 1950s, including Senator Joseph McCarthy's anti-Communist campaign, the Rosenberg trial, and the Alger Hiss–Whittaker Chambers case. Following critics such as Merrill and Seed, students can investigate these events and Heller's transformation of them. In Heller's parodic version, the famous pumpkin at the center of the Hiss-Chambers case becomes a plum tomato that provides the crucial evidence that the chaplain is guilty of theft. Or, as his interrogator puts the matter: "Then why are you acting so guilty if you didn't steal it?" Such logic characterizes a whole series of episodes: the Glorious Loyalty Oath Campaign, Clevinger's trial, and the plight of Major Major, who is not allowed to sign a loyalty oath but whose failure to sign becomes proof of his disloyalty.

4. Catch-22, the rule that gives the novel its title, embodies all of these themes and provides the conceptual lens and defining metaphor of the work. In its basic form the rule requires airmen who desire to stop flying combat missions to request an evaluation of their mental fitness; but the request itself shows a rational regard for one's own safety and thereby proves one's sanity and fitness to keep flying the missions. As critics have long noted, Catch-22 demonstrates the extent to which the novel is about language and its misuses. Heller scatters miniature versions of the paradox throughout the novel: "Dunbar was working so hard at increasing his lifespan that Yossarian thought that he was dead"; Yossarian curses "Catch-22 vehemently . . . even though he knew there was no such thing." For Heller, Catch-22 exemplifies, to borrow William Blake's formulation, society's "mind-forged manacles." Students can use the Catch-22 paradox and Heller's self-negating sentences to learn much about the ways in which Heller's style communicates his vision. On the one hand, Heller repeats patterns of language and plot structures to emphasize the sameness of apparently disparate situations. On the other hand, he also uses language to transform. Language has a talismanic quality, altering the things it represents. For example, Doc Daneeka contrives to have his name listed in the flight logs of planes so that he can collect combat pay; one of the planes crashes, killing all aboard. From then on, all of the other characters treat him as if he were dead.

5. For readers of the 1960s and 1970s *Catch-22* became a way to explain the dilemmas of the Vietnam War. Such famous statements as the one by the briefing officer who claimed, "It became necessary to destroy the village in order to save it," seemed as if they had been invented by Heller's fertile imagination. Students may wish to research the history of the novel's reception, especially its connection to the Vietnam War and the antiwar movement. Such an investigation could document one of the ways in which Catch-22—the concept and the novel—has furnished a vehicle to explain and interpret the contradictory demands of contemporary life.

RESOURCES

Primary Works

Catch-22: A Dramatization (New York: Delacorte, 1973).
The Yossarian plot recast as a drama.

Catch as Catch Can: The Collected Stories and Other Writings (New York: Simon & Schuster, 2004).
Includes various works that directly bear on *Catch-22:* the short stories that preceded the novel; four essays, most notably "*Catch-22* Revisited"; the story "Love, Dad"; and the play *Clevinger's Trial.*

Closing Time (New York: Simon & Schuster, 1994).
The sequel in which Heller reprises Yossarian, Milo, and Chaplain Tappman in a fin de siècle continuation of the novel's principal plotlines.

Conversations with Joseph Heller, edited by Adam Sorkin (Jackson: University Press of Mississippi, 1993).
Comprises thirty-one interviews, and essays based on them, spanning Heller's career prior to *Closing Time.*

Now and Then: From Coney Island to Here (New York: Knopf, 1998).
Memoir of Heller's youth on Coney Island that also includes a brief account of his war years and discusses some of the people and events that serve as inspiration for episodes in *Catch-22*, including the Snowden death scene.

"Yossarian Survives: A Missing Chapter of Catch-22," *Playboy,* 34 (December 1987): 144–146, 184, 186.
Material cut from *Catch-22* set at Lowry Field, including the earliest hospital episode.

We Bombed in New Haven (New York: Knopf, 1968).
Antiwar play that extends the themes of *Catch-22* and illuminates the Vietnam War era during which the novel gained such prominence.

Bibliography

Matthew J. Bruccoli and Park Bucker, *Joseph Heller: A Descriptive Bibliography* (Pittsburgh: University of Pittsburgh Press, 2002).
The most recent and comprehensive bibliography of Heller.

Criticism

David M. Craig, *Tilting at Mortality: Narrative Strategies in Joseph Heller's Fiction* (Detroit: Wayne State University Press, 1997).
Locates the novel between the unpublished Avignon stories and other manuscript material that preceded *Catch-22* and "'Catch-22' Revisited," which followed and which explicates Heller's war with mortality, especially as it is figured in his dead-child story.

Robert Merrill, *Joseph Heller* (Boston: Twayne, 1987).
Provides a valuable analysis of *Catch-22* while placing the novel against the literary traditions on which Heller drew.

James Nagel, ed., *Critical Essays on Joseph Heller* (Boston: G. K. Hall, 1984).
Includes a representative selection of essays on *Catch-22*.

Sanford Pinsker, *Understanding Joseph Heller* (Columbia: University of South Carolina Press, 2009).
Explores the repetitive structure that Heller uses in *Catch-22* and argues that the work constitutes a new kind of war novel.

Judith Ruderman, *Joseph Heller* (New York: Continuum, 1991).
Provides an overview of the themes and characters of *Catch-22* and argues that the novel reveals the limitations of language.

David Seed, *The Fiction of Joseph Heller: Against the Grain* (New York: St. Martin's Press, 1989).
Explores Heller's themes and techniques and demonstrates how the novel reflects the Cold War context in which it was written.

—*David M. Craig*

Ernest Hemingway, *The Old Man and the Sea*
(New York: Scribners, 1952)

The reputation of Ernest Hemingway (1899–1961) rests on his deftly crafted short stories; his three masterful novels, *The Sun Also Rises* (1926), *A Farewell to Arms* (1929), and *For Whom the Bell Tolls* (1939); and his novella, *The Old Man and the Sea* (1952), which won the Pulitzer Prize in 1953 and contributed to Hemingway's winning the Nobel Prize in literature the following year. It remains one of his most read and beloved works.

According to the publisher, Charles Scribner Jr., the novella had its origins in "On the Blue Water: A Gulf Stream Letter," a travel piece Hemingway wrote for *Esquire* magazine in 1936. In the article Hemingway tells about an old Cuban fisherman who caught a great marlin but lost it to the sharks during his return to land. Hemingway wrote to his editor, Maxwell Perkins, three years later, that he intended to expand the anecdote into a piece to be included in a book of short stories. But the Spanish Civil War and World War II intervened, and Hemingway did not begin to work on the "Santiago story" until January 1951—fifteen years after the *Esquire* piece. On 5 October 1951 Hemingway wrote to Scribner that it was a book that he had "been working on all my life" and that it "should read easily and simply and seem short and yet have all the dimensions of the visible world and the world of man's spirit." Critics generally agree that he succeeded in that aim.

The Old Man and the Sea is the story of Santiago, an old Cuban fisherman who has had "no luck"—no catches—for eighty-four days. On the eighty-fifth day he ventures out beyond the normal fishing grounds and hooks a gigantic marlin that tows him into the Gulf Stream, beyond the sight of land. Santiago defeats the marlin; but because the fish is so large, he cannot haul it into his skiff but must tie it to the side. As Santiago returns to the mainland, sharks begin to attack the marlin. Santiago battles them until his strength and his weapons are used up and he must let the sharks have their fill of the great fish's flesh. He returns with only the head and skeleton of the marlin and goes to his shack, where he is tended to by Manolin, the boy who is the old man's friend and companion, and falls asleep.

The novel was a critical success, became a best seller overnight, and has been made into at least three notable movie versions. Perhaps the best known is the almost word-for-word retelling of the story starring Spencer Tracy that was released in 1958. A made-for-television version starring Anthony Quinn was broadcast in 1990. Finally, a Russian animated version directed by Alexsander Petrov was released in 1999.

Before reading the novella, the student is advised to read Scribner's introduction to the eBook edition for information about the history of the composition of the work. After reading the novella, the student may wish to consult Bickford Sylvester's "Hemingway's Extended Vision: *The Old Man and the Sea*" and *"The Old Man and the Sea* and the American Dream," by Delmore Schwartz, for insights into the larger themes in the novella and their relationship to American attitudes and culture; both are included in *Twentieth Century Interpretations of* The Old Man and the Sea: *A Collection of Critical Essays* (1968), edited by Katharine T. Jobes. Gerry Brenner's The Old Man and the Sea: *Story of a Common Man* (1991) is a thorough study of the novella.

TOPICS FOR DISCUSSION AND RESEARCH

1. A rewarding inquiry could begin with an exploration of the character of Manolin, the boy who is Santiago's only friend. At the end of the novella Manolin sits beside Santiago as the old man dreams, once again, of the lions. The boy tends to Santiago's needs, bringing him food, water, and newspapers. Students might locate the definition of *confidant* in a dictionary of literary terms and discuss how Manolin functions as the confidant in Hemingway's novel.

2. Manolin may also be viewed as Santiago's pupil. Throughout the adventure on the sea Santiago says, "I wish the boy were here." He means not only that Manolin could help him in his work but also that the boy could learn from the experience of catching the big fish. As Santiago is about to go to sleep at the end of the novella, the boy says to him, "You must get well fast for there is much that I can learn and you can teach me everything. How much did you suffer?" The question "How much did you suffer?" indicates that Manolin understands that he is to learn not only the art of fishing but also the art of living from Santiago. What values and beliefs might Hemingway wish to convey through Santiago?

3. Another interesting and revealing investigation could be a comparison of the relationship between Santiago and Manolin with that of the Boy and the Father in Cormac McCarthy's apocalyptic novel *The Road* (2006). At the end of the work the Father instructs the Boy, "You have to carry the fire." The "fire" is the values and ideals that represent what is good about humanity. Students might compare and contrast the values the Father teaches the Boy in McCarthy's novel with those taught to Manolin by Santiago in *The Old Man and the Sea*. Both works deal with the idea of "fatalism": How does one live properly in a world that is either dead or without meaning? What other great works of literature involve mentor relationships like that in *The Old Man and the Sea*? In what ways can they be compared and contrasted to Hemingway's novella?

4. Closely allied to these ideas is the notion that *The Old Man and the Sea* is, perhaps, Hemingway's "purest" demonstration of "The Code": his definition of how to live the proper kind of life in a world that is without meaning. Most of Hemingway's famous protagonists have some psychological or physical incapacity, but Santiago does not suffer from such hindrances. Thus, he can act on his beliefs without the burdens that plague Hemingway's other heroes. What are these beliefs? The student could begin by considering the themes of honor and dignity.

5. Another dimension to the novella is nature. Is Santiago's relationship to the sea symbolic of humanity's relationship to the natural world? A fruitful exercise could be a comparison of the attitudes toward nature of the protagonists of *The Old Man and the Sea* and Hemingway's short story "Big Two-Hearted River" (1925), which also deals with a fishing expedition. Why does each protagonist feel both competent in and awed by the natural world?

6. Finally, critics have made much of the Christian symbolism in the novella: the three-day trip on the sea, analogous to the three days between the Cruci-fixion and Resurrection; the crosslike mast that Santiago carries as he stumbles up the hill to his shack after the ordeal at sea. Christ, however, was not a fisherman; the disciples were literal fishermen, and their call from Christ was "Come, follow me, and I will make you fishers of men" (Matt. 4:19). Most of the disciples were also crucified. Is it possible that Santiago is not a Christ figure but a disciple? A disciple is an individual who not only embodies but also spreads the word about the proper way to live. The student might explore the idea of Santiago not as the Messiah but as a disciple.

RESOURCES

Primary Works

Conversations with Ernest Hemingway, edited by Matthew J. Bruccoli (Jackson: University Press of Mississippi, 1986).
Includes a helpful introduction by the editor, forty profiles and interviews spanning the years from 1919 to 1965, and Hemingway's Nobel Prize acceptance speech.

In Our Time (New York: Boni & Liveright, 1925).
Includes "The Big Two-Hearted River: Part Two," another Hemingway story involving a fishing trip that one might compare to *The Old Man and the Sea*.

Selected Letters: 1917–1961, edited by Carlos Baker (New York: Scribners, 1981).
An enthralling body of personal, professional, and literary correspondence.

Bibliography

Audre Hanneman, *Ernest Hemingway: A Comprehensive Bibliography* (Princeton: Princeton University Press, 1967).
The standard Hemingway bibliography.

Hanneman, *Supplement to Ernest Hemingway: A Comprehensive Bibliography* (Princeton: Princeton University Press, 1975).
Updates Hanneman's earlier work with nearly two decades of scholarship.

Biography

Carlos Baker, *Ernest Hemingway: A Life Story* (New York: Scribners, 1966).
The standard Hemingway biography.

Richard O'Connor, *Ernest Hemingway* (New York: McGraw-Hill, 1971).
A carefully considered biography.

Robert W. Trogden, ed., *Dictionary of Literary Biography*, volume 210: *Ernest Hemingway: A Documentary Volume* (Detroit: Bruccoli Clark Layman / Gale Group, 1999).

Criticism

Carlos Baker, *Hemingway: The Writer as Artist* (Princeton: Princeton University Press, 1963).
Explores the biblical allusions in the novella and their connection with Samuel Taylor Coleridge's *The Rime of the Ancient Mariner*. Both the Mariner and Santiago feel great "compassion" for the creations of nature.

Susan F. Beegel, "Santiago and the Eternal Feminine: Gendering *La Mar* in *The Old Man and the Sea*," in *Ernest Hemingway*, edited by Harold Bloom, Bloom's Modern Critical Views (Philadelphia: Chelsea House, 2005), pp. 193–217.
Proposes that far from being a "masculine" parable, *The Old Man and the Sea* features the sea as a character. The Spanish word for "sea," *la mar*, is feminine; thus, in the novella "the true sin is masculinizing nature."

Gerry Brenner, The Old Man and the Sea: *Story of a Common Man* (New York: Twayne, 1991).

A full-length study of the novel from both a literary and a historical stand-point, combined with a close reading of the text.

Leo Gurko, *Ernest Hemingway and the Pursuit of Heroism* (New York: Crowell, 1968).
Sees Santiago as "the clearest representation of the hero" because he "has not been permanently wounded or disillusioned."

Earl Rovit, *Ernest Hemingway* (Boston: Twayne, 1963).
Explores the "three open-ended allegorical readings" of the novel: the "religious," the "introspective journey," and the "aesthetic."

Delmore Schwartz, "*The Old Man and the Sea* and the American Dream," in *Twentieth Century Interpretations of* The Old Man and the Sea: *A Collection of Critical Essays*, edited by Katharine T. Jobes (Englewood Cliffs, N.J.: Prentice-Hall, 1968), pp. 97–102.
Argues that the novel gives the reader "an intensified awareness of . . . the kingdom of Heaven which is within us" and is made up of "moral stamina alone, and experience, stripped of illusion."

Charles Scribner Jr., "Introduction: The Ripening of a Masterpiece," in *The Old Man and the Sea*, by Ernest Hemingway (New York: Scribner eBook Edition, 2002).
Provides essential biographical information concerning Hemingway's approach to and writing of the novella and his concerns as his story developed.

Samuel Shaw, *Ernest Hemingway* (New York: Ungar, 1973).
Considers the novella as Hemingway's "clearest assertion of evil" (the Portuguese man-of-war, the sharks) and as a work in which Hemingway shows a "balanced vision of the human condition."

Bickford Sylvester, "Hemingway's Extended Vision: *The Old Man and the Sea*," in *Twentieth Century Interpretations of* The Old Man and the Sea: *A Collection of Critical Essays*, edited by Jobes (Englewood Cliffs, N.J.: Prentice-Hall, 1968), pp. 81–96.
Argues that the novella represents Hemingway's "discovery" that the world is not meaningless but a "reflection of the natural law man is permitted to follow."

Philip Young, *Ernest Hemingway*, University of Minnesota Pamphlets on American Writers, no. 1 (Minneapolis: University of Minnesota Press, 1965).
Brief but succinct analysis of *The Old Man and the Sea* that clearly states the background and major themes of the novel.

—*Bob Bell*

Jack Kerouac, *On the Road*

(New York: Viking, 1957)

Jack Kerouac (1922–1969) was a prolific writer of journals, letters, poems, essays, and novels, but he is best known for his breakthrough novel *On the Road* (1957), a lightly fictionalized account of his travels across the United States. Today readers tend to associate him with adventurous living on the fringes of 1950s American society: hitching rides on highways, hopping between jazz clubs, and smoking marijuana. He sought, instead, to be known as a literary innovator who developed modern forms of prose.

Kerouac grew up in the working-class town of Lowell, Massachusetts, during the Depression years when the cotton mills along the rivers were falling into decline. His parents were devout Catholics of French Canadian heritage, so Kerouac grew up steeped in the religious imagery of the Catholic Church and in the French language that his family spoke at home. Kerouac did not develop confidence in speaking English until he was in junior high school, but he was a good student and an exceptional athlete. On graduating from Lowell High School in 1939, he accepted a football scholarship to attend Columbia University. In New York his restless nature met the city that never sleeps.

Within a few years Kerouac met two men with whom he would share life-long literary aspirations: Allen Ginsberg, also a Columbia student, and William S. Burroughs, a Harvard graduate. Kerouac's first published novel, *The Town and the City* (1950), traces a fictionalized version of his move from Lowell to New York; seven years passed before he published another novel. During this time he wrote *On the Road* and a series of other works that appeared only after the success of that novel: the novels *Visions of Cody* (written in 1951–1952, published in 1972), *Doctor Sax* (written in 1952, published in 1959), *Maggie Cassidy* (written in 1953, published in 1959), *The Subterraneans* (written in 1953, published in 1958), *Tristessa* (written in 1955, published in 1960), *Visions of Gerard* (written in 1956, published in 1963), and *Desolation Angels* (first half written in 1956, second half in 1961, published in 1965), and a book-length poem, *Mexico City Blues* (written in 1953, published in 1959).

Kerouac wrote *On the Road* in 1951 in an attempt to convey the spirit of his travels with his friend Neal Cassady, named Dean Moriarty in the novel. At the beginning of the novel Sal Paradise (the first-person narrator, based on Kerouac) is listless, bored, and despondent following a broken marriage. Dean arrives in New York City and stirs up commotion and inspiration. His presence catalyzes Sal: "I was beginning to get the bug like Dean. He was simply a youth tremendously excited with life." Sal soon heads out on his own adventures, beginning as a tender-foot who finds himself stranded beside the road in the rain; before long, though, he grows more road savvy. The book covers a series of trips—with and without Dean—back and forth across the United States and into Mexico. Observing Dean's manic engagement with the world, Sal becomes open to new experiences. He meets random friends and lovers and generally finds inspiration in music and simple pleasures but also resorts to using drugs and committing petty crimes.

The book received a celebratory review in *The New York Times*, which called it a "major novel" and hailed its publication as "a historic occasion." The review also claimed that the book would be regarded as a testament to the "Beat Generation," an association that ignited controversy. Kerouac had coined the phrase as early as 1948 to describe the generation that had been born during the Great Depression and had come of age during World War II. He claimed that he intended the phrase to convey a general sense of being tired and down and out; but he also asserted a connection to Jesus' Sermon on the Mount, generally known as the Beatitudes, in that the hipsters, hustlers, bums, and struggling artists of the generation exemplified a spirit of being blessed and sanctified. Magazines and newspapers ran articles on the Beat Generation, often equating this group with juvenile delinquency, crime, and decadence; after *On the Road* entered the best-seller lists, a full-scale media blitz ensued, a result that Kerouac decried and regretted. Before long the "Beatniks," as this group came to be called, devolved in media portrayals from a criminal threat to a silly stereotype of the unshaven, work-shirking "cat" and the leotard-clad, bongo-banging "chick."

The flurry of novels Kerouac published in the five years following *On the Road* overloaded some readers, but three of them are especially helpful for students who wish to understand the scope of his artistic vision as expressed initially in *On the Road*. *Visions of Cody*, written shortly after *On the Road*, revisits the same material in Kerouac's newly developed writing style, a jazzy, exploratory prose technique crafted under the influence of James Joyce and William Faulkner that he called "spontaneous prose." Kerouac believed that in *Visions of Cody*, of which only an excerpt was published during his lifetime, he rendered more effectively the depths and insights of his traveling adventures and the spirit of his friend Cassady, whom he saw as a new—and Beat—American hero. Students will also benefit from *The Subterraneans*, a barely fictionalized account of a romance. Finally, if *On the Road* begins the journey outward toward adventure and the possibilities of freedom, then *Big Sur* (1962) ends the ride. Here Kerouac recounts an alcoholic breakdown precipitated by his fame as a Beat writer. He provided general outlines of his prose technique in two articles, "Essentials of Spontaneous Prose" (1957) and "Belief & Technique for Modern Prose" (1959). Students might also consult the various biographies of Kerouac to compare the actual events to Kerouac's accounts of them and also to follow his arduous path of literary development.

TOPICS FOR DISCUSSION AND RESEARCH

1. One of the reasons for the success and continuing popularity of *On the Road* is the character Dean Moriarty. Some 1950s reviewers declared his behavior aberrant to a psychotic degree, but from Sal's point of view Dean provides a way out of the rigid, generally negative atmosphere that pervades the start of the novel. Many readers in 1957 identified with Sal's state. Students might research the social norms and shared patterns of the postwar era in the United States in David Halberstam's *The Fifties* (1993), William H. and Nancy K. Young's *The 1950s* (2004), or Martin Halliwell's *American Culture in the 1950s* (2007). What were some of the effects of the generation's military involve-

ment? Millions of Americans had worn uniforms during the war, and afterward many went to college on the GI Bill or took jobs with large corporations. How did the development of the suburbs and planned communities such as Levittown, New York, featuring a television in every living room (broadcasting news reports on the threat of atomic warfare), change the way that typical Americans saw themselves? Many among the youth began to feel that they were missing some vital element of life; in what ways might *On the Road* have provided a road map toward fulfillment for them? Sal sees that Dean needs only a car, a few dollars, and girl at the end of the line. Everything in between is "kicks." In what ways do Dean and Sal offer an alternative to the mainstream corporate life? Students interested in the contemporary view on the growing corporate culture should read Sloan Wilson's *The Man in the Grey Flannel Suit* (1955) or William H. Whyte's *The Organization Man* (1956); suburban staleness defeats a young couple in Richard Yates's novel *Revolutionary Road* (1961). How do these "insider" views contrast with the vision of an alternative lifestyle presented in *On the Road?*

2. For many readers in the late 1950s *On the Road* was a revelation with its depictions of jazz, fast cars, sex, and marijuana. Is it reasonable to conclude that the novel advocates hedonism and narcissistic pleasure? How do Dean and Sal contrast with one another in their essential views regarding their adventures on the road? Is one more reactive, more visceral, while the other is more reflective, more romantic by nature? Is there a threat that readers might perceive only the adventures and miss the goal that both Dean and Sal assure themselves that they are seeking? Is the appeal of the novel based on physical pleasures or on spiritual values? Many readers note elements of spiritual exploration. Therefore, comparisons to the American Transcendental movement can be especially enlightening, particularly in regard to such lesser-known Transcendentalists as Jones Very (1813–1880). Can Very be regarded as a kind of Beat artist? What traits does he share with the characters in *On the Road?*

3. Students might also want to look at the treatment in the novel of women, homosexuals, and people of color. Kerouac's depiction of women in *On the Road* has been attacked by some critics as chauvinistic, conveying the impression that women are desirable as sex objects or homemakers but not as equal companions. Students might investigate the courtship and marriage practices and career expectations of women of the 1940s and 1950s in such books as Beth L. Bailey's *From Front Porch to Back Seat: Courtship in Twentieth-Century America* (1988). Why might women readers find the novel liberating for them? Kerouac includes brief scenes involving homosexuality; these passages were quite toned down in the published version as compared to his first drafts of the novel. How openly was homosexuality portrayed in the literature and the news of the 1950s? In terms of ethnicity, Sal, of Italian descent, compares himself several times in the novel to the Mexicans with whom he works and lives for a time, and at one point wishes that he were "a Negro, feeling that the best the white world had offered was not enough ecstasy for me, not enough life, joy, kicks, darkness, music, not enough night." These forays into race issues predate the Civil Rights movement and place Kerouac as essentially a white observer

(he was French Canadian) of terrain generally inaccessible to white readers. What race and ethnicity issues were debated in the 1950s?

4. Kerouac portrays the United States as a unique geographical space, treating the country's landscape as a character in itself. How has the development of the interstate highway system changed the nature of travel, including the restaurant and motel businesses? Sal and Dean drove cross-country in the later 1940s; by the time *On the Road* appeared in print in 1957, the routes they had driven and crossed, such as the fabled Route 66, were being bypassed by the long stretches of high-speed interstates spotted with fast-food chains. How has the passing of Route 66 changed the way Americans regard travel and the scope and character of the country itself?

RESOURCES

Primary Works

"Belief & Technique for Modern Prose," *Evergreen Review*, 3 (April 1959): 57.
Article in which Kerouac lists the "essentials" for spontaneous prose. The piece is reprinted in his *Good Blonde & Others*, edited by Donald Allen (San Francisco: Grey Fox Press, 1993) and in *The Portable Jack Kerouac*, edited by Ann Charters (New York: Viking, 1995).

Big Sur (New York: Farrar, Straus & Cudahy, 1962).
Novel that recounts Kerouac's battles with alcoholism and fame.

"Essentials of Spontaneous Prose," *Black Mountain Review*, 7 (Autumn 1957): 226–228.
Article in which Kerouac defines his method of writing. This piece has been reprinted in *Good Blonde & Others* and *The Portable Jack Kerouac*.

Jack Kerouac: Selected Letters, 1940–1956, edited by Ann Charters (New York: Viking, 1995).
A thorough selection of Kerouac's letters as he developed as a writer and worked on *On the Road*.

Visions of Cody (New York: McGraw-Hill, 1972).
Kerouac's "spontaneous prose" recasting of his road material. Kerouac preferred this far more complex work, which was published posthumously, to *On the Road*.

Bibliography

Ann Charters, *A Bibliography of Works by Jack Kerouac (Jean Louis Lebris De Kerouac), 1939–1975* (New York: Phoenix Bookshop, 1975).
Lists primary publications: books, pamphlets, broadsides, periodical and anthology contributions, translations, recordings, and interviews.

William Lawlor, *The Beat Generation: A Bibliographical Teaching Guide* (Lanham, Md.: Scarecrow Press, 1998).
Indispensable guide to works by and about Kerouac, as well as other Beat writers. It includes "Topics for Investigation and Writing."

Robert Milewski, *Jack Kerouac: An Annotated Bibliography of Secondary Sources, 1944–1979* (Metuchen, N. J.: Scarecrow Press, 1981).
A fine source for articles about Kerouac up to 1979.

Biography

Ann Charters, *Kerouac: A Biography* (San Francisco: Straight Arrow, 1973; New York: St. Martin's Press, 1994).
The first biography of Kerouac. Charters worked with Kerouac on his bibliography.

Dennis McNally, *Desolate Angel: Jack Kerouac, the Beat Generation, and America* (New York: Random House, 1979).
Ties the events in Kerouac's life to his contemporary culture.

Gerald Nicosia, *Memory Babe: A Critical Biography of Jack Kerouac* (New York: Grove, 1983; revised edition, Berkeley: University of California Press, 1994).
Carefully researched study that includes critical analysis of Kerouac's works.

Criticism

Tim Hunt, *Kerouac's Crooked Road: Development of a Fiction* (Hamden, Conn.: Archon, 1981).
Insightful analysis of Kerouac's development as a prose stylist.

Warren Tallman, "Kerouac's Sound," *Tamarack Review,* 11 (Spring 1959): 58–74.
Early and astute examination of Kerouac's prose style and themes.

Matt Theado, *Understanding Jack Kerouac* (Columbia: University of South Carolina Press, 2000).
Biographical and literary analysis of Kerouac's work, with chapters on *On the Road* and *Visions of Cody.*

Regina Weinreich, *The Spontaneous Poetics of Jack Kerouac: A Study of the Fiction* (Carbondale: Southern Illinois University Press, 1987).
A thorough examination of Kerouac's prose method.

—*Matt Theado*

Ken Kesey, *One Flew Over the Cuckoo's Nest*
(New York: Viking, 1962)

Ken Kesey (1935–2001), whose classic novel *One Flew Over the Cuckoo's Nest* epitomizes the ethos of the 1960s American counter culture, grew up on a dairy farm in La Junta, Colorado, and moved to Springfield, Oregon, with his family after World War II. Kesey was an accomplished high-school athlete, later wrestling for the University of Oregon at Eugene, where he became involved in creative writing and graduated in 1957 with a degree in speech and communication. In 1958–1959, he received a Woodrow Wilson Fellowship to study in the creative-writing program at Stanford University, where he joined Larry McMurtry, Ernest J. Gaines, Tillie Olson, and Robert Stone. Kesey adopted a bohemian lifestyle for which he became renowned; he was heavily influenced at this time by the Beat writers, such as Jack Kerouac and Allen Ginsberg, living and writing mostly in San Francisco.

Kesey's first published novel, *One Flew Over the Cuckoo's Nest*, set in a mental asylum in Oregon, tells the story of the conflict between a new patient, Randle P. McMurphy, and the head nurse for dominion over the ward. It is narrated by another inmate, Chief Bromden—who progresses from a near veg-etative state to one of self-determination, as a result of the inspiration of the rebellious McMurphy. The often humorous story is also painful and sad, and Kesey successfully balances the personal, character-driven story with his larger social criticisms.

Two of the clearest points of origin for the setting and events in *One Flew Over the Cuckoo's Nest* were Kesey's introduction to LSD in 1959 and the time that he spent working at the Veterans Administration (VA) hospital in Menlo Park, California, in 1961. Though Kesey became a vocal advocate for the rec-reational use of LSD, his first exposure to it came through paid drug trials, in which he was given psychotropic drugs. Kesey worked in the psychiatric ward at the VA hospital as a night aide, a job similar perhaps to that of Mr. Turkle in the novel. His time on the psychiatric ward allowed Kesey to observe the day-to-day operation of a mental facility and granted him the opportunity to get to know some of the patients. Kesey took the responsibility of accurately rendering the experiences of mental patients seriously, even enduring a voluntary round of electroshock therapy in order to correctly describe the process in the novel.

Students working with the novel will benefit from consulting several other sources. While Kesey continued writing for decades after the publication of *One Flew Over the Cuckoo's Nest*, none of his other works gained the same degree of critical or popular acclaim. His second novel, *Sometimes a Great Notion* (1964), came the closest, and many of the same themes and topics appear, making it a useful companion in the study of Kesey's first novel. Tom Wolfe's *The Electric Kool-Aid Acid Test* (1968) provides an intimate, firsthand description of Kesey and his "Merry Pranksters," the group Kesey traveled across the country with in a psy-chedelically painted school bus; Mark Christensen's *Acid Christ* is the most thor-ough biography, and is the only one published since Kesey's death. Among the best critical sources regarding the novel are One Flew Over the Cuckoo's Nest: *Rising to Heroism*, by Gilbert M. Porter, and Stephen L. Tanner's *Ken Kesey*. The following collections of essays are also valuable: *Ken Kesey's* One Flew Over the Cuckoo's Nest (2002; new edition 2008), both editions edited by Harold Bloom; *Readings on* One Flew Over the Cuckoo's Nest, edited by Lawrence Kappel; and *A Casebook on Ken Kesey's* One Flew Over the Cuckoo's Nest, edited by George J. Searles. The most thorough Kesey bibliography can be found at the *Literary Kicks* website at <http://www.litkicks.com/Biblio/KeseyBiblio.html>.

TOPICS FOR DISCUSSION AND RESEARCH

1. Perhaps the most significant theme in *One Flew Over the Cuckoo's Nest* is that of the sacrificial hero—in fact, McMurphy is often described as a Christ figure. McMurphy has the chance to escape at the end of the novel as the party on the ward comes to a close; yet, he chooses not to, which leads directly to his forced lobotomy and death. When McMurphy first comes on the ward, he is like an alien to the other patients and the staff; he laughs, swears, and causes trouble seemingly for the fun of it. As time progresses and McMurphy brings the other patients out of their shells, the Chief notices that McMurphy's inner strength begins to wane. In other words, as the other patients grow stronger, McMurphy grows weaker and eventually succumbs to the power of the Big Nurse and the Combine, while the Chief escapes. Early in the novel, Nurse Ratched makes it clear that McMurphy is not an altruistic person—he is a con man, in her opinion. One might discuss whether McMurphy is a con man, a savior, or both, using multiple episodes from the text as evidence.

2. Issues of sanity and insanity loom large in this novel. Supposedly, the patients on the ward are insane, though readers may have differing opinions on this by the end of the novel. When McMurphy discovers that most of the patients are on the ward by choice, not by force, he has trouble understanding why, and none of the patients can give him an explanation that makes sense to him. Billy Bibbit tries to, saying, "I could go outside to-today, if I had the guts." McMurphy argues with the men, saying that they're not "*nuts.*" On some level, being sane or insane in this novel seems to come down to confidence—"guts." McMurphy undoubtedly commits some of the most socially unacceptable acts in the novel; yet, he is unapologetic: he stands behind his actions and usually gets away with them. The other men on the ward, on the other hand, are made to feel ashamed for the slightest "abnormal" thought or behavior. One may take on this topic by first posing the question of what counts as sane or insane: is there a clear line of distinction, or are there gray areas? Are any of the "insane" in any way more rational than the "sane"?

3. On a similar note, the themes of freedom versus control are important in this work. In most instances during the novel, the outside world that the Chief describes represents freedom. His recollections of childhood among his Native American relatives stand in sharp contrast to the world on the ward. Bromden's father is a Native American; his mother is white. In many ways, his parents symbolize the two worlds and sets of values that the Chief is pulled between. Often, Bromden describes how the Combine, the huge organization that seeks to control the whole world, implements and exacts that control over people and things. The ward and Nurse Ratched are specific examples of the Combine. McMurphy's entire character works as a counterbalance to the Combine. At one point, the Chief says that somehow McMurphy was able to escape the Combine's grasp and was completely free. Take note of how carefully Kesey works to describe McMurphy and Nurse Ratched in oppos-

ing ways: she is like a porcelain doll; he is red and rough. The novel might be interpreted as a mythic battle between two powerful forces, one representing control and the other freedom. How does the ending confound or complement this interpretation?

4. Some scholars have been critical of Kesey's characterization of women in the novel, a topic that invites discussion. Few women are present in the novel, and nearly all of them are significantly flawed. For the most part, they are either controlling, domineering "ball-cutters" like Nurse Ratched or immoral prostitutes like Candy. The one exception is the Japanese nurse on the Disturbed Ward, who is unable actually to effect any change to the situation. Taking this into consideration, are women somehow naturally at fault in the novel? If not, why is there not a strong, positive female presence in the book? What effects might such a character have had on the story?

5. The 1975 movie version of *One Flew Over the Cuckoo's Nest* stars Jack Nicholson and won five Academy Awards. While the movie is an artistic success in its own right—though Kesey disliked it—it should not be viewed as a substitute for the novel, because there are many differences. Perhaps most significant, the perspective of the movie is moved from Chief Bromden to McMurphy, which creates a completely different narrative arc. Is the casting appropriate? Kesey spends a lot of time and space describing the physical qualities of both McMurphy and Nurse Ratched, and neither of the actors in these parts seem to match up to their descriptions. Any number of angles may be employed to compare the novel and film, but the most logical starting point would be to create a list of what was omitted or significantly changed from page to screen, then to evaluate the implications of these editorial choices.

RESOURCES

Bibliography

Literary Kicks <http://www.litkicks.com/Biblio/KeseyBiblio.html> [accessed 5 October 2009].
A comprehensive primary and secondary bibliography that includes books, short stories, articles, audio recordings, and movie listings.

Biography

Mark Christensen, *Acid Christ: Ken Kesey, LSD, and the Politics of Ecstasy* (Tucson, Ariz.: Schaffner, 2010).
The only biography of Kesey published since his death.

Tom Wolfe, *The Electric Kool-Aid Acid Test* (New York: Farrar, Straus & Giroux, 1968).
A firsthand account of Kesey's LSD-fueled cross-country trip with his band of "Merry Pranksters" on the psychedelically painted school bus. Describes in particular Kesey's political aims for the trip.

Criticism

Harold Bloom, ed., *Ken Kesey's* One Flew Over the Cuckoo's Nest (Philadelphia: Chelsea House, 2002).
A collection of quality essays on the novel, most of which focus on the thematic and literary aspects of the novel.

Bloom, ed., *Ken Kesey's* One Flew Over the Cuckoo's Nest (New York: Infobase, 2008).
A new collection of criticism that includes a completely different set of essays. Focuses mostly on the social and literary impact of the novel.

Barry H. Leeds, *Ken Kesey* (New York: Ungar, 1981).
A brief but helpful bio-critical assessment of Kesey up to 1980 that focuses mainly on his writing. The book begins with a short introduction, then is organized around Kesey's major works.

M. Gilbert Porter, One Flew Over the Cuckoo's Nest: *Rising to Heroism* (Boston: Twayne, 1989).
Provides an overview and a comprehensive literary analysis of the novel, which is broken down in terms of historical context, importance, reception, plot, symbolism, point of view, and characterization.

George J. Searles, ed., *A Casebook on Ken Kesey's* One Flew Over the Cuckoo's Nest (Albuquerque: University of New Mexico Press, 1992).
A varied collection of essays that cover several different topics, including its literary elements, social context, connection with other works, and translation to film.

Stephen L. Tanner, *Ken Kesey* (Boston: Twayne, 1983).
An excellent overview of Kesey's work, which devotes a chapter to *One Flew Over the Cuckoo's Nest*.

—*David Wright*

Harper Lee, *To Kill a Mockingbird*

(Philadelphia: Lippincott, 1960)

The facts regarding the early life of Harper Lee (1926–) suggest that the settings and many of the characters in her only published novel, *To Kill a Mockingbird* (1960), are based on actual places and people. Nelle Harper Lee grew up in Monroeville, a town in the southern part of Alabama much like the fictional Maycomb in *To Kill a Mockingbird*. Like Atticus Finch, Lee's father was a lawyer and a member of the state legislature. Though he never defended an African American man charged with rape, he did defend two black men charged with murdering a local merchant. Like Atticus, Lee's father lost the case; the men were hanged in the Monroeville jail. Her father published a newspaper, *The Monroeville Journal,* which may be represented in the novel by *The Maycomb Tribune.* The editor of the fictional paper, Mr. Underwood, is often cast in a positive light in the novel: his editorials do not shy away from the truth—no matter how unpopular—and he is ready to use violence to defend Atticus from the lynch mob that is out to get Tom Robinson in chapter 15. In addition to her father as the inspiration for both Atticus Finch and Mr. Underwood, most experts agree that the character Dill is based largely on Lee's lifelong friend, the Southern writer Truman Capote. Unquestionably, the character of Scout is based on the young Harper Lee. Like Scout, Lee has been noted for being a tomboy, an early and precocious reader, and somewhat of a social outcast. From an early age, she enjoyed writing—first with Capote as a child and then in high school and in college. During part of her undergraduate career at the University of Alabama she was an editor of the college's satirical magazine, the *Rammer-Jammer.*

One of the true hallmarks of Harper Lee's *To Kill a Mockingbird* is its popularity. A year after its publication, it had sold half a million copies, been translated into ten languages, and been awarded the Pulitzer Prize. The novel, which has never been out of print, had sold more than thirty million copies and been translated into forty languages by 2009. As a further testament to the influence of Lee's book, President George W. Bush awarded Lee the Presidential Medal of Freedom, the United States' highest civilian honor, in 2007. Perhaps another indication of the continued relevance of the novel is its regular appearance on proposed banned-books lists owing to its racial and sexual themes, language, and imagery.

While Lee herself has been notoriously reclusive and silent regarding her writing, secondary sources on Lee and *To Kill a Mockingbird* are widely available. *Mockingbird: A Portrait of Harper Lee* (2006), by Charles J. Shields, is the only biography available that is not written for young adults. Students should also consult the several collections of criticism regarding the novel: *Harper Lee's* To Kill a Mockingbird, updated edition (2007), edited by Harold Bloom; *Understanding* To Kill a Mockingbird: *A Student Casebook to Issues, Sources, and Historical Documents* (1994), edited by Claudia Durst Johnson; *Racism in Harper Lee's* To Kill a Mockingbird (2008), edited by Candice Mancini; *Readings on* To Kill a Mockingbird (2000), edited by Terry O'Neill; and *On Harper Lee: Essays and Reflections* (2007), edited by Alice Hall Petry. A bibliography of articles and books on the novel and author can be found at the website of *The Society for the Study of Southern Literature Bibliography.*

TOPICS FOR DISCUSSION AND RESEARCH

1. One avenue for discussion that *To Kill a Mockingbird* opens up concerns life in the South during the Great Depression. The novel attempts to capture a moment in the development of Southern American society through the eyes of a child. It is a classic example of a bildungsroman, or coming-of-age story: in such a work the protagonist undergoes some important development in intellect or character. Such a process certainly takes place in Scout. In the

beginning she is intimately familiar with Maycomb's unwritten codes, because she has grown up within them. Her first-grade teacher, on the other hand, is an outsider and, thus, not able to deal with various issues that arise on the first day of school. During the course of the novel Scout becomes increasingly aware of the world around her by observing events that occur around her and her family. She also learns and grows through her regular, humorous transgressions of social norms regarding dress, speech, and action, and she discovers some of the darker truths about her society from which she had previously been shielded. Students might consider the ways in which Scout's view of the world changes significantly. For instance, how does her understanding of Boo Radley and Atticus change? What lessons does she ultimately learn through Atticus's teaching and example? Students might also discuss how the novel could represent not only Scout's growth as an individual but also the coming of age of the American South as a region.

2. Race and racism are perhaps the most commonly encountered topics of discussion concerning this novel. The most blatant instance of racism in the novel is, of course, Tom Robinson's unjust trial, conviction, and death, but racist language, attitudes, and actions occur throughout the work. For instance, Calpurnia, the Finches' African American housekeeper, has great influence over the children, for whom she is almost a surrogate mother. In chapter 12 Calpurnia takes Scout and Jem to her church, which is clearly an uncommon practice. Fascinated by the differences between the services at the black church and the white one she attends, Scout hopes to go back to Calpurnia's church; but Aunt Alexandra forbids it, because such interracial socializing is not "proper." Since the late 1960s many people have objected to the book being read in public schools, much as objections have been raised to Mark Twain's *The Adventures of Huckleberry Finn* (1884). While advocates of these novels do not deny that racism is depicted in them, they argue that the books do not promote racism but instead demonstrate the follies of such thinking. Students can examine this question: is *To Kill a Mockingbird* critical of racism, or is it racist itself? Are the two mutually exclusive, or could the novel be both?

3. Another key theme in *To Kill a Mockingbird* is the highly subjective treatment of justice in Scout's isolated world. Obviously, Atticus's positions as a lawyer and a representative in the legislature bring in concerns of actual law and order, as does the trial of Tom Robinson. Perhaps the more interesting questions of justice in the novel, however, revolve around issues that never see the inside of a police station or courtroom. On the one hand, the children's concerns and games involve a certain sense of justice and morality; on the other hand, as they begin to enter into the adult world, their sense of justice and morality begins to change, as well. For instance, Scout is confused and concerned when Jem becomes distraught over the result of Tom Robinson's trial; but Atticus recognizes that Jem is trying to align his childish sense of justice with the "justice" of the world. How does the changing and uncertain idea of justice in the novel work concerning Boo Radley? Is Mr. Ewell's death justified? Should Boo Radley have been held accountable?

4. Even though *To Kill a Mockingbird* revolves around the gravest issues, it is full of humor—most of which arises from Scout's unusual way of seeing, describing, and interacting with the world around her. A careful reading of the dialogue cannot help turning up laugh-out-loud reactions throughout; for instance, at the end of the novel, in one of its most tense scenes, Scout's repeated inquires to Dr. Reynolds about Jem—"Then he's not dead?"—add a dash of humor to an otherwise melodramatic moment. Humor also occurs because of some of the adventures in which Scout, Jem, and Dill involve themselves; a common characteristic of the bildungsroman is for a young protagonist to get in over his or her head and use wit and luck to get out safely. Students might locate the moments of humor that strike them the most and discuss their relationship to the overall meaning of the novel.

5. The immense popularity of the novel may be rivaled by that of popularity of the 1962 film version. The movie was nominated for eight Academy Awards and won three; Gregory Peck's Oscar for his portrayal of Atticus was the only one of his career. Students should be able to make many worthwhile connections and comparisons between the novel and the film, discussing what is left out of the movie and what effect the omissions have on the story. Also, students might compare their interpretations of the characters as they are presented in the novel with the choices that the filmmakers made concerning the appearance and speech of the principal characters.

RESOURCES

Primary Work
"Christmas to Me," *McCall's,* 89 (December 1961): 63.
The story of how friends gave Lee a year's salary as a Christmas gift, allowing her to complete *To Kill a Mockingbird*.

Bibliography
The Society for the Study of Southern Literature Bibliography <http://www.missq. msstate.edu/sssl> [accessed 4 December 2009].
Includes approximately thirty scholarly articles on *To Kill a Mockingbird* and Harper Lee.

Biography
Charles J. Shields, *Mockingbird: A Portrait of Harper Lee* (New York: Holt, 2006). A well-researched biography, written without Lee's cooperation but still helpful to one's understanding of the author, her novel, and her friendship with Truman Capote.

Criticism
Harold Bloom, ed., *Harper Lee's* To Kill a Mockingbird, updated edition, Bloom's Modern Critical Interpretations (New York: Chelsea House, 2007).

Eleven essays, including an introductory one by Bloom, covering a variety of literary and social topics regarding *To Kill a Mockingbird*.

Claudia Durst Johnson, *Understanding* To Kill a Mockingbird: *A Student Casebook to Issues, Sources, and Historical Documents* (Westport, Conn.: Greenwood Press, 1994).
Comprehensively situates *To Kill a Mockingbird* within the social and literary landscape of its historic period by excerpting a wide variety of historical and literary documents. Johnson also looks at the issue of censorship and the novel.

Candice Mancini, ed., *Racism in Harper Lee's* To Kill a Mockingbird (Farmington Hills, Mich.: Greenhaven, 2008).
Provides various perspectives on racism in the novel and also connects the novel to current issues of race.

Terry O'Neill, ed., *Readings on* To Kill a Mockingbird (San Diego: Greenhaven, 2000).
A survey of major points of interest about the novel, including its critical reception, its literary techniques, and the social issues it treats.

Alice Hall Petry, ed., *On Harper Lee: Essays and Reflections* (Knoxville: University of Tennessee Press, 2007).
A combination of academic essays and personal reflections on Lee and *To Kill a Mockingbird*.

—David Wright

⸎

Norman Mailer, *The Naked and the Dead*
(New York: Rinehart, 1948)

Norman Mailer (1923–2007) was a major novelist and creative nonfiction writer whose career spanned nearly six decades. Raised in Brooklyn, Mailer began writing at a very early age. His precociousness was evident to his family, and his admission to Harvard in 1939 introduced him to the work of a range of intellectual and artistic influences, including Ernest Hemingway, John Steinbeck, John Dos Passos, and James T. Farrell, which shaped his writing for the rest of his life. The distinctive styles of these writers and their treatment of the theme of human suffering inspired Mailer. At eighteen, he published a short story in the Harvard *Advocate*, "The Greatest Thing in the World," which won the *Story* magazine prize for best short story by an undergraduate in 1941. In September of that year, Mailer completed, but never published, his first novel, "No Percentage."

Mailer's classic World War II novel, *The Naked and the Dead*, is often considered one of the three great Realistic American war novels of the twentieth century. (See studies by Philip Bufithis and Robert Alter listed below for analyses of the elements of Realism.) The other two are *A Farewell to Arms* (1929), by

Ernest Hemingway, and *From Here to Eternity* (1951), by James Jones. Mailer was drafted into military service near the end of World War II. He refused the opportunity to become an officer, as was the norm for Harvard graduates. Mailer entered the army with the rank of private, and his job as infantryman was the only full-time employment Mailer would ever hold, except for his lifelong occupation as a writer.

Hemingway and Jones were both wounded in military action, and they saw the grim realities of war that fed their powerful novels. Mailer drew much of his material from the brief time he spent in the Pacific near the Philippines. He enlisted in the army in the summer of 1944. After completing basic training, he was assigned in spring 1945 to a unit responsible for searching out the remaining Japanese soldiers on a small island in the Pacific. Although Mailer did not see much combat, he did see death, and his acute, creative imagination was already distilling the meticulous notes he took about his fellow soldiers. This record was the basis for *The Naked and the Dead,* which remained on the best-seller list for sixty-three consecutive weeks and established Mailer, only twenty-five years old, as one of America's most promising young writers.

Mailer was always interested in conflict, and a duality of forces exists in nearly all of his writing. At one level, he emphasizes the continuing struggle between good and evil, as developed in his last novel, *The Castle in the Forest* (2007). At another level, Mailer captures the tension between ideas, individuals, and cultures and creates portraits that are profound and probing. Mailer offers powerful character portraits, as well as psychological and physical descriptions, that energize both his fiction and nonfiction. *The Naked and the Dead* reveals, for example, tensions between institutions (the army) and individuals (soldiers). Readers are given a glimpse into the anxiety-ridden, competing temperaments: characters obsessed with power versus individuals who believe in individual freedom. (See Ihab Habib Hassan's discussion of institutional authority.) The brutality of war is coupled with flashbacks of characters' premilitary experiences that shape their beliefs and behavior. Mailer's body of writing reveals, again and again, his interest in many of the fundamental tensions of life and how these tensions are so necessary for characters (and readers) to develop and express the values they come to hold.

Early in his career Mailer was a prominent member of a small group of America's premier writers, including Saul Bellow, Truman Capote, Joan Didion, Philip Roth, John Updike, and Kurt Vonnegut. Mailer's mastery of complex metaphor and his inexhaustible range of topics have attracted generations of readers. Mailer was also an ardent sports fan, having written, for example, about boxing in *The Fight* (1975), an account called one of the greatest sports books ever written on the heavyweight championship bout between Muhammad Ali and George Foreman. He has written in-depth character studies, in the form sometimes called creative nonfiction, of well-known personalities, including Pablo Picasso, Gary Gilmore, Lee Harvey Oswald, and Marilyn Monroe.

Mailer wrote more than forty books over his career and directed four films. He was awarded both the National Book Award and the Pulitzer Prize for *The Armies of the Night* in 1968, and in 2005 he received the National Book Foundation Medal for Distinguished Contribution to American Letters. His career as a novelist, essayist, journalist, poet, playwright, screenwriter, public intellectual, and man of letters inspired the founding of *The Mailer Review* in 2007, a journal dedicated to the life and work of Mailer.

TOPICS FOR DISCUSSION AND RESEARCH

1. *The Naked and the Dead* is a Naturalistic war novel, as Donald Pizer explains, but it is also much more than a war chronicle. Mailer is a philosophical writer. *The Naked and the Dead* is a complex novel that examines human relationships in the overall context of human experience. For Mailer, all humans are unavoidably and continually locked into a series of tense, challenging situations. Sometimes the struggles are with outside forces (for example, American GIs confronting enemy soldiers). On other occasions they illustrate rifts between individuals that should be together (soldiers who dislike one another, like General Cummings and Lieutenant Hearn). Oftentimes conflicts are within a person; for example, the psychological demons plaguing Sergeant Croft. Students might identify ideological conflicts in one or more of the major characters. In considering ideological objectives and power, students should consult Nigel Leigh's 1990 study of Mailer's novels.

2. Strife within, between, and among characters is representative of the general tension that permeates the novel. First, there is the obvious conflict between nations at war. This struggle is represented by the army unit searching for a relatively small group of steadfast Japanese soldiers who remain on the island, presenting a danger to American forces. Second, there is the conflict between some soldiers and their respective personal philosophies. General Cummings is a power-obsessed fascist who believes in the importance of dominating others. His distaste for Lieutenant Hearn is representative of the contempt the general has for the average person, for men who are different from him. The ongoing rift between the general and the lieutenant dramatizes Mailer's concern for showing how the desire to control others is a fundamental part of human behavior. Further, such obsessive behavior is made possible by being part of an institutional structure—in this case, the army, which protects the general and his obsessions. Generals are very powerful, and Mailer's novel emphasizes the psychology of the men who want power. *The Naked and the Dead* encourages readers to think about power and the abuse of power. After reading the novel, students might consider the following: What are some of the possible dangers of power being concentrated in the hands of the few? How do configurations of power relate to conditions of war?

3. It is sometimes said that Mailer is a believer in Manichaeism, a philosophy that posits a core concept of opposing principles (good and evil, for example). General Cummings and Sergeant Croft are represented as unrestrained followers of their worst instincts. Lieutenant Hearn is an opposing force to Cummings and Croft, a thoughtful and empathetic individual who is more humane than his opposites. Hearn is despised by Cummings and Croft. His kindness and intellectual honesty is taken as a sign of weakness rather than strength.

Power-obsessed, inhumane individuals like Cummings and Croft instinctively and ruthlessly seek out the destruction of characters like Hearn. Is there an identifiable source of the evil in Cummings and Croft? What might it be?

4. Mailer creates powerful metaphors in *The Naked and the Dead*. He also reveals a love for parable and allegory, as discussed in the work of Robert Begiebing. What metaphors are particularly memorable and meaningful in the novel, and what is the source of their power? Parables and allegories are representations of ideas beyond the surface meaning of a story. Which characters and situations in the novel suggest something larger than themselves? How might these be interpreted?

5. Mailer addresses the importance of sensitivity in his introduction to the fiftieth-anniversary reprinting of the novel: "Compassion is of value and enriches our life only when compassion is severe, which is to say when we can perceive everything that is good and bad about a character but are still able to feel that the sum of us as human beings is probably a little more good than awful. In any case, good or bad, it reminds us that life is like a gladiators' arena for the soul and so we can feel strengthened by those who endure, and feel awe and pity for those who do not." *The Naked and the Dead* is a novel about suffering and survival. Mailer's words establish him as an affirmative writer, one who believes that humans can endure, perhaps even thrive, because of their capacity to learn and grow. The struggles illustrated in the travails of the soldiers in *The Naked and the Dead* are a parable for the struggle of life itself. The novel raises many questions for students to ponder. All individuals struggle, but is there value in suffering? Does one learn something of sympathy and empathy as he engages conflict in the lives of fictional characters?

RESOURCES

Primary Work

The Naked and the Dead: Fiftieth Anniversary Edition (New York: Holt, 1998).
Important for Mailer's new introduction, which comments on his debt to Tolstoy and the significance of compassion. Mailer offers a candid assessment of his achievement.

Interviews

J. Michael Lennon, ed., *Conversations with Norman Mailer* (Jackson: University of Mississippi Press, 1988).
A series of interviews conducted with Mailer between the late 1940s and the late 1980s.

Bibliography

J. Michael Lennon and Donna Pedro Lennon, *Works and Days* (Shavertown, Pa.: Sligo Press, 2000).
A detailed listing of works by and about Mailer through 1998.

Phillip Sipiora, ed. *The Mailer Review,* cosponsored by the University of South
    Florida and The Norman Mailer Society.
An annual journal devoted to the life and work of Mailer. The first issue, published in 2007, includes a complete Mailer bibliography through 2006, which
subsequent issues update.

Biography

Mary Dearborn, *Mailer: A Biography* (Boston: Houghton Mifflin, 1999).
Provides articulate analyses of Mailer's work and includes a consideration of the
sensual side of the creative artist.

Peter Manso, *Mailer: His Life and Times* (New York: Simon & Schuster,
    1985).
Draws on interviews with over one hundred individuals who knew Mailer.

Hilary Mills, *Mailer: A Biography* (New York: Empire Books, 1982).
The first Mailer biography, which examines the influences in Mailer's life that led
to the writing of *The Naked and the Dead.*

Car Rollyson, *The Lives of Norman Mailer* (New York: Paragon House, 1991).
Presents Mailer's eccentricities without exaggeration and integrates his life and
work better than the other biographies. It shows how Mailer the creative writer
is integrated into his narratives.

Criticism

Robert Alter, "The Real and Imaginary Worlds of Norman Mailer," in his *Motives
    for Fiction* (Cambridge, Mass.: Harvard University Press, 1984), pp. 46–60.
Alter selects a variety of texts, including *The Naked and the Dead,* to explore how
various writers approach "reality" and its representations.

Robert J. Begiebing, *Acts of Regeneration: Allegory and Archetype in the Works of
    Norman Mailer* (Columbia: University of Missouri Press, 1980).
Examines Mailer's philosophical issues as they are illustrated by parables and
allegories in several works, including *The Naked and the Dead.*

Philip H. Bufithis, *Norman Mailer* (New York: Ungar, 1978).
Looks at *The Naked and the Dead* as a work that exemplifies Realistic
Naturalism.

Ihab Habib Hassan, "Encounter with Necessity," in *Critical Essays on Norman
    Mailer,* edited by J. Michael Lennon (Boston: G. K. Hall, 1986), pp. 91–98.
Analyzes *The Naked and the Dead* in terms of its representations of structures of
power and the ways in which individuals relate to institutional authority.

Nigel Leigh, *Radical Fictions and the Novels of Norman Mailer* (New York: St.
    Martin's Press, 1990.)
Focuses on the author's concern for power relationships, particularly as they relate
to ideological objectives.

Robert Merrill, "*The Naked and the Dead:* The Beast and the Seer in Man," in his *Norman Mailer Revisited* (New York: Twayne, 1992), pp. 11–29.
Merrill takes a formal approach to Mailer's work, examining the different depictions of action in the novel.

The Norman Mailer Society Homepage <http://normanmailersociety.org/> [accessed 24 November 2009].
The official website of the Norman Mailer Society, frequently updated with information about Mailer's life and work.

Donald Pizer, "The Naked and the Dead," in his *Twentieth-Century American Literary Naturalism: An Interpretation* (Carbondale: Southern Illinois University Press, 1982), pp. 90–114.
Analyses Mailer's use of Naturalism in *The Naked and the Dead.*

—Phillip Sipiora

〜✕〜

Carson McCullers, *The Member of the Wedding*
(Boston: Houghton Mifflin, 1946)

Carson McCullers (1917–1967) began to conceive the story that became *The Member of the Wedding* (1946) as early as the fall of 1939, but she had not solved the problems of the narrative until Thanksgiving of the following year. McCullers drew on her past, growing up in the small town of Columbus, Georgia, for the novel. In her article "How I Began to Write," published in the September 1948 issue of *Mademoiselle,* McCullers describes her childhood as a time of restlessness: "The firelight on the walnut folding doors would sadden me, and the tedious sound of the old swan clock. I dreamed of the distant city of skyscrapers and snow, and New York." And yet, McCullers admits that it was "our Georgia rooms, the marvelous solitary region of simple stories and the inward mind" that became the staples of her fiction, and so one finds many parallels between McCullers's life and the life of Frankie Addams portrayed in the novel. McCullers, like Frankie, was "gray-eyed" and restless. Like Frankie, her father was a hardworking jeweler. And while she claimed that the cook, Berenice, was modeled after Dilsey from William Faulkner's *The Sound and the Fury* (1929), she also displays a striking resemblance to the McCullers's cook, Lucille.

While McCullers's fiction is often classified as Grotesque or Southern Gothic, *The Member of the Wedding* is essentially a novel of psychological Realism. Told almost exclusively from the perspective of Frankie, the novel takes place during three days at the end of August 1944 in a small, unnamed Alabama town. Part one of the novel takes place mostly in the Addams's kitchen, and Frankie is characterized as a restless twelve-year-old who does not know what to do with herself in these late summer days full of loneliness and repetition. She is too old for children's play and too young to join the "older" girls who have formed a "club."

Throughout the novel, Frankie attempts to find an outlet for her dreams, which are impeded by the stultifying small-town atmosphere. When she tries to escape by attempting to join her brother and his wife on their honeymoon, the attempt fails, and she runs away from home only to be picked up by a policeman in a GI bar where she has had a dangerous flirtation with a soldier. For Frankie, there is no escape. In the novel's denouement, it is fall and Frances has returned to school. John Henry, her young friend and cousin in part one, has died; Berenice, the wise African American cook, has decided to get married and leave the family; the house that Frances and her father lived in is for sale, and they are moving. Everything has changed; yet, nothing has changed. The world that Frankie inhabited at the beginning of the novel is now gone; she must face her new situation at school. She is preoccupied with her nascent friendship with Mary Littlejohn, with whom she shares a newfound interest in art and poetry and who serves as a substitute for the deceased John Henry and Berenice, whom she seems to dismiss from her mind as she naively anticipates the promise of adolescence. Yet, the novel is full of unfulfilled dreams, and Frankie—now, in the autumn, "Frances"—continues to dream of a life outside the small Southern town, imagining for the time being that she and Mary Littlejohn will someday be world travelers.

The Member of the Wedding remains one of McCullers's most popular successes and has had several incarnations. In 1950 a stage version ran for 501 performances. The play was made into a 1952 movie and a television version in 1997. Further, the short stories "Breath from the Sky" and "Wunderkind" share strong affinities with *The Member of the Wedding,* as they also deal with lonely young characters on the verge of self-discovery.

Several other primary and secondary sources will help students better understand *The Member of the Wedding.* "Loneliness . . . An American Malady," collected in *The Mortgaged Heart* (2005), is an essential resource. In this essay, McCullers explains how loneliness is inherent in the American character. Virginia Spenser Carr's works are excellent, particularly her biography and introduction to the *Collected Stories.* Useful criticism can be found in Sarah Gleeson-White's *Gender and Identity in the Novels of Carson McCullers* and Barbara A. White's "Loss of Self in *The Member of the Wedding.*" These works concentrate on Frankie and the problem of growing up female.

TOPICS FOR DISCUSSION AND RESEARCH

1. One of the most obvious features of *The Member of the Wedding* is its three-part structure, and within each part Frankie has a different name: Frankie in part one, F. Jasmine in part two, and Frances in part three. These name changes reflect a change in the way Frankie perceives the world, while at the same time they reflect a change in her personality. Using these ideas as a base, students might explore what Frankie learns in each of the sections of the novel—if she learns anything. A good focus would be Frankie's dreams, ambitions, desires, and how her attitude toward them changes, does not change, or is modified throughout the narrative.

2. McCullers frequently treats the subject of the adolescent female coming to grips with her life. A productive analysis can be made by comparing and contrasting the characters of Mick Kelly in *The Heart Is a Lonely Hunter* (1940), Constance in the short story "Breath from the Sky," and Frankie in the short story "Wunkerkind." Although these characters inhabit different settings (even different time periods), what is it that unites them? How does each help to convey the common themes found in McCullers's fiction?

3. Consider the setting in *The Member of the Wedding*. What part does the "hot house" atmosphere play in McCullers's novel? It is the hottest part of the summer in Alabama, and the nights are as warm and steamy as the days. How does the setting and her journey through it reflect Frankie's desires and ambitions? Does the setting represent an escape that Frankie feels she must make, or is it the setting that nurtures her dreams? Finally, can one find a universal meaning in the novel's setting?

4. In many of McCullers's narratives, the female character is an adolescent sitting on the cusp between childhood and adulthood; this is marked by McCullers's use of male-female names, such as Mick or Frankie, for her protagonists. An important investigation might center on Frankie as an emerging woman: What are her dreams and ambitions before and after her discovery that she is a woman? Are these dreams suppressed in order for her to "fit into" society, or are they put aside until the time when she is an adult, so they can be brought back out, dusted off, and worked toward?

5. In an unkind and stilted review of *Illumination and Night Glare* in the January 2000 issue of *The New Criterion*, Brooke Allen called McCullers an "emotional vampire": She "had a devouring wish for love, and her love object, once attained, would in turn be devoured and drained by her voracious needs." Whether this is true of McCullers is problematic. However, taking the definition that Allen gives of an emotional vampire, can that definition be applied to the character of Frankie? Looking at Frankie's character through the eyes of the definition, what does this tell us about McCullers's characterization of her and her relationships with others? Analyzing these features, the student may argue whether the definition is reflected in Frankie's character.

6. Central to the novel is the theme of loneliness. In an essay published in the 19 December 1949 edition of *This Week* magazine called "Loneliness . . . An American Malady," McCullers wrote that loneliness, in America, is "essentially . . . [a] quest for identity." McCullers claims in the American consciousness there is a constant conflict between the "dual motives" of "identity" and "the will . . . to belong." She goes on to say that Americans desire both a "sense of separateness" and a sense of belonging "to something larger and more powerful than the weak, lonely self." In this context, she mentions Frankie in *The Member of the Wedding*. Explore this essential duality in the character of Frankie in the novel: Is she successful, by novel's end, in achieving a balance (uneasy or otherwise) between these two essential elements in the American character? Students might consult the section titled "*Fear of Independence: 'The We of Me,'*" in chapter 5 of Margaret B. McDowell's critical study for help with this topic.

RESOURCES

Primary Works

The Collected Stories of Carson McCullers, edited by Virginia Spencer Carr (Boston: Houghton Mifflin, 1998).
Includes *The Member of the Wedding*, *The Ballad of the Sad Café*, and several short stories that share the similar themes and situations.

Illumination and Night Glare: The Unfinished Autobiography of Carson McCullers, edited by Carlos L. Dews (Madison: University of Wisconsin Press, 1999).
Contains the narrative of how McCullers found the "solution" to the novel and letters to Reeve McCullers during World War II.

"Loneliness . . . An American Malady," in *The Mortgaged Heart: Selected Writings of Carson McCullers*, edited by Margarita G. Smith (Boston: Houghton Mifflin, 2005).
An essential essay. McCullers clearly explains how "loneliness" in built into the American character. It is a central theme that appears in most of her fiction.

Biography

Virginia Spencer Carr, *The Lonely Hunter: A Biography of Carson McCullers* (New York: Carroll & Graf, 1985).
An excellent biography of McCullers with many references to *The Member of the Wedding*.

Oliver Evans, *The Ballad of Carson McCullers: A Biography* (New York: Coward-McCann, 1965).
A literary biography with a summary and analysis of *The Member of the Wedding*. Sees Frankie Addams as a representation of McCullers and "a particularly eloquent symbol of human loneliness."

Josyane Savigneau, *Carson McCullers: A Life*, translated by Joan E. Howard (Boston: Houghton Mifflin, 2001).
A literary biography. Chapter 5, "Frankie 'The European,'" deals directly with *The Member of the Wedding*.

Sherill Tippins, *February House* (Boston: Houghton Mifflin, 2005).
A history of the house at 7 Middagh Street in Brooklyn where McCullers lived off and on from 1940 to 1941 while writing *The Member of the Wedding*.

Bibliography

Judith Giblin James, *Wunderkind: The Reputation of Carson McCullers, 1940–1990* (Columbia, S.C.: Camden House, 1995).
A series of bibliographic essays dealing with the works of McCullers. Chapter 5 is devoted to *The Member of the Wedding*.

Criticism

Richard M. Cook, *Carson McCullers* (New York: Ungar, 1975).
Sees the novel as "inward," as concerning Frankie's world: "She cannot afford to take up pressing social issues outside of Frankie's ken."

Thadious M. Davis, "Erasing the 'We of Me' and Rewriting the Racial Script: Carson McCullers's Two *Member(s) of the Wedding*," in *Critical Essays on Carson McCullers*, edited by Beverly Lyon Clark and Melvin J. Friedman (New York: G. K. Hall, 1996), pp. 214–219.
Compares the handling of race and gender identification in the novel and the stage version of *The Member of the Wedding;* unlike the novel, the play "succumbed to the then popular images of blacks."

Sarah Gleeson-White, *Strange Bodies: Gender and Identity in the Novels of Carson McCullers* (Tuscaloosa: University of Alabama Press, 2003).
Argues that Frankie defies the standard "binarism" of gender and is "suspended" between male and female.

Margaret B. McDowell, *Carson McCullers* (Boston: Twayne, 1980).
Includes chapter 5, which deals with *The Member of the Wedding*. McDowell sees the novel as balanced between "the turmoil and self-centered egotism of Frankie with the agony, courage, and cynical humor of Berenice."

Barbara A. White, "Loss of Self in *The Member of the Wedding*," in *Modern Critical Views: Carson McCullers*, edited by Harold Bloom (New York: Chelsea House, 1986), pp. 125–142.
Sees the novel as an "initiation into acceptance of *female* limits." At the end of the novel Frankie transforms her dreams from those of boys and men to the acceptance of her place in the world as a girl and a woman.

—Bob Bell

Arthur Miller, *The Crucible*

(New York: Viking, 1953)

When *The Crucible* premiered at the Martin Beck Theater in New York City on 22 January 1953, Arthur Miller was already regarded, along with Tennessee Williams, as one of the most important American playwrights of his time. He had won a Pulitzer Prize for *Death of a Salesman* (1949), two Drama Critics' Circle Awards, for that play and for *All My Sons* (1947); *The Crucible* won an Antoinette Perry (Tony) Award and ran for 197 performances.

Miller was regarded as a moral playwright whose work addressed the difficult choices conscientious people are forced to make in modern society. Thus, critics were initially surprised that he had set his new play in seventeenth-century New England. The political significance of his theme, however, quickly became clear. Indeed, Miller was denied a passport to see the London opening in 1954 because the play was considered hostile to the interests of the U.S. government.

The Crucible deals with the 1692 Salem, Massachusetts, witch trials, in particular with a family devastated by adultery and charges of witchcraft. Amid the hysteria of the day Abigail Williams, who had been dismissed from her duties as a servant of John and Elizabeth Proctor when Elizabeth discovered an adulterous relationship between her and John, is arrested as a witch possessed by the devil. Angry about her dismissal, Abigail claims to have been bewitched by Elizabeth and implicates others, as well. A trial ensues, at which the judge and deputy governor refuse to admit any exculpatory evidence and urge the accused to confess to save their lives. To save his wife, John calls Abigail a whore and confesses to adultery but refuses to testify about others. When his wife, unaware of John's admission, is questioned about the matters to which her husband confessed, she lies to protect him and thereby complicates his situation. At the end of the play John refuses to name others as witches and tears up his confession. He is sentenced to hang along with the other defendants.

In 1953 both the House Committee on Un-American Activities (HCUA) and the Senate Subcommittee on Government Operations were conducting investigations of Communist activity among Americans. Suspect witnesses were called to testify with the understanding that they could avoid further accusation and punishment if they cooperated by naming other people known or thought to be Communists. As Miller was beginning his research on *The Crucible,* his friend, director Elia Kazan, was called to testify and named names to save his career. Other friends of Miller's made the same decision, including Lee J. Cobb, who had played Willy Loman in *Death of a Salesman.* Miller felt that they had failed a test of their character. When Miller himself was called to testify before the House committee in 1956, he testified about his own activities but refused to name others. He was tried on two counts of contempt of Congress and found guilty; his conviction was overturned on appeal in 1958.

One must be aware of the political situation of the 1950s to respond fully to *The Crucible.* There are several histories of the HCUA and McCarthy hearings. One of the most accessible is Stefan Kanfer's *A Journal of the Plague Years* (New York: Atheneum, 1973). Victor Navasky's *Naming Names* (New York: Viking, 1980) is a decidedly leftist account that discusses Miller's testimony and his relationships with those who did name names, particularly Kazan. Miller's own statement about the play and his intentions can be found in the introduction to his *Collected Plays* (1957). Miller gave frequent interviews in which he discussed his plays; Matthew C. Roudané's 1987 collection is the recommended source. After the play itself and Miller's introduction to his *Collected Plays,* Christopher Bigsby's 2009 biography is the clear best choice for students interested in learning about Miller's approach to his work. There are collections of essays on *The Crucible* by Harold Bloom (1999 and 2004) and John H. Ferres (1972), and James J. Martine provides particularly sound approaches to the play.

TOPICS FOR DISCUSSION AND RESEARCH

1. In an interview with Matthew C. Roudané, Miller said, "In The Crucible we see the fate of the society from a religious, moral point of view; its merged sublime and political powers forcing the transmission of a man's conscience to others and then of the man's final immortal need to take it back." Discuss how that statement applies to the social situation of the early 1950s and of other periods, as well. What does Miller mean by "transmission of a man's conscience to others"? Does *The Crucible* have universal application? Is it relevant to the national and international situation today? Dennis Welland addresses this topic in his chapter on *The Crucible*.

2. The Salem witch trials of 1692 are well documented, and the characters in Miller's play are based on real people whose testimony in the trials is preserved. But Miller has been accused of playing loose with the facts regarding the trial. Why might he have altered the historical facts, and what effect did those alterations have on the meaning of his play? Read Miller's "Journey to *The Crucible*" (1953), James W. Douglas's "*The Crucible:* Which Witch Is Which?" (1953), and, for a politically conservative perspective, Donald Lyons's "Othertimes, Otherwheres" (1992) before you formulate an answer.

3. *The Crucible* is a politically charged play. Consider how the responses to it might be affected by the political predisposition of critics or readers. Would a committed Democrat read the play differently than a conservative Republican, for example? Read reviews of the Broadway revivals of the play in 1964, 1972, 1991, and 2002 in *The New York Times* or another source. Do critics' responses change with the political and social climate? See Tetsumaro Hayashi's bibliography (1976) for help in identifying critical responses.

4. Miller called his play a tragedy, a form that has particular traditional significance with regard to drama. Review the formal definition of tragedy in a reliable source, such as C. Hugh Holman's *A Handbook to Literature* (New York: Macmillan / London: Collier-Macmillan, 1992), and then read Miller's comments about *The Crucible* in Roudané's collection of interviews. How does Miller's play qualify as a tragedy? What are the elements necessary to a tragedy? Does *The Crucible* embody those elements?

5. Consider the role of religion in the play. Miller reverses what might be regarded as the normal moral situation: traditionally, societies have turned to religious authorities for guidance about moral questions; but in *The Crucible* the religious authorities are villainous, seeking to force people to act against their consciences to save themselves—to sacrifice their souls to save their bodies in the name of fighting the devil. Research Puritan religious beliefs—the Cotton Mather entry in *Research Guide to American Literature: Colonial Literature, 1607–1776* is a good starting place—to attempt an explanation of the court's motivation in the witch trials. Does Miller fairly portray the religious sentiments of the period?

RESOURCES

Primary Works

Collected Plays (New York: Viking, 1957).
Includes an introduction in which Miller makes an important statement on *The Crucible* and what he hoped to achieve with the play.

"Journey to *The Crucible*," *New York Times*, 8 February 1953, p. X3.
Miller's account of his visit to Salem to research his play.

Bibliography

Tetsumaro Hayashi, *An Index to Arthur Miller* Criticism (Metuchen, N.J.: Scarecrow Press, 1976).
The most reliable bibliography of secondary sources.

Biography

Christopher Bigsby, *Arthur Miller: 1915–1962* (Cambridge, Mass.: Harvard University Press, 2009).
The definitive biography of Miller, meticulously researched and drawing on previously unavailable material.

Matthew C. Roudané, ed., *Conversations with Arthur Miller* (Jackson: University Press of Mississippi, 1987).
A collection of the best of Miller's frequent interviews.

Criticism

Claudia Durst Johnson and Vernon E. Johnson, *Understanding* The Crucible: *A Student Casebook to Issues, Sources, and Historical Documents* (Westport, Conn.: Greenwood Press, 1998).
Interdisciplinary casebook that provides a rich variety of primary historical documents and commentary on *The Crucible* in the context of the Salem witch trials of 1692 and the "Second Red Scare" of the 1950s.

Harold Bloom, ed., *Arthur Miller's* The Crucible, Bloom's Modern Critical Interpretations (Philadelphia: Chelsea House, 1999).
Bloom, ed., *Arthur Miller's* The Crucible, Bloom's Guides (Philadelphia: Chelsea House, 2004).
Two collections of essays on the play with completely different contents.

James W. Douglas, "*The Crucible:* Which Witch Is Which?" *Renascence*, 15 (Spring 1953): 145–151.
Examines the historical accuracy of *The Crucible*.

John H. Ferres, ed., *Twentieth Century Interpretations of* The Crucible: *A Collection of Critical Essays* (Englewood Cliffs, N.J.: Prentice-Hall, 1972).
Nineteen essays on issues related to the play.

Donald Lyons, "Othertimes, Otherwheres," *New Criterion*, 10 (January 1992): 54–57.
Argues from a conservative political position that Miller makes false comparisons between the Salem witch trials and McCarthyism.

James J. Martine, The Crucible: *Politics, Property, and Pretense* (New York: Twayne, 1993).
An excellent, readable guide to the play and its major themes.

Dennis Welland, *Miller, the Playwright,* third revised edition (London & New York: Methuen, 1985).
Includes a chapter on *The Crucible* that offers interesting commentary, particularly regarding the political implications of the play.

—Charles Puckett

Arthur Miller, *Death of a Salesman*
(New York: Viking, 1949)

Arthur Miller (1915–2005) was one of the most prolific playwrights of his day, with a career that spanned some sixty years. His magnum opus, *Death of a Salesman*, is his finest work and is a signal play in the history of American drama. Miller was born in Harlem and moved to Brooklyn as a teenager, where he played football and graduated from Abraham Lincoln High School. He attended the University of Michigan, where he twice won the prestigious Avery Hopwood Award for drama. In his youth Miller experienced the economic collapse of the Great Depression, a president who declared that the "business of America is business," and the ever-optimistic mantras of self-made millionaires such as John D. Rockefeller, who declared that "the most essential quality of success is perseverance." All of these elements helped shape *Death of a Salesman*, which Miller wrote in six weeks in the tiny studio he had built with his own hands in rural Connecticut. *Death of a Salesman* received instant acclaim, ran for over seven hundred performances, and received the Pulitzer Prize, the New York Drama Critics' Circle Award, and the Antoinette Perry (Tony) Award, among others. Two years after *Death of a Salesman* premiered, Miller met Marilyn Monroe. Miller married three times, but it was his second wife, Monroe, who eclipsed his considerable fame. He was haunted by her memory (mainly because of her suicide and his inability to keep her from it), and she became the subject of two of his later dramas. Miller continued to write for more than fifty years after *Death of a Salesman*, producing celebrated works, including his most performed play, *The Crucible* (produced, 1953), *A View from the Bridge* (produced, 1955) the short story "The Misfits" (1957—later produced as a film starring Marilyn Monroe), the film script for *Everybody Wins* (1990), *Broken Glass* (1994), and *Finishing the Picture* (2004).

Students are often confused by Miller's unusual depiction of time in *Death of a Salesman*. Willy's past and present frequently blend into one, but Miller cautions the reader not to see this strange merging of time as some sort of mental collapse. While it is clear that Willy is suffering under the strain of a world that no longer makes sense to him, the reality that he constructs in his "conversations" with himself is a world he has created to mask the suicide that beckons him. The scenes from the past are not true "flashbacks" per se but should be read as the "past breaking in on the present" for a suffering man who sees them as a continuum, not discrete entities. Miller's use of time is one of the play's many innovative—and oft-overlooked—elements that also include the use of language that ranges from the banal to the poetic and music that is haunting and evocative of a bygone era.

The depth and complexity of *Death of a Salesman* can be challenging, and readers should turn to other works by and about Miller to aid them in fully appreciating this monumental drama. Miller's autobiography, *Timebends*, is an especially helpful text, as Miller details the inspiration for the play, its first production, and many of the insights that he and others have expressed about the play over the years. It is here, for example, that Miller describes how he initially struggled to write the play, then saw Tennessee Williams's *A Streetcar Named Desire*, which gave him "license to speak at full throat." After that he easily completed the drama. Miller's introductions to the play (in both volumes of *Collected Plays*) offer two excellent analyses for students. His essay "Tragedy and the Common Man" is also an essential perspective for any serious student of this drama. Miller was far more intentional about writing a classically-inspired drama when he wrote *A View from the Bridge*, and students will recognize the framework for tragedy in that play. The father-son relationship and play-ending suicide in his earlier play *All My Sons* will provide readers with an interesting comparison to *Death of a Salesman*. Sue Abbotson's *Student Companion to Arthur Miller* gives readers excellent insights into Willy Loman's life and times, with useful supporting documents. Considering that Willy's life spans both world wars and the Great Depression, the context for Willy's milieu will help students make important connections. By quoting Horatio Alger, Dale Carnegie, and others from the era, Abbotson helps establish the context for Willy's insistence on being "well-liked," maintaining a positive attitude, and his dogged belief in the importance of making a good impression. *Echoes Down the Corridor: Collected Essays*, edited by Steve Centola, is an excellent resource that includes many of Miller's theories on the role of drama in America, including some specific reminiscences of *Death of a Salesman*. Harold Bloom's excellent collection of critical essays includes new material on Miller, and the bibliography is solid. Christopher Bigsby's *Arthur Miller: The Definitive Biography* is precisely as advertised: the most comprehensive biography on one of America's greatest playwrights, written by the man who may well have known him better than anyone else.

TOPICS FOR DISCUSSION AND RESEARCH

1. In his introduction to the play, Miller admits that "*Death of a Salesman* is a slippery play to categorize because nobody in it stops to make a speech objectively stating the great issues which I believe it embodies." Perhaps the most often dis-

cussed "issue" has been whether or not the play rises to the level of a classic tragedy as defined by Aristotle. Willy is clearly not "of noble birth"; yet, from Miller's
perspective, his little salesman from Brooklyn is a tragic figure because he "refuses
to settle for half," and will—like Jay Gatsby—carry a luminous dream to his grave.
While Miller was convinced that the common man was as fitting a subject for
tragedy as any king, most critics believe that the play falls short of those heights
because Willy, unlike tragic heroes such as Oedipus and Hamlet, never comes to
self-knowledge. Instead, Willy's pervasive denial follows him to his death, as he
refuses to be labeled as "a dime a dozen." Students might consider what elements
of *Death of a Salesman* align it with any of the great Shakespearean tragedies. How
might the play be considered a tragedy in the classic sense? Miller's essay "Tragedy and The Common Man" is a helpful starting point for this inquiry.

2. The drama is often cited as an open critique of the American dream, as Willy
   Loman (the "low-man" in a society that promises prosperity to all) becomes the
   embodiment of one who carries the delusion of success with him so fully that it
   becomes lethal. Miller called the Great Depression the "most influential event"
   in his life, and to him—like many others of this era—it reflected the failure
   of a competitive system that was at odds with the promise of true community
   in America. In *Death of a Salesman* Willy's brother, Ben, embodies a ruthless,
   capitalistic drive to succeed at all costs, while Dave Singleman, the beloved
   salesman for whom the play is titled, represents an irretrievable past where one
   is respected and helped and loved by others. Ben trips his own nephew and
   then warns him to "never fight fair with a stranger, boy." He is the epitome of
   the brutal businessman who tears the natural resources out of the jungle and
   comes out rich. Dave Singleman does business in his famous green slippers, and
   when he dies, people flock to his funeral—a clear sign to Willy that the man
   was loved. Willy is seduced by his brother's success but chooses instead the life
   of a salesman—which he believed would be far more satisfying. Yet, Willy will
   never realize his "American Dream" of success; he will carry his false hope with
   him to the grave. Though many may be able to pull themselves up from their
   bootstraps and succeed in America, Willy is thwarted time and again. Students
   might discuss whether the American dream is achievable or simply a facade.
   Some argue that Americans' individual drive for financial success keeps them
   from building community values. To what extent does *Death of a Salesman*—or
   your own personal observations—refute or substantiate this claim?

3. *Death of a Salesman* is also a sharp indictment of the American family, and—
   considering the time it was published—the Lomans are a vivid precursor of
   the now-familiar phrase "dysfunctional family." Willy was abandoned by his
   salesman-father, a "footloose pioneer," and still feels "kind of temporary" about
   himself. This rootlessness is passed on in his treatment of his sons. He entreats
   his brother, Ben, to help him make sure that he is raising them right, but Willy
   cannot instill any sense of morality in them. One is a petty thief and the other
   a philanderer. Willy is unable to guide them morally, and they are metaphori-
   cally abandoned before they literally abandon Willy near the end of the play
   as he raves alone in a restaurant restroom. His wife, Linda, is seen by some
   as the typical faithful housewife of her era and as an "enabler" by others, who

condemn her for not forcing Willy to face his shortcomings. She allows him to continue in his delusion of grand sales and many friends, though she knows better than anyone how little he truly earns and how alone and desperate he is. Who—if anyone—is to blame for the Lomans' tragic fate as a family? Should Linda have confronted Willy with the truth? What evidence in the play suggests that Willy's sons are to blame for never growing up or that, perhaps, Willy prevented them from becoming productive adults?

4. The play finally suggests that the very world that Willy has known has changed; perhaps it has disappeared forever. Linda tells us that Willy's old friends are all either dead or retired, and the buyers he could always count on have been replaced by others who see him as a stranger. The "progress" that has come with modern industrial life comes at a cost: we have begun to treat people like commodities, and men like Willy Loman are often unnoticed; they pass through life and—despite Linda's famous plea that "attention must be paid"—simply fade away. Willy's world has indeed changed: the people have changed; the fact that he named his current boss does not keep him from firing Willy. In fact, the scene in which Willy is fired by his new boss, Howard, illustrates how Willy cannot cope with the changes that have come with the twentieth century. Howard's new "wire recorder" becomes the symbol of a new, incomprehensible era, and Willy is "frightened" by the new machine and begs Howard to turn it off. In Willy's world the cars have changed, the people have changed, and the very landscape has changed—the pastoral beauty he once knew has now been transformed into the forbidding apartment buildings of a new age that choke out the sunlight, overshadow his home, thwart his gardening, and menace his very existence. In what way might current technological advances threaten our society the way that growing industrialization may have threatened Willy's?

RESOURCES

Primary Works

Conversations with Arthur Miller, edited by Matthew C. Roudané (Jackson: University of Mississippi Press, 1987).
Includes thirty-nine interviews and is the best collection of Miller interviews currently available.

Echoes Down the Corridor: Collected Essays, 1944–2000, edited by Steven R. Centola (New York: Viking, 2000).
A collection of fifty of Miller's essays that illuminate his life and work.

The Theater Essays of Arthur Miller, edited by Robert A. Martin, second edition (London: Methuen, 1994).
Includes "*Death of a Salesman* to *A View From the Bridge:* Tragedy and the Common Man" among other important Miller essays.

Timebends: A Life (New York: Grove, 1987).
Miller's underrated autobiography.

Bibliography

Harold Bloom, ed., *Arthur Miller's* Death of a Salesman: *Modern Critical Interpretations* (New York: Chelsea House, 2007).
Updated edition, with fine essays spanning the breadth of Miller's most celebrated work. In addition, the bibliography is as outstanding and as comprehensive as any on the play.

Biography

C. W. E. Bigsby, *Arthur Miller: The Definitive Biography* (London: Weidenfeld & Nicolson, 2008).
The most recent and thorough biography, carefully researched and expertly written by a leading Miller scholar.

Criticism

Susan C. W. Abbotson, *Student Companion to Arthur Miller* (Westport, Conn.: Greenwood Press, 2000).
Offers a strong overview of Miller's primary themes with a particularly good analysis of *Death of a Salesman*.

C. W. E. Bigsby, *Arthur Miller: A Critical Study* (Cambridge, England: Cambridge University Press, 2005).
Outstanding analysis of works in the context of Miller's life. The chapter on *Death of a Salesman* is a detailed study.

Stephen A. Marino, editor, *"The Salesman Has A Birthday": Essays Celebrating the Fiftieth Anniversary of Arthur Miller's* Death of a Salesman (Lanham, Md.: University Press of America, 2000).
Features many new, solid essays on Miller's greatest play.

—*Carlos Campo*

⌒❲❳⌒

N. Scott Momaday, *House Made of Dawn*
(New York: Harper & Row, 1968)

N. Scott Momaday (1934–) gathered much of the material for *House Made of Dawn* from childhood memories, many of which came from stories his parents told him. He was born on a Kiowa Indian reservation in Lawton, Oklahoma, and his family soon moved to the American Southwest, where his mother, an author of children's books, and his father, a painter, taught at several reservation schools, exposing him to Navajo, Apache, and Jamez Pueblo cultures. Momaday has pointed out that Abel, his protagonist, is not based on a single person he met but on "a composite of several people that I knew when I was living in Jemez, New Mexico." Yet, Momaday also befriended Hispanic and white families, and his multicultural perspective was certainly broadened during his own early school-ing, which took place in reservation schools as well as public and private schools, including a Virginia military academy. In 1958 he earned a B.A. in political science from the University of New Mexico. And after briefly studying law at the University of Virginia, he earned an M.A. in creative writing in 1960 and a Ph.D. in English in 1963, both from Stanford University, where the poet and critic Yvor Winters served as his dissertation adviser. In 1969 Momaday won the Pulitzer Prize in fiction for *House Made of Dawn,* helping to bring Native American literature into the mainstream. He went on to publish fiction, poetry, and essays while teaching variously at such institutions as the University of California, Santa Barbara and Berkeley; Stanford University; and the University of Arizona. In 2007 Momaday was awarded the National Medal of Arts by President George W. Bush, and in the same year he began a two-year term as poet laureate of Okla-homa. Contemporary Native American writers, such as Sherman Alexie, continue to acknowledge the influence of Momaday's work.

House Made of Dawn is a complex, unconventional novel: like his grandfather, the protagonist has no last name; the novel begins at the end; events happen in a nonlinear sequence; the point of view changes; long sermons appear at odd times; and some of the major events that occur seem to be without motivation. Yet, there is little denying that the novel is a modern masterpiece for all its lack of traditional narrative structure and characterization. The plot is impressionistic, with one event often suggesting the one that follows without the usual causal relationships. Woven within these events is a pastiche of moments and memories, sacrifices and sermons that often resemble a meditation.

The novel tells the story of Abel, a Native American, who, having being drafted into the U.S. Army, returns from World War II an alcoholic, rudderless, and unable to reestablish a place for himself within the Native American culture of the reservation. At its most basic level, the novel conveys Abel's search for identity, for a connection to the life he finds after his return. There is little sense that Abel sees himself as belonging in any of the different cultural settings within the novel. The plot, however, is only the bare bones of the piece; woven within is the continual, steady drumbeat of belonging—what it means to the individual and how it is achieved—in a world that seemingly has no place for those who are different. Even the reservation's white priest, Father Olguin, is torn by conflicting loyalties to the culture of the Native Americans, his own religious principles, and the history of the church that he serves. Those who are adjusted—such as Ben Benally—live a life balanced between their Native American heritage and the contemporary white world, a life that is tenuous at best. John Big Bluff Tosamah is the character Momaday uses as a reminder of the Native American traditions within the white world. The settings of his two sermons—a storefront temple and a hill overlooking Los Angeles—represent the two places where the traditions must be kept alive: within the urban walls and outside amid the natural world. While Momaday has acknowledged that John Big Bluff Tosamah, the Priest of the Sun, is his mouthpiece in the novel, he has also noted that Abel represents a number of veterans who returned from the war and experienced problems read-justing to American, let alone Native American, society.

Students should begin research on the novel by consulting Momaday's own reflections regarding his work: "The American West and the Burden of Belief" and "The Place of Words in a State of Grace," both contained in *The Man Made of Words: Essays, Stories, Passages*. These essays provide insight into his creative process and the intentions behind the novel. They also discuss the sources from which Momaday drew inspiration, particularly for the character Abel. In addition, Laura Coltelli's interview with Momaday in *Winged Words: American Indian Writers Speak* gets to the heart of the novel and the issues that it raises about cultural disjunction. Charles Woodard's *Ancestral Voice: Conversations with N. Scott Momaday* is an excellent collection of interviews in which Momaday (perhaps because he is also a teacher) is forthcoming and articulate about the meaning of the novel. Finally, Charles Larson's chapter on *House Made of Dawn* in *American Indian Fiction* points out not only the novel's central concerns but also the problems brought about by its complexity.

TOPICS FOR DISCUSSION AND RESEARCH

1. Students might compare and contrast John Big Bluff Tosamah and Father Olguin, who not only represent differing religious outlooks but also represent the way in which two cultures view one's spiritual life. What do these two characters have in common? Students might consider their attitudes toward the past and analyze the way the Native Americans on the reservation respond to Father Olguin. What kinds of adjustments do they make in their worship and their attitudes toward the divine? What might these changes reveal?
2. Two other characters who might be compared and contrasted are Milly, the social worker, and Angela St. John, the woman who comes to the reservation, has an affair with Abel, and ultimately rescues him from his beating and arranges for his hospitalization. In particular, to what social class does each of these women belong, and how does each react toward Abel? What does he represent in each of their lives?
3. The characterization of Ben Benally provides insight into an individual who has adapted to "the ways of the white man." Yet, he also experiences the pull of his native Navajo heritage. How does he handle the transition to the modern world of Los Angeles and the new lifestyle that it represents? Also, what is Momaday implying about the mingling of races through Ben's obvious attraction to Milly and the attention he gives her after Abel has left? Finally, Ben narrates the third part of the novel, "The Night Chanter." Should readers trust him as a narrator since this is where they get an "outside" look at the way Abel operates in the world? What is it about his character that allows him to adjust to the white man's lifestyle and culture?
4. Of central importance to the novel are the two sermons preached by John Big Bluff Tosamah, one of which is "The Way to Rainy Mountain." Read both sermons carefully, asking what, specifically, is Tosamah suggesting about Native American culture and its relationship to modern culture? Most important, what does Tosamah say about the past? Has it disappeared, or is it part of a "livable" past that can help each Native American find his or her place within the dominant, white culture?

5. The past dominates the novel. Significantly, the past is lodged within the mind of Abel's grandfather, Francisco. The action begins with Francisco's moving through the reservation on his way to meet Abel's bus. His and Abel's memories form a significant part of the first half of the novel. How are these memories similar? Why is Abel incapable of seeing the connection between his cultural past and the present? He is, after all, living within the Native American culture on the reservation. What is it about the present that does not allow him to feel a sense of belonging while Francisco exists contented within the reservation?

RESOURCES

Primary Work

N. Scott Momaday, *The Man Made of Words: Essays, Stories, Passages* (New York: St. Martin's Press, 1997).

Contains two crucial essays regarding *House Made of Dawn*. "The American West and the Burden of Belief" discusses Momaday's ideas on the ways in which white men view the West, using George Armstrong Custer and Buffalo Bill as illustrations. Momaday provides insight into the novel by analyzing the way in which Native Americans and whites view and create the landscape. The other, "A Divine Blindness: The Place of Words in a State of Grace," focuses on language, one of the central issues in the novel. Momaday says, "Language is the context of our experience. We know who we have been, who we are, and who we can be in the dimension of words, of language." Momaday compares stories from modern authors such as Jorge Luis Borges to the ancient songs and rituals of Native Americans.

Bibliography

Andrew Wiget, *Native American Literature* (Boston: Twayne, 1985).

Although dated, a good starting point for research. It contains a primary and extensive secondary bibliography.

Biography

Matthais Schubnell, *N. Scott Momaday: The Cultural and Literary Background* (Norman: University of Oklahoma Press, 1985).

Carefully chronicles Momaday's life and traces the influences on his work.

Criticism

Laura Coltelli, *Winged Words: American Indian Writers Speak* (Lincoln: University of Nebraska Press, 1990).

Includes an extensive interview with Momaday in which he talks frequently about *House Made of Dawn*. Speaking of Abel, he says, "He represents a great many people of his generation, the Indian who returns from the war." Abel, then, "represents" a "dislocation of the psyche in our time."

Charles R. Larson, *American Indian Fiction* (Albuquerque: University of New Mexico Press, 1978).
A thorough analysis of the work that Larson claims is "the most complex and the most obscure novel written by an American Indian." Larson's central thesis is that Momaday sees the future of the Native American experience pessimistically. That is, the characters in the novel are "the last members of a dying race."

Suzanne Evertsen Lundquish, *Native American Literatures: An Introduction* (New York: Continuum, 2004).
Analyzes the novel in terms of time and space. "Conceptions of space and time are of particular relevance in a post-Einsteinian time frame," writes Lundquish. "Momaday's novel speaks to these reconceptions as they resonate with Native cosmology."

H. S. McAllister, "Be a Man, Be a Woman: Androgyny in *House Made of Dawn*," *American Indian Quarterly*, 2 (Spring 1975): 14–22.
Explores the androgynous character Father Nicolas, the priest whom Father Olguin replaces. Momaday uses Father Nicolas and Father Olguin, McAllister says, "as an analogy to Abel" since both face the problems of "integration" of their personalities into the cultural setting with Abel attempting to "create a unified personality" from the "dual cultural" heritages he faces.

Charles L. Woodard, *Ancestral Voice: Conversations with N. Scott Momaday* (Lincoln: University of Nebraska Press, 1989).
An essential resource that draws on interviews with Momaday concerning Abel's alienation from his language. Woodard also provides excellent criticism of the novel concerning "Abel's rediscovery of his native sense of the appropriate through the experience of his grandfather's death." Woodard continues, "In the end he is running sacrificially in the dawn, investing himself in the natural world to become one with it, as it is right for him to do."

—Bob Bell

Vladimir Nabokov, *Lolita*
(New York: Putnam, 1955)

Russian-born writer Vladimir Nabokov (1899–1977) had already published nine novels in his native Russian language before World War II compelled him to switch to English in hopes of expanding his readership. It is all the more astounding, then, that his third novel in his new tongue, *Lolita* (1955), the lyrical story of an expatriate's doomed love for a twelve-year-old American girl, remains one of the most remarkable literary achievements of the twentieth century and a miracle of English prose.

Russian and English were only two of the three languages in which Nabokov was fluent; the third was French, a language long associated with the Russian aristocracy of which Nabokov was a member. Born, he said, on William Shakespeare's birthday in St. Petersburg in 1899, Nabokov spent his lavish Tolstoyan boyhood on a sprawling estate, surrounded by governesses and numerous artifacts of English culture, as his father, a prominent Russian politician, was something of an Anglophile. Early on, Nabokov discovered the three lifelong passions that would shape his career: literature, chess, and butterflies. Fleeing the violence of the Russian Revolution, his family moved to England, where Nabokov attended Trinity College, Cambridge. After his graduation in 1922, Nabokov, essentially destitute, moved to Berlin to join that city's burgeoning Russian expatriate community. Under the pseudonym Sirin he published the Russian novels *Mashen'ka* (1926; translated as *Mary*, 1970) and *Zashchita Luzhina* (1930; translated as *The Defense*, 1964), which were read only by a select group of Russian-speaking exiles.

The rise of the Nazis forced Nabokov and his wife and child to relocate first to France and in 1940 to the United States. For the next decade Nabokov spent the fall, winter, and spring teaching college literature and the summer hunting butterflies, all the while producing a steady stream of fiction and criticism in English. He composed much of *Lolita* on four-by-six-inch note cards while on butterfly-hunting expeditions. Because of the controversial subject matter—pedophilia—he published the book with Olympia, a small French press that specialized in racy fiction for English-language readers. Within a year of its appearance in 1955, several major literary figures, including Graham Greene, praised the literary qualities of the novel; and when it was published in the United States in 1958, *Lolita* was a best seller. The financial windfall freed Nabokov from university life and allowed him to move to Switzerland, where he remained from 1961 until his death in 1977.

Although its subject matter is shocking, *Lolita* reaches the summit of artistic excellence. The narrator, an erudite madman named Humbert Humbert, relates his story in a soaring, lyrical prose style that is rich in puns, allusions, and self-reflective gestures, all of which mark the book as an early instance of Postmodernist metafiction—that is, fiction that calls attention to its own status as fiction. Humbert's hilariously ornate voice and heightened literary sensibility stand in sharp contrast to Lolita herself, the gum-chewing, wisecracking twelve-year-old "nymphet" (a word Nabokov coined) who has sent him into raptures. To remain close to her, Humbert marries her boorish, bourgeois mother; but after the mother is removed from the picture by a fatal accident—which Nabokov stages with artful self-consciousness—Humbert unexpectedly finds himself alone with his love. The two commence a restless itinerant life of constant travel, during which time Humbert begins to suspect that a rival named Clare Quilty is on his trail. Eventually, he loses Lolita, vowing from that moment on to exact his revenge on the man who took her away—a man who may or may not be Nabokov himself.

Most editions of *Lolita* include an afterword by Nabokov, "On a Book Entitled Lolita," which is an indispensable addendum to the novel. There Nabokov explains, "The first throb of *Lolita* went through me in late 1939 or early 1940, in Paris." He goes on to reveal that he wrote an early novella-length version of the story that he later "destroyed"—untrue, as that work is now available in English as *The Enchanter* (1986). Students should also consult *The Annotated Lolita* (1991), edited by Alfred Appel Jr., which includes 150 pages of footnotes detailing the dense and intricate pattern of allusions, linguistic puns, and formal puzzles in the novel. Nabokov's autobiography, *Speak, Memory* (first published as *Conclusive Evidence*, 1951), widely acknowledged as a masterpiece of the genre, provides a wealth of insight into the particulars of his art. Nabokov has also been the subject of several biographies, the most complete being Brian Boyd's two-volume work (1990, 1991); of particular interest to readers of *Lolita* is the second volume, *The American Years*, which includes an exhaustive bibliography. Although *Lolita* has attracted a prodigious amount of sophisticated attention from literary critics, some of the best sources for initiates include Carl Proffer's *Keys to Lolita* (1968), Michael Wood's *The Magician's Doubts: Nabokov and the Risks of Fiction* (1994), and Lance Olsen's *Lolita: A Janus Text* (1995).

TOPICS FOR DISCUSSION AND RESEARCH

1. A contemporary of James Joyce and William Faulkner, Nabokov outlived both and, even more important, continued to produce innovative fiction until the 1970s, when the vogue for Postmodernist metafiction was at its zenith. As a result, he occupies the unique position among major twentieth-century writers of straddling the Modernist and Postmodernist periods. Yet, his career cannot be subdivided into Modernist and Postmodernist phases, as the signatures of his art remained consistent throughout. As is true of all of Nabokov's mature fiction, *Lolita* unfolds within a self-contained verbal realm where coincidences, patterns, and artifice all point to a world beyond the text in accordance with his desire, as he explains in his Russian novel *Dar* (1937–1938; translated as *The Gift*, 1963), to create a form of fiction that exists "on the brink of parody" while at the same time maintaining "an abyss of seriousness" so that it straddles "the narrow ridge between [his] own truth and a caricature of it." Exploring how—and why—*Lolita* balances atop this narrow ridge is the first point of entry for any serious interpretation of the novel.

2. As evidenced by *The Annotated Lolita*, in which the footnote section is half as long as the novel itself, nearly every sentence in *Lolita* includes some buried treasure: a pun, an allusion, or an image that points backward or forward to some key theme or trope—a density of design that not only needs unpacking for its own sake but also needs addressing in more-general terms. In other words, what is the purpose of all of this elaborate formal play in a novel about pedophilia? Students will find an enigmatic answer to this question in Nabokov's afterword, where he archly insists, "*Lolita* has no moral in tow," but then explains, "For me a work of fiction exists only insofar as it affords me what I shall bluntly call aesthetic bliss, that is a sense of being somehow, somewhere, connected with other states of being where art (curiosity, tenderness, kindness, ecstasy) is the norm." Students might explore what Nabokov means by

"aesthetic bliss" and how this idea can be applied to the curious experience of reading *Lolita*, which has left many readers deploring Humbert Humbert for the damage he inflicts on the girl and yet loving the book itself.

3. Although *Lolita* has safely achieved the status of a literary classic, questions about its possible obscenity remain, and students should not feel dissuaded from tackling this subject head-on. Midway through the novel, after he and Lolita have consummated their relationship, Humbert Humbert declares, "I am not concerned with so-called 'sex' at all. Anybody can imagine those elements of animality. A greater endeavor lures me on: to fix once and for all the perilous magic of nymphets." Students might wish to explore exactly how Nabokov depicts sexuality in the novel, and whether the novel conforms in any way to the famous description of obscenity coined by U.S. District Judge James Woolsey (and quoted in *Lolita*). In his 1933 decision lifting the obscenity ban on Joyce's *Ulysses* (1922) Woolsey declared that that novel's frank depiction of various acts did not "stir the sex impulses or to lead to sexually impure or lustful thoughts." Is Judge Woolsey's definition adequate? How does Nabokov's novel measure up by this standard? Students will benefit from researching the book's use of allusions and will find a rich set of literary source texts, including Edgar Allan Poe's poem "Annabelle Lee" (1849), which Humbert Humbert invokes as early as the first page, and Lewis Carroll's *Alice's Adventures in Wonderland* (1865), which provides a fascinating analogue for the "looking-glass" narrative strategy of *Lolita*. Poe and Carroll shared Humbert Humbert's obsession with "nymphets." What is the function of the allusions?

4. *Lolita* offers an unexpectedly rich and vivid portrait of post–World War II America that invites a variety of interpretive possibilities. Throughout the book Humbert Humbert records, with bemused fascination, the full range of Lolita's pop-culture consumption, from songs to movie-star magazines, franchise restaurants, and self-help manuals. He even surmises that "she it was to whom ads were dedicated: the ideal consumer, the subject and object of every foul poster." In this sense the character of Lolita can be read as an emblem of Cold War consumerism writ large. Students might explore the connections between Lolita's status as a targeted-market consumer and the current-day explosion of sexually suggestive "tween" products such as Bratz dolls and midriff-baring teen pop singers.

RESOURCES

Primary Works

The Annotated Lolita: Revised and Updated, edited by Alfred Appel Jr. (New York: Vintage, 1991).
Includes 150 pages of exhaustive, indispensable footnotes tracing Nabokov's intricate system of allusions, puns, and formal surprises.

The Enchanter, translated by Dmitri Nabokov (New York: Putnam, 1986).
Nabokov's novella-length first attempt to capture the "throb" that later became *Lolita*.

Lectures on Literature, edited by Fredson Bowers (New York: Harcourt Brace Jovanovich/Bruccoli Clark, 1980).
A collection of Nabokov's lectures from his famous Cornell University classes on the European novel. The lectures provide key insights into the author's conception of the novel and his ideas on reading in general.

Lolita: A Screenplay (New York: McGraw-Hill, 1974).
The unproduced screenplay that Nabokov submitted to Stanley Kubrick, director of the first of two film adaptations of *Lolita.*

Selected Letters, 1940–1977, edited by Dmitri Nabokov and Matthew J. Bruccoli (New York: Harcourt Brace Jovanovich/Bruccoli Clark, 1989).
A judicious selection of Nabokov's letters to friends, editors, and fellow literary giants during the years of his English-language triumph.

Speak, Memory: An Autobiography Revisited (New York: Putnam, 1966).
Revised edition of Nabokov's classic collection of autobiographical essays, originally published in 1951 as *Conclusive Evidence.*

The Stories of Vladimir Nabokov (New York: Knopf, 1995).
A 650-page collection of every short story Nabokov published, arranged in chronological order.

Strong Opinions (New York: McGraw-Hill, 1973).
An entertaining collection of prickly interviews, articles, and editorials in which the author famously proclaims, "I think *like* a genius, I write *like* a distinguished author, and I *speak like a child.*"

Bibliography

Zembla: The Vladimir Nabokov Site <http://www.libraries.psu.edu/nabokov/zembla.htm> [accessed 28 July 2009].
The most complete Nabokov site on the World Wide Web, with links to online bibliographies and the *Nabokov Online Journal.*

Biography

Brian Boyd, *Vladimir Nabokov: The American Years* (Princeton: Princeton University Press, 1991).
The second volume of Boyd's two-volume biography, which covers Nabokov's life and career from his arrival in New York in 1940 to his death in Switzerland in 1977. Dedicated Nabokovians will also want to read the first volume, *Vladimir Nabokov: The Russian Years* (1990).

Criticism

Harold Bloom, ed., *Vladimir Nabokov's* Lolita (New York: Chelsea House, 1987).
Includes a selection of key essays on the novel by leading Nabokov scholars.

Lance Olsen, *Lolita: A Janus Text* (New York: Twayne, 1995).
Part of Twayne's Masterwork Studies series. This slim but helpful volume out-lines the basic themes of the novel, situates the work in its historical context, and lists additional primary and secondary sources.

Carl Proffer, *Keys to Lolita* (Bloomington: Indiana University Press, 1968).
A good source for readers new to the novel.

Michael Wood, *The Magician's Doubts: Nabokov and the Risks of Fiction* (Prince-ton: Princeton University Press, 1994).
One of the better book-length studies of Nabokov. Wood addresses the oblique ways in which Nabokov's aesthetically daunting novels approach ethical issues.

—*Marshall Boswell*

Flannery O'Connor, *Wise Blood*
(New York: Harcourt, Brace, 1952)

Flannery O'Connor (1925–1964) published some of the most enduring short stories of the late twentieth century, and her novel *Wise Blood* (1952) continues to intrigue readers and invite scholarly attention. O'Connor was born in Savan-nah, Georgia, and moved with her parents to her mother's childhood home in Milledgeville during her early teens. In 1945 she graduated from Georgia State College for Women in Milledgeville and enrolled in the Writers' Workshop at the University of Iowa, where she began writing *Wise Blood*. She received an MFA in creative writing in 1947. In 1950, while living in Connecticut, she was diagnosed with lupus, the disease that had claimed her father's life nine years earlier, and she returned to the South to live with her mother. During the next thirteen years she published her only two novels, *Wise Blood* and *The Violent Bear It Away* (1960), and a short-story collection, *A Good Man Is Hard to Find* (1955). Her second collection of stories, *Everything That Rises Must Converge* (1965), was published after her death. Three of the stories in that book—"Greenleaf," "Revelation," and the title piece—were first-place recipients of the O. Henry Award. In 1972 *The Complete Stories of Flannery O'Connor* (1971) won the National Book Award.

   Wise Blood introduces the first of a line of proud, ornery, self-deluded protagonists whose misadventures are the focus of O'Connor's fiction. Having entered World War II a God-fearing future preacher, Hazel Motes has returned to his rural Tennessee home jaded and eager to embark on a worldly adventure. In the opening pages of the novel he heads to the city, intending to "do some things I never had done before." Unable to resist the need to preach, he begins his outrageous "Church of Christ Without Christ." Though O'Connor was wary of the classification, *Wise Blood*, like all of her fiction, typifies the genre known as Southern Gothic; it therefore invites comparisons with the work of William Faulkner and Carson McCullers, who also make use of grotesque characters and bizarre situations as a way of exploring Southern mores. Like the novels of Faulkner and McCullers, O'Connor's fiction is pervaded by universal moral concerns that have allowed her to transcend the status of a Regional writer. Her moral outlook, however, is informed by her steadfast Roman Catholic beliefs. Students, like early critics of *Wise Blood*, often overlook the urgent spiritual concerns beneath the surface of her fiction, which is generally marked by moral corruption and violence. Aware that many readers had misinterpreted the plight of Hazel Motes, O'Connor provided a note to the second edition of *Wise Blood* (1962): "That belief in Christ is to some a matter of life and death has been a stumbling block for readers who would prefer to think it a matter of no great consequence." The consequence of not believing in Christ is the idea that plagues Hazel, who futilely attempts to free himself of moral responsibility by denying the existence of a soul. Despite the grave moral concerns at its heart, however, *Wise Blood* is a comic novel following in the tradition of Nathanael West, whose black humor appealed to O'Connor. Yet, while West, a pessimist, dooms his protagonists, O'Connor allows for redemption—but at a price. For O'Connor mystery and grace are vital forces in the world despite modern humans' attempts to distract themselves from them. Hazel tries to prove his disbelief in Christ but proves instead, as O'Connor has noted, to be a Christian despite himself, resulting in his grueling atonement.

Students will gain a deeper understanding of *Wise Blood* by reading other works by O'Connor. Four short stories that O'Connor modified slightly and incorporated into *Wise Blood* are collected in *The Complete Stories of Flannery O'Connor:* "The Train" (1948), "The Heart of the Park" (1949), "The Peeler" (1949), and "Enoch and the Gorilla" (1952). These stories trace the genesis of *Wise Blood* and O'Connor's aesthetic and philosophical development. The stories collected in *A Good Man Is Hard to Find* and *Everything That Rises Must Converge*, though generally more subtle in their treatment of Christian themes—they often make no explicit reference to Christ—are nonetheless highly useful companions to *Wise Blood*. In the former book "Good Country People," with its seemingly nihilistic protagonist, best elucidates Hazel's crisis. In the latter collection "Greenleaf," "Revelation," and the title story, with their arrogant protagonists, reconsider themes first encountered in *Wise Blood*. O'Connor's other novel, *The Violent Bear It Away*, is also highly recommended, as its young hero attempts a similar evasion of an innate religious calling. O'Connor's letters, collected in *The Habit of Being* (1971), are an indispensable source of insight into the author's thinking, while *Mystery and Manners* (1969), a collection of essays, provides helpful commentary on her creative process. Dorothy Tuck McFarland's *Flannery O'Connor* (1976), Margaret Early Whitt's *Understanding Flannery O'Connor* (1995), Miles Orvell's *Flannery O'Connor: An Introduction* (1991), and Dorothy Walters's *Flannery O'Connor* (1973) each devote an excellent chapter of analysis to *Wise Blood*. The most authoritative O'Connor biography is Brad Gooch's *Flannery: A Life of Flannery O'Connor* (2009). Finally, *The Society for the Study of Southern Literature Bibliography* website provides the most up-to-date secondary bibliography.

TOPICS FOR DISCUSSION AND RESEARCH

1. In addition to being a religious novel, *Wise Blood* is a deeply philosophical one. O'Connor's introductory note to the second edition makes it clear that, contrary to the understanding of many early readers, she intended the novel to be an assault on philosophical materialism and nihilism. Hazel expresses his insistence on a purely material world when he asserts that it is wrong to believe in things that "you couldn't see or hold in your hands or test with your teeth." By extension, he contends that there is no inherent meaning or value in the universe. In his preaching he paraphrases—certainly unwittingly—the proclamation of the nihilist philosopher Friedrich Nietzsche, "God is dead." Students might consider how O'Connor uses symbols to satirize and convey the shortcomings in Hazel's outlook. They might also compare Hazel's newly acquired worldview to that of Hulga Hopewell in "Good Country People," considering at what points each character accepts and renounces material-ism and nihilism and how O'Connor renders these changes symbolically through such items as Hazel's rat-colored car, Enoch Emory's gorilla costume and obsession with the zoo, or the stuffed figure from the museum that will become "the new Jesus."

2. Another philosophical approach to *Wise Blood* might be to consider O'Connor's preoccupation with the dual physical and spiritual nature of human beings, an idea that is fundamental to both Eastern and Western religious thought and is at the heart of Hazel's dilemma. Consequently, duality and opposition pervade *Wise Blood*—beginning with the title, which, combining the idea of wisdom with that of instinct, underscores O'Connor's theme that attraction toward the holy is innate. In addition, consider the dual meaning of the concepts of *sight* and *home:* by blinding himself, Hazel can *see* more clearly and finds his way not to his physical *home* but to his spiritual one. What other dualities does O'Connor include? Perhaps attention might be given to characters who serve as foils or doppelgängers, an idea touched on in chapter 2 of Whitt's *Under-standing Flannery O'Connor*.

3. *Wise Blood* can profitably be read as a Christian allegory in which Hazel's trip to Taulkinham is a journey toward personal salvation. It thus has much in common with Dante's fourteenth-century epic *The Divine Comedy* and with John Bunyan's *A Pilgrim's Progress* (1678). Like Bunyan, O'Connor gives apt names to her characters and places. Students should consult the Bible for the source of Hazel's surname; they should further consider the implications of his nickname, "Haze." Other characters have biblically derived names as well, and they are often laden with irony: Enoch Emery, Sabbath Lily, Asa Hawks, and Mrs. Flood, for example. Even the name of the city Taulkinham contains one of O'Connor's perennial symbols for the soulless human: the pig ("talkin' ham"). Like Dante, O'Connor represents sin by means of animal imagery. What are some examples of this tactic?

4. On a similar note, O'Connor's use of the grotesque is an essential element in her fiction. "I am interested in making a good case for distortion," O'Connor stated, "as I am coming to believe it is the only way to make people see." Her

characters often suffer physical afflictions that symbolize spiritual depravity: Hazel is one of many whose heads jut forward and whose walk is reminiscent of lower primates. Students might analyze other descriptions, as O'Connor's characters are hardly attractive. Her use of fights, arguments, murders, arrests, and sexual encounters in *Wise Blood* could also be analyzed for the symbolic implications beneath their dark comic surface.

5. O'Connor painstakingly crafted her fiction, claiming to have a clear intention behind the placement of each sentence. Thus, *Wise Blood* provides an excellent means for studying the connection between structure and content. A second reading of the novel will reveal overlooked patterns. For example, Mrs. Wally Bee Hitchcock's inquiry in the opening pages as to whether Hazel is "going home" is echoed in the final pages when Mrs. Flood comments, "I see you've come home." Descriptions of Hazel at the beginning are also repeated nearly verbatim at the end. Students should consider the implications of Hazel's archetypal journey with regard to the circular structure of the work as a whole.

6. *Wise Blood* can also be read as O'Connor's view of post–World War II America. She told the novelist John Hawkes that she was gravely concerned with "the conflict between an attraction for the Holy and the disbelief in it that we breathe in with the air of the times." Students might consider how this conflict plays out in Hazel and how other characters, such as the phony preacher, the potato-peeler merchant, and the promiscuous Sabbath Lilly, could provide further comment on attributes of modern American culture.

7. O'Connor disapproved of the lifestyle of her contemporaries, the Beat writers, whose spirituality she found facile. "They call themselves holy but holiness costs and so far as I can see they pay nothing," she wrote. Students should consider what O'Connor believed constitutes a "holy" life. To what degree is Hazel's atonement an exaggeration of O'Connor's edict "holiness costs"? Students should also research the backgrounds of major Beat figures such as Allen Ginsberg and Jack Kerouac, whose major works—*Howl* (1956) and *On the Road* (1957), respectively—make frequent use of the word *holy*. How is the Beat concept of holiness at odds with the worldview O'Connor evokes in *Wise Blood*?

RESOURCES

Primary Works

The Complete Stories of Flannery O'Connor (New York: Farrar, Straus & Giroux, 1971).
Includes all of O'Connor's collected and uncollected short stories in chronological order.

The Habit of Being, edited by Sally Fitzgerald (New York: Farrar, Straus & Giroux, 1971).
An exhaustive collection of O'Connor's correspondence with friends, readers, and other literary personalities.

Mystery and Manners, edited by Robert Fitzgerald and Sally Fitzgerald (New York: Farrar, Straus & Giroux, 1969).
A collection of O'Connor essays that is especially helpful in understanding her role and intentions as a Southern Catholic writer.

The Violent Bear It Away (New York: Farrar, Straus & Giroux, 1960).
O'Connor's second novel, which concerns the young protagonist's attempts to follow in the footsteps of his uncle, a nihilist, rather than in those of his late grandfather, a preacher.

Bibliography

The Society for the Study of Southern Literature Bibliography <http://www.missq. msstate.edu/sssl> [accessed 30 July 2009].
Includes more than seventy scholarly articles on *Wise Blood* and hundreds on O'Connor and her other works.

Biography

Brad Gooch, *Flannery: A Life of Flannery O'Connor* (New York: Little, Brown, 2009).
The most recent and thorough biography, carefully researched and successful at tying much of O'Connor's work to her life.

Criticism

Miles Orvell, *Flannery O'Connor: An Introduction* (Jackson: University Press of Mississippi, 1991).
Provides an aesthetic, religious, and regional context for O'Connor's work and a thorough discussion of the background, motifs, characters, and themes in *Wise Blood*.

Dorothy Tuck McFarland, *Flannery O'Connor* (New York: Ungar, 1976).
Offers a helpful overview of O'Connor's concerns in the introduction and a concise, yet penetrating, analysis of *Wise Blood*.

Dorothy Walters, *Flannery O'Connor* (New York: Twayne, 1973).
An excellent analysis of *Wise Blood*, with particular attention to biblical connections and symbolism.

Margaret Earley Whitt, *Understanding Flannery O'Connor* (Columbia: University of South Carolina Press, 1995).
Includes a useful overview of *Wise Blood* with in-depth character analyses and a discussion of the novel as Southern literature.

—John Cusatis

Eugene O'Neill, *Long Day's Journey into Night*
(New Haven, Conn.: Yale University Press, 1956)

Never published or produced in his lifetime, *Long Day's Journey into Night* solidified the reputation of Eugene O'Neill (1888–1953) as the greatest American
dramatist with its 1956 premiere in Sweden. Written in "tears and blood," this
highly autobiographical play examines in a single summer day the doomed fates
and ruined fortunes of the four members of the Tyrone family. O'Neill grew up in
a family haunted by regrets and recriminations. His father, James O'Neill, a promising Shakespearean actor, wasted his talent by continuously touring in a lucrative
melodrama, *The Count of Monte Cristo*. O'Neill was conceived by his parents as a
replacement for an infant son, Edmund, who died after being exposed to measles
by his older brother James Jr. Complications following Eugene O'Neill's birth
led his mother Ella to become addicted to morphine. As a young man O'Neill
traveled the world as a merchant seaman where he contracted tuberculosis, a
potentially fatal disease. O'Neill's experience of returning to his family's summer
home before entering a sanitarium provides the play's biographical impetus. A
major discrepancy between the play and O'Neill's biography is that the playwright
had a brief marriage before he contracted tuberculosis; Edmund Tyrone never
mentions being married.

O'Neill's recovery sparked his ambition to become a writer. While on summer holiday in Massachusetts, he joined The Provincetown Players, a group of
avant-garde artists and writers who sought to create a mature American theatre.
O'Neill's plays attracted critical attention and later became very successful on the
New York stage. He experimented with dramatic forms and psychological themes
throughout the 1920s in such plays as *Emperor Jones* (produced 1920), an expres-
sionistic nightmare; *The Great God Brown* (produced 1926), in which contemporary characters wear masks; and *Strange Interlude* (produced 1928), a nine-act play
punctuated with characters speaking interior monologues. He demonstrated his
deep interest in classical Greek tragedy in *Mourning Becomes Electra* (produced
1931), in which he updated Aeschylus's *Oresteia* to post–Civil War America. He
completed his two greatest dramas, *The Iceman Cometh* (produced 1946) and *Long
Day's Journey into Night*, in 1940 while listening to devastating news of the war
in Europe. He won a record four Pulitzer Prizes and the 1936 Nobel Prize in
literature; he was the only American dramatist ever to receive the award.

The play traces the events of one day in summer 1912 in which the four
characters revisit the tragic events of their individual and communal existence.
As with most other tragedies, the play begins happily, with Mary Tyrone recently
released from a sanitarium, ostensibly cured of her drug addiction. She relapses
during the course of the play to escape her fear that her son Edmund has
contracted tuberculosis, the disease that killed her father. The confirmation of
Edmund's diagnosis brings the play to its crisis, forcing each family member to
confront his or her role in contributing to the family's tragedy.

Students will gain a deeper understanding of O'Neill's play by reading a few
of the author's other works. You might compare James Tyrone to the protagonists

in *Emperor Jones* and *A Touch of the Poet* (produced 1957), both boastful poseurs, and Mary Tyrone to Nina in *Strange Interlude,* a wife/mother who commands the attentions and loyalties of the doomed men around her. Edmund resembles many O'Neill young poets, particularly Robert Mayo in *Beyond the Horizon* (produced 1920). Students should consider his speeches about the sea in connection with O'Neill's early sea plays such as *Bound East for Cardiff* (produced 1916) and *Anna Christie* (produced 1921). Students can also compare the play with O'Neill's Freudian drama *Desire Under the Elms* (produced 1924). Jamie Tyrone appears as a leading character in *A Moon for the Misbegotten* (produced 1947), in which he details the events of Mary Tyrone's death. Students will also benefit from contrasting the tragedy of *Long Day's Journey into Night* with O'Neill's only full-length comedy, *Ah, Wilderness!* (produced 1933), the playwright's idealized version of his doomed family.

As O'Neill drew heavily from his personal biography for the subject matter of his plays, students will find *Selected Letters of Eugene O'Neill* an excellent source for the playwright's own comments on his life and work. Arthur and Barbara Gelb's *O'Neill* provides the best single-volume biography of the author, and their *O'Neill: Life with Monte Cristo* is the first volume of a planned three-volume biography that offers many new details on the playwright's early life and career. Travis Bogard's *Contour in Time: The Plays of Eugene O'Neill* provides the best book-length critical study. The most authoritative primary bibliography is *Eugene O'Neill: A Descriptive Bibliography,* by Jennifer McCabe Atkinson. *Eugene O'Neill: An Annotated International Bibliography,* 1973 through 1999, by Madeline Smith and Richard Eaton, provides the most recent secondary bibliography. Students can also consult excellent databases and source material at *eOneill.com: An Electronic Eugene O'Neill Archive* (<www.eoneill.com>).

TOPICS FOR DISCUSSION AND RESEARCH

1. As with most other tragedies, *Long Day's Journey into Night* examines how past events and choices dictate present-day decisions and options. O'Neill described his play as occurring on a "day in which things occur which evoke the whole past of the family and reveal every aspect of its interrelationships. A deeply tragic play, but without any violent dramatic action. At the final curtain, there they still are, trapped within each other by the past, each guilty and at the same time innocent, scorning, loving, pitying each other, understanding and yet not understanding at all, forgiving but still doomed never to be able to forget." Although each of the Tyrones experiences a tragedy, the play centers on Mary as the ghostly heart of the haunted family. She delivers the play's thesis when, urged by her husband to forget the past, she responds, "How can I? The past is the present, isn't it? It's the future too. We all try to lie out of that but life won't let us." She also ends the play in a delusional monologue in which she isolates the tragic turning point of her life when she fell in love and married James Tyrone—forsaking her religious faith, family, and artistic ambitions—and was "so happy for a time." What might be the tragic turning points for the other three characters?

2. Following classic guidelines, O'Neill places his play in a single setting and within a single day. According to the classical formula for tragedy, the protagonist's tragic flaw of hubris (intense pride or arrogance) contributes to his or her own destruction. Each of the four Tyrones possesses traits that necessitate his or her own downfall: Mary's fear of reality condemns her to a ghost-like existence of drug addition; Tyrone's fear of poverty makes him a miser, denying his family proper medical care and support; Jamie's jealousy of his younger brother drives him into slothful alcoholism; and Edmund's morbidity compels him to the brink of suicide and despair, forever haunted by the realization that his birth resulted in his family's doom. Each character confesses his or her culpability, but to what effect? Is there reason to believe any of the characters can change or alter his or her course?

3. Students will notice that O'Neill employs sea imagery throughout the play as a metaphor for his tragic vision. The evening fog represents the self-delusions that blind the Tyrones to reality. Edmund relates a brief moment while serving as a seaman that he had a glimpse of the divine meaning of the universe. While alone on deck he communed with the sea and saw "the veil of things as they seem drawn back by an unseen hand. For a second you see—and seeing the secret, are the secret. For a second there is meaning! Then the hand lets the veil fall and you are alone, lost in the fog again and you stumble on toward nowhere, for no good reason." As indicated by the "unseen hand," O'Neill also exploits religious imagery in Mary's frequent evocation of Mary, Mother of God. Students might explore the play for other religious or supernatural imagery and analyze its significance.

4. As O'Neill is the first mature American dramatist, students should consult non-American texts for influences on his work. From the beginning of his career O'Neill took ancient Greek tragedy as his model, particularly the work of Aeschylus, the first great Greek tragic author. He also subscribed to the Greek belief of inherited sin. Students might compare the curse on the House of Atreus in the *Oresteia* to the damnation of the Tyrones. As the son of a great Shakespearean actor, O'Neill knew the plays of William Shakespeare intimately and quotes from them often in *Long Day's Journey into Night*. Students will benefit from comparing the Tyrone's situation to Shakespeare's tragic families in *Hamlet, Othello,* and *Macbeth*. Students might also consult Henrik Ibsen's *Ghosts* (1881) and August Strindberg's *The Ghost Sonata* (1907). Nondramatic influences for O'Neill include the sea fiction of Joseph Conrad and the poetry of Algernon Charles Swinburne and Oscar Wilde (both quoted heavily in the play). O'Neill drew much of his philosophy from the writings of Friedrich Nietzsche and Sigmund Freud. He places many of his sources onstage as represented by two bookshelves—one, belonging to Tyrone, houses well-read volumes of Shakespeare, Alexandre Dumas *père*, and Victor Hugo. It is in visual conflict with Edmund's bookshelf that holds books by "modern" authors such as Ibsen, Swinburne, Wilde, Dante Rossetti, and Karl Marx. Students might discuss what the family's competing bookcases reveal about character.

5. Students should note that as the product of a theatrical family, O'Neill uses his play as a bitter commentary on the role of the artist. All four Tyrones fail

as creative or interpretive artists. Mary laments her girlhood desire to be a concert pianist, focusing at the play's conclusion on her crippled hands, playing the family piano like a clumsy amateur. James mortgaged his theatrical ambitions as a serious actor for the easy money of a cheap melodrama. Jamie plays the Broadway sport and appears to have some natural talent but squanders it though alcoholic loafing. Edmund shows the greatest artistic promise of the family but rejects his poetic gifts as substandard. He complains that he only has the "*makings* of a poet . . . like the guy who is always panhandling for a smoke. He hasn't even got the makings. He's got only the habit." What role does art play in the tragedy? Can it be considered a curse or a salvation?

RESOURCES

Primary Works

Complete Plays: 1913–1920; 1920–1931; 1932–1943, 3 volumes (New York: Literary Classics of the United States, 1988).
Collects all of O'Neill's published plays with a chronology and explanatory notes by leading O'Neill critic Travis Bogard.

Conversations with Eugene O'Neill, edited by Mark W. Estrin (Jackson: University Press of Mississippi, 1990).
Interviews with the playwright from newspapers and journals. The work includes a chronology.

Selected Letters of Eugene O'Neill, edited by Travis Bogard and Jackson R. Bryer (New Haven, Conn.: Yale University Press, 1988).
Compiles more than five hundred letters from the playwright to family members, friends, and critics, providing many biographical details.

Bibliography

Jennifer McCabe Atkinson, *Eugene O'Neill: A Descriptive Bibliography* (Pittsburgh: University of Pittsburgh Press, 1974).
Detailed illustrated primary bibliography of every edition of the playwright's works. Also includes bibliography of O'Neill's appearances in periodicals and books by other authors.

eOneill.com: An Electronic Eugene O'Neill Archive <http://www.eoneill.com> [accessed 6 October 2009].
Provides many electronic texts of O'Neill's early plays, as well as biographical and critical databases. The site includes a link to library-finding aids.

Jordan Y. Miller, *Eugene O'Neill and the American Critic: A Bibliographical Checklist* (Hamden, Conn.: Archon, 1977).
Annotated secondary bibliography limited to English-language works.

Madeline Smith and Richard Eaton, *Eugene O'Neill: An Annotated International Bibliography, 1973 through 1999* (Jefferson, N.C.: McFarland, 2001).

Biography

Stephen A. Black, *Eugene O'Neill: Beyond Mourning and Tragedy* (New Haven, Conn.: Yale University Press, 2002).
Psychological examination of the playwright in relationship to his work.

Arthur Gelb and Barbara Gelb, *O'Neill*, enlarged edition (New York: Harper, 1973).
The best and most thorough single-volume biography.

Gelb and Gelb, *O'Neill: Life with Monte Cristo* (New York: Applause, 2000).
First volume of a planned trilogy. The authors examine the playwright's early life and career in great detail.

Criticism

Travis Bogard, *Contour in Time: The Plays of Eugene O'Neill*, revised edition (New York: Oxford University Press, 1988).
Excellent book-length study of O'Neill's plays, including extensive production information.

Michael Manheim, *The Cambridge Companion to Eugene O'Neill* (Cambridge, England: Cambridge University Press, 1998).
Collects essays from several prominent O'Neill scholars. The book includes a chronology and primary bibliography.

—Park Bucker

Walker Percy, *The Moviegoer*
(New York: Knopf, 1961)

Walker Percy (1916–1990) secured his place among the most notable twentieth-century American writers when *The Moviegoer*, his first published novel, won the National Book Award for Fiction in 1962, beating other finalists such as Joseph Heller's *Catch-22* and J. D. Salinger's *Franny and Zooey*. Being an author was not, however, his first intention. Percy studied medicine, but after contracting tuberculosis during a pathology internship his promising medical career was derailed. Rather than practicing medicine, he became a patient in a TB sanatorium, giving him a two-year period to study the human condition in an entirely different way. This time in the Trudeau Sanatorium in Saranac Lake, New York, may have saved his life in more ways than one, as it not only gave him time to be cured but also gave him time to reflect upon the forces that had shaped his beliefs. He left the sanatorium determined to be a philosopher and novelist rather than a doctor, and at the time of his death he had lived longer than any other male Percy.

Percy's first writing, however, was not fiction. Instead, he wrote on philosophy and language, publishing his writing in journals. Eventually, he turned to writing fiction to express his philosophy more fully. An early attempt, "The Gramercy Winner," read too much like a philosophical treatise, and it was never published. In *The Moviegoer* he found his own style, a mixture of wryness and reflection, and introduced the first of the Percyan heroes. The novel opens the week before Mardi Gras with its protagonist, Binx Bolling, determined to resume a search for meaning that first occurred to him on the battlefields of Korea. Much to the disappointment of his aunt, who raised him following his father's death, he is neither doctor nor lawyer, as his social class dictates; instead, he is a stockbroker who fills his days with the pursuit of money and his evenings with the pursuit of his secretaries and the distraction of the movies. That week, however, proves to be a crucial week in Binx's life. He awakens from the complacency of his everydayness, and by the novel's end he has committed to a course of action which brings true meaning to his life while, as a bonus, pleasing his aunt.

In many ways Binx is modeled after Percy himself. After his father's suicide and his mother's death, his father's bachelor cousin, William Alexander Percy, adopted Percy and his brothers, bringing them to his home in Greenville, Mississippi. The boys adored "Uncle Will," who was very much a Southern aristocrat: although he published poetry and his memoirs, he was a practicing lawyer; he was a disciple of Marcus Aurelius Antoninus, the Roman emperor and Stoic philosopher; and he was a lover of literature and classical music. His influence over Percy can be seen in the character of Aunt Emily, who sends Will a quote from Marcus Aurelius's *Meditations* and plays Chopin for him on the piano. Percy said, in fact, that Aunt Emily's rant in part 5 was pure Uncle Will, and it is easy to imagine that this might have been Will Percy's reaction to Walker's abandonment of medicine, had Will not died in 1941.

During Percy's time in the sanatorium, his exposure to other thinkers began to balance the influence of Uncle Will. He read voraciously during that period, having no other pursuits available to him, devouring the philosophy of writers such as Søren Kierkegaard, Gabriel Marcel, Albert Camus, Martin Heidegger, Charles Sanders Peirce, and Ludwig Wittgenstein. While glimmerings of Marcel, Camus, and Heidegger can be seen in *The Moviegoer,* the strongest influence on Percy's own developing philosophy at that point was Kierkegaard, whom he juxtaposes against the Stoicism of Marcus Aurelius. As Binx's ultimate choices, seen in the epilogue, reveal, Percy sides with Kierkegaard's Christianity, abandoning the philosophy of the aristocrats as he abandoned their professions.

Finally, his conversion to Catholicism provided him with a new way of understanding himself and his role in the world. For this reason, the time frame of the novel should be seen as carrying religious, not merely cultural, significance. However, students of Percy are likely to miss the religious and philosophical underpinnings of *The Moviegoer* if they do not attend carefully to the details. As Binx reports in the epilogue, "[I]t is not open to me even to be edifying . . ." However, becoming more familiar with Percy's work can be helpful. *The Last Gentleman* (1966) and *Love in the Ruins* (1971) share many of the themes of *The Moviegoer,* despite the marked difference in subject matter. Additionally, many of the interviews in *Conversations with Walker Percy* focus on *The Moviegoer,* and Percy patiently and repeatedly explains the connections to his adoptive father as well as to Kierkegaard and other philosophers. Jay Tolson's *Pilgrim in the Ruins: The Life of Walker Percy* is the most helpful literary biography, and Linda Hobson's *Understanding Walker Percy* provides a readable and enlightening critical overview.

TOPICS FOR DISCUSSION AND RESEARCH

1. In an interview, Walker Percy said of William Alexander Percy, "The whole idea of the Greek-Roman Stoic view, the classical view, was exemplified in him more than in any other person I ever knew." This view regards an honor system, *noblesse oblige,* above all else, and agrees with the Romans of old that it is better to fall upon one's sword than to be dishonored. Readers of Percy sometimes mistakenly infer that he espouses this belief system because he presents it with such vigor in characters such as Aunt Emily. In contrast, his Christianity is more subtly drawn, and readers must be alert to the signs. Percy's Christianity is Catholic in its orientation; therefore, the symbolism of the Eucharist, the references to Ash Wednesday, and other aspects of Catholicism should be seen as having great weight. Students may want to discuss Binx's spiritual development, using the symbols mentioned above to guide their study. Additionally, by focusing on the differing reactions of Emily and Binx to the deaths of Scotty and Lonnie, students might discuss the philosophical differences between the two.

2. While Percy is unmistakably Catholic in his views, his belief system cannot be so neatly categorized. His encounters with the Christian existentialists— Kierkegaard and Marcel, particularly—shaped his view of humanity. He argues in both essays and interviews that man is *homo viator,* a wayfaring stranger, displaced from his true home. This theme, which is present in all of his fiction, is a focal point in *The Moviegoer.* In his essay "The Message in the Bottle" he compares mankind's existence to that of Robinson Crusoe, who found himself stranded on an island in search of signs and messages from his home. Consider Binx, who reads *Arabia Deserta* and embarks on a search. What signs does he see, what messages does he receive that remind him of his true identity, and how does his search end? Students should also consider "rotation" and "repetition" and how those techniques relate to the search.

3. Kierkegaard's stages of life are crucial to understanding Binx's development. Kierkegaard argued that people travel through three stages: the aesthetic, the ethical, and the religious. The aesthetic stage is characterized by the pursuit of pleasure, whether it be the enjoyment of Chopin's music or the desire for physical love. The ethical stage is marked by the movement from a pleasure-driven existence to a duty-driven existence. A person in the ethical stage is concerned with faithfully performing the duties of a good citizen. The final stage is the religious stage. Kierkegaard asserts that the religious

stage is often hidden by an exterior that seems to be ethical. The movement to this stage is internal, and it is one that cannot be easily discussed by the person in the religious stage. This reticence is caused by the absurdity of believing that which is entirely illogical and of following commands which may not make sense in an ethical universe. Lonnie exists in the religious stage, and his belief in his own sin provides an excellent example of the tension between the ethical stage and the religious stage; Aunt Emily, on the other hand, is wholly in the ethical stage. Beyond these examples, many of the other characters can be identified as occupying a particular stage. Binx, however, moves between stages, making progress and then backsliding, leaving critics undecided about the stage he is in at the novel's end. Students can seek to answer that question by studying Binx's possessions, his actions, and his interactions with others.

4. An important aspect of waking up to one's existence, to undertaking the search, and to making the movement to the religious stage, according to Percy, is being aware of despair. The novel's epigraph from Kierkegaard's *The Sickness Unto Death* provides an important clue: ". . . the specific character of despair is precisely this: it is unaware of being despair." Percy is not concerned with typical sadness or depression. Instead, he relies upon an unwritten context created by his reference to Kierkegaard: despair is the state of all people who are separated from Christ. The greater the separation is, the greater the despair is. That separation also creates an obtuseness, making sufferers ignorant of their state. Students may want to determine what Percy is ultimately saying about the role of despair in the spiritual development of people by focusing on Binx's concern with the malaise, with living death, and with what he terms "everydayness," a term he borrows from Heidegger.

5. Percy's concern with consumerism, the media, and the way these forces formulate self-perception, reality, and identity is a worthy topic. Students may want to consider how the various characters in the novel attempt to create identity. Does the consumption of media itself and the products advertised in the media help people to understand themselves and the world in which they find themselves, or is the identity they fashion one which masks their authentic selves?

RESOURCES

Primary Works

Conversations with Walker Percy, edited by Lewis A. Lawson and Victor A. Kramer (Jackson: University Press of Mississippi, 1985).

A collection of interviews in the first half of which various scholars and journalists prompt Percy to discuss the origins—biographical, philosophical, and artistic—of *The Moviegoer*, along with themes, characters, symbolism and other features of the novel.

Lost in the Cosmos: The Last Self-Help Book (New York: Farrar, Straus & Giroux, 1983).

An ironically subtitled collection of essays on philosophical topics, the best of which combine elements of fiction with philosophical musings, as in "The Last Donahue Show."

Bibliography

The Society for the Study of Southern Literature Bibliography <http://www.missq. msstate.edu/sssl> [accessed 9 October 2009].
Contains more than forty entries on *The Moviegoer* and nearly four hundred on Percy.

Biography

Jay Tolson, *Pilgrim in the Ruins: The Life of Walker Percy* (New York: Simon & Schuster, 1992).
Of the three biographies on Percy, offers the most interpretive look at his life and his work.

Bertram Wyatt-Brown, *The House of Percy: Honor, Melancholy, and Imagination in a Southern Family* (New York: Oxford University Press, 1994).
Examination of the Percy family that offers surprising insight into Percy's literary and philosophical endeavors.

Criticism

Panthea Reid Broughton, ed., *The Art of Walker Percy: Stratagems for Being* (Baton Rouge: Louisiana State University Press, 1979).
Includes three essays on *The Moviegoer* that offer excellent insights, with the Hobbs essay applying Kierkegaard's stages to Binx Bolling proving particularly helpful.

Linda Hobson, *Understanding Walker Percy* (Columbia: University of South Carolina Press, 1988).
A comprehensive overview of Percy's fiction in which Hobson clarifies his major themes in direct, understandable language free of jargon and specialized literary theories.

Lewis A. Lawson, *Following Percy: Essays on Walker Percy's Work* (Troy, N.Y.: Whitston, 1988).
A book by perhaps the most perceptive of Percy's critics, who has devoted a life's work to the critical analysis of Percy's work.

Martin Luschei, *The Sovereign Wayfarer: Walker Percy's Diagnosis of the Malaise* (Baton Rouge: Louisiana State University Press, 1972).
Provides excellent biographical information, offering a different angle from Tolson's biography and clear analysis of the first three Percy novels.

—Rhonda McDonnell

Thomas Pynchon, *The Crying of Lot 49*
(Philadelphia: Lippincott, 1966)

The life of Thomas Pynchon (1937–   ) has been the object of speculation since he published his first novel, *V.*, in 1963. Some of what is known about his life is echoed in *The Crying of Lot 49*. For example, he studied engineering physics at Cornell and worked for two years at Boeing Aircraft in Seattle as a technical writer and engineering aide. In the novel the protagonist, Oedipa Maas, begins her quest in San Narciso, the headquarters of "the Galactronics Division of Yoyodyne, Inc., one of the giants of the aerospace industry," and Maxwell's Demon operates on the principle of entropy, a theory of physics. For several years after he left Boeing, Pynchon spent time between California and Mexico. The novel is set in California and Mazatlán, Mexico, where the character Pierce takes Oedipa while they are lovers. Oedipa and Pierce also share a sunrise on Library Hill on the campus of Cornell when they are still together; and during their "songfest" the shareholders at Yoyodyne sing a hymn that is "to the tune of Cornell's alma mater." Perhaps most important, Pynchon graduated from Cornell with a degree in English, and this perhaps accounts for the numerous literary allusions—both real and imaginary—that are sprinkled throughout the novel. Most notable is Pynchon's creation of *The Courier's Tragedy*, which parodies such Jacobean revenge tragedies as *The Duchess of Malfi* and *The Revenger's Tragedy*. Very little, however, is actually known about the details of Pynchon's life. There have been numerous "sightings" of him, and today it is assumed he lives in New York with his wife and children. The most reliable accounts of his life are found in his introduction to *Slow Learner* (1984), an anthology of his short stories, and the introduction to Richard Farina's novel *Been Down So Long It Looks Like Up to Me* (1966). Pynchon has become an anticelebrity celeb.

The Crying of Lot 49 tells the story of Oedipa Maas and the quest that develops when she is summoned to execute the will of her former lover, Pierce Inverarity. "As things developed," the narrator predicts, "she was to have all manner of revelations. Hardly about Pierce Inverarity, or herself. . . ." As she immerses herself in the web of Inverarity's interests, she discovers the Tristero System, an underground mail service that has existed in one form or another for hundreds of years. The quest's main concern, caught by Pynchon in the symbol of Maxwell's Demon, is the answer to the question: What is the connection—if any—between Inverarity's "empire" and the "silent empire" of the Tristero System? Since the structure of the novel resembles that of a classical romance, as the essential quest—the search for the connection—continues, there are stories within stories within stories and twists and turns of the plot that at times seem bewildering. However, there are two touchstones that can bring focus to the details of what critics accurately characterize as the dense narrative style of Pynchon. The first, which occurs near the middle of chapter 3, is the detailed account of the plot of *The Courier's Tragedy*, which not only gives insight into the history and nature of the Tristero System but also develops many of the central motifs of the novel. The second—occurring near the beginning of chapter 5—is Oedipa's encounter with John Nefastis and Maxwell's Demon, which focuses on the idea of entropy. For Oedipa, the piling up of details and evidence throughout the novel leads to an information overload. There is too much data for her to sort out. Oedipa, in the end, must decide whether everything that she has experienced is real or whether everything that she has experienced has either "a transcendent meaning" or is "only the earth." Oedipa decides to continue the quest as she "settled back, to await the crying of lot 49." But while the novel is about Oedipa's quest, on a deeper level, as in all of Pynchon's major works, it is about the search for the meaning of America: "There either was some Tristero beyond the appearance of the legacy America, or there was just America and if there was just America then it seemed the only way she could continue . . . was as an alien . . ."

Criticism of Pynchon and his work is extensive, with much of it being as esoteric as his novels. Before reading the novel, students are advised to read Pynchon's introduction to *Been Down So Long It Looks Like Up to Me*, "Is It OK to Be a Luddite?," and, especially, his introduction to *Slow Learner*. After reading, the student can find solid approaches to the novel in Edward Mendelson's "The Sacred, the Profane, and *The Crying of Lot 49*," Molly Hite's *Ideas of Order in the Novels of Thomas Pynchon*, and Thomas Schaub's "Influence and Incest: Relations between *The Crying of Lot 49* and *The Great Gatsby*."

TOPICS FOR DISCUSSION AND RESEARCH

1. Because of the complexity of the plot, a good way to approach what Pynchon is trying to do and say in the novel is by analyzing its motifs—for example, his use of the labyrinth. Such images as webs, circuits, freeways, the "swirl" of suburban land tracts, and Inverarity's multiple "empires" are all images that describe the labyrinthian nature of Oedipa's quest. Labyrinths are objects that have to be traveled through that often contain dead ends and false paths and are usually without road maps (another labyrinth), and often they are designed by someone known or unknown. Students might trace one of these "web" images through the novel and examine whether or not it "fits" or comes to a satisfactory conclusion. Or does the image reach, perhaps like Oedipa, a dead end?

2. Other motifs Pynchon employs represent communication: the attempt to communicate or the attempt to understand what is being communicated. This image is closely connected with the image of the labyrinth, and is caught nicely in the analogy of the landscape of San Narciso and the "transistor radio" circuit that Oedipa once saw. They both revealed to her an outward clarity—a "hieroglyphic" (another image of communication)—a message that floats "just past the threshold of [Oedipa's] understanding." From Inverarity's phone call at three in the morning as he assumes different voices, through the aboveground and belowground mail systems, to Maxwell's Demon, to the eventual "crying" of the stamp lot, Oedipa experiences attempts to communicate throughout the novel. One special element that continually attempts to communicate to Oedipa is the "landscape": San Narciso and San Francisco provide opportunities for Oedipa to "listen" to what the landscape is telling her. Can Oedipa "read" what the landscape is trying to tell her, or does it, like the transistor circuit, pass just beyond the threshold of her understanding? See Mendelson for help with this topic.

3. Silence, too, plays a crucial role in the novel. There are important moments when—amid the clang and clatter of the plot—things fall silent; things come to a standstill. These moments are carefully marked out by Pynchon. An exploration of how the central themes are carried out when nothing is happening will prove a rewarding exploration.

4. The novel was published in the middle of the 1960s, and like many other novels during these years, the plot speculates on the direction America is taking or is going to take. The core of the novel can be found by exploring the vision of America it contains. Exploring what Pynchon is saying is the nature of American culture, and what that culture has to offer the individual in terms of comprehending its ebb and flow is a major concern within the novel. If the legacy of Pierce Inverarity is the legacy of America, what is that legacy, and where is it going? Have things changed since its publication, or is Pynchon's characterization of America still contemporary?

5. *The Crying of Lot 49* is a Postmodern novel. Students can grasp the structure of the novel by exploring the elements of Postmodernism. Rather than entering into the labyrinth of books and articles concerning what Postmodernism is, a student might consult a good, recent dictionary of literary terms, find the definition of *Postmodernism,* and apply the elements mentioned to the novel, especially focusing on how Pynchon handles his material.

RESOURCES

Primary Works

Slow Learner: Early Stories (Boston: Little, Brown, 1984), pp. 79–98.
Contains the story "Entropy," which not only explores the idea of entropy but also explores the themes of isolation and chaos also found in *The Crying of Lot 49.* The introduction provides autobiographical information, along with helpful ideas regarding the development of Pynchon's themes and style. The introduction also discusses the idea of entropy.

Introduction, in Richard Fariña, *Been Down So Long It Looks Like Up to Me* (New York: Viking, 1983).
Helpful for biographic information, especially Pynchon's California experience.

"Is It O.K. to Be a Luddite?" *New York Times Book Review,* 28 (October 1984), pp. 1, 40–41 <http://www.themodernword.com/Pynchon/pynchon_essays_luddite.html> [accessed 4 December 2009].
Discusses Pynchon's attitudes and ideas about technology and America's attitude toward technology.

Bibliography

Kerry J. Grant, *A Companion to* The Crying of Lot 49 (Athens: University of Georgia Press, 1994).
A chapter-by-chapter reference guide explaining everything from Oedipa's name to the "crying" of the stamp lot. The book contains an excellent bibliography.

Criticism

Diana York Blaine, "Death and *The Crying of Lot 49*" in *Thomas Pynchon: Reading from the Margins*, edited by Niran Abbas (Madison, N.J.: Fairleigh-Dickinson University Press, 2003), pp. 51–70.

Explores Oedipa as one who seeks to understand "the nature of human mortality." Even though she "dreads finding it," she continues on her quest to seek knowledge of it.

Judith Chambers, *Thomas Pynchon* (New York: Twayne, 1992).

Includes chapter 4, "*The Crying of Lot 49:* The Word in Ruins." Chambers claims that Pynchon's language destroys the concrete quality of words while at the same time his language is "evocative" in its "power." She also deals with the archetype of the White Goddess as it relates to Oedipa.

Molly Hite, *Ideas of Order in the Novels of Thomas Pynchon* (Columbus: Ohio State University Press, 1983).

Includes chapter 3, which argues that the novel's construction is a world unto itself, that communication does exist among the isolates in the novel. Like Oedipa, Pynchon projects a world—the novel—where "events do not have to be explained by reference to an ultimate purpose." Thus, the novel itself becomes a kind of art object.

Stefan Mattissich, *Lines of Flight: Discursive Time and Countercultural Desire in the Work of Thomas Pynchon* (Durham, N.C.: Duke University Press, 2002).

Includes chapter 2, which deals with the novel's focus on "the double bind" of America's "market culture," concluding that there is no answer at the end of the novel—there is not "even a simple way out."

Edward Mendelson, "The Sacred, the Profane, and *The Crying of Lot 49*," in *Thomas Pynchon*, edited by Harold Bloom (New York: Chelsea House, 2003), pp. 11–42.

Particularly good at analyzing the motif of communication that runs throughout the novel and is one of its major concerns.

Robert D. Newman, *Understanding Thomas Pynchon* (Columbia: University of South Carolina Press, 1986).

Includes chapter 4, which explores the novel as a commentary on American culture and "an investigation into the uses and misuses of metaphor."

Pierre-Yves Petillon, "A Re-cognition of Her Errand into the Wilderness," in *New Essays On* The Crying of Lot 49, edited by Patrick O'Donnell (Cambridge, England: Cambridge University Press, 1991).

Connects the novel to other American works. Petillon sees the novel as influenced by works ranging from Jack Kerouac's *On the Road* to the novels and style of Henry James.

Thomas Schaub, "Influence and Incest: Relations between *The Crying of Lot 49* and *The Great Gatsby*," in *Thomas Pynchon: Readings from the Margins*, edited

by Niran Abbas (Madison, N.J.: Fairleigh-Dickinson University Press, 2003),
pp. 139–153.
Despite the daunting title, offers an intriguing Freudian approach to the two
novels. Freudian aspects aside, the comparison-contrast of other aspects of the
two novels is interesting and solid.

—*Bob Bell*

Philip Roth, *Goodbye, Columbus*
(Boston: Houghton Mifflin, 1959)

Published when Philip Roth (1933–) was only twenty-seven, *Goodbye, Columbus*
won the National Book Award in 1960. Comprising a novella (the title piece) and
five additional stories, the book, Roth's first, not only established him as a major
American writer but also earned the ire of Jewish intellectuals and religious readers, sparking a controversy about Roth's depiction of Jews that continued to shape
the direction of his career for decades.

Born in 1933 to an insurance salesman and a doting, loving mother, Roth and
his older brother grew up in the mostly Jewish Weequahic area of Newark, New
Jersey. A gifted student, Roth graduated from high school at the age of sixteen,
after which he spent a year at the Newark branch of Rutgers University before
transferring to Bucknell University in Pennsylvania. Following his graduation,
he entered the Ph.D. program in English literature at the University of Chicago
before halting his studies to serve his required term in the U.S. Army. In the mid
1950s he returned to Chicago as a writing instructor and wrote several of the
stories and the novella that are included in *Goodbye, Columbus*. During this period
he also met Saul Bellow, who became a key early supporter. The title novella,
"Conversion of the Jews," and "Epstein" all appeared originally in *The Paris
Review*, while "Defender of the Faith," which draws upon Roth's army experience,
appeared originally in *The New Yorker* in 1959, where it ignited the first wave of
controversy that would engulf the book when it was published later that year.

The title piece is a love story between a working-class Jewish college graduate, Neil Klugman, and an affluent Radcliff student named Brenda Patimkin,
whose family, following the first major wave of Jewish assimilation after World
War II, has moved from Newark, New Jersey (both Klugman's and Roth's
hometown), into the once all-Protestant suburb of Short Hills. Neil and Brenda
struggle against not only the constraints of Brenda's moralizing parents but also
the class differences that separate them. Throughout, Roth trains a caustic, satirical eye on the gaucheness of the newly minted Patimpkins, as when Neil inven-
tories the untouched contents of the Patkimpkins' brand-new basement bar, on
the back shelf of which stand "two dozen bottles—twenty-three to be exact—of
Jack Daniels, each with a little booklet tied to its collared neck informing patrons
how patrician of them it was to drink the stuff."

In the five remaining stories, Roth depicts a range of memorable young Jewish heroes caught between the desire to assimilate into what he elsewhere calls "the country's much proclaimed, self-defining heterogeneity" and the pressure to maintain ethnic and religious solidarity. In the most famous of these five stories, the much anthologized "Conversion of the Jews," twelve-year-old Ozzie Freedman asks an oppressive rabbi named Binder why God couldn't "let a woman have a baby without having intercourse," while in "Defender of the Faith," a Jewish sergeant named Marx finds himself torn between his allegiance to the army and the dishonest demands of a fellow Jew in his charge.

Roth's gift for damning detail earned him early comparisons to such American satirists as Sinclair Lewis and Mark Twain. The book's vivid writing, slapstick humor, and crisp contemporaneity also set it apart from the work of such Jewish American masters as Bernard Malamud and Isaac Bashevis Singer, whose stories and novels often focus on the unique particulars of life amid the Eastern-European Jewish immigrants of New York. Instead, Roth's style owed more to the free-wheeling exuberance of his mentor Saul Bellow's *The Adventures of Augie March* (1953) and to the mannered precocity of J. D. Salinger. Meanwhile, Roth's detractors in the Jewish community—a group that included both rabbis and literary critics—accused the book of confirming negative Jewish stereotypes, with some even accusing Roth of "Jewish self-hatred." Although Roth addressed the controversy directly in his essay "Writing About Jews," later reprinted in *Reading Myself and Others* (1974), he has also made oblique use of it in his numerous novels about his fictionalized alter ego, the Jewish American novelist Nathan Zuckerman. In *The Ghost Writer* (1979), Roth introduces Nathan Zuckerman at the very beginning of his writerly career, just as his first book, *Higher Education*, is starting to attract the exact same accusations that greeted *Goodbye, Columbus*. Meanwhile, in *The Counterlife* (1986), Roth boldly satirizes the charge that his work is somehow "dangerous" when he depicts Zuckerman, while on a plane flight out of Israel in the late 1970s, being recruited into a hijacking by a radical Jewish terrorist who tells Zuckerman, "Every idea I ever had, I got from your books!"

Because of the sheer size of Roth's published canon—thirty books and counting—it is easy to get lost in the rapidly expanding world of Roth criticism. The clearest and most direct readings of the stories in *Goodbye, Columbus* can be found in the first chapter of Murray Baumgarten and Barbara Gottfried's *Understanding Philip Roth*. Brief though it is, Hermione Lee's consideration of the collection in her slim 1982 monograph *Philip Roth* remains an indispensable starting point for students interested in the book's major themes and social context.

TOPICS FOR DISCUSSION AND RESEARCH

1. Although *Goodbye, Columbus* can be read as a complete work or as a series of self-contained shorter pieces, most critics separate it into the title novella and the five stories that follow it. What unifies the collection is Roth's fresh approach to the dilemma facing Jews of his generation, many of whom, like Roth, were the U.S.-born children of first- and second-generation immigrants. Ozzie Freedman, in "The Conversion of the Jews," captures Roth's theme when he asks "how Rabbi

Binder could call the Jews 'The Chosen People' if the Declaration of Independence claimed all men to be created equal." Students might consider not only the various ways Roth dramatizes this conflict but also the way his humor and irony invite misinterpretation. For instance, at the end of "The Conversion of the Jews," Ozzie stands on the roof of the building housing his Hebrew school and demands that his mother, his rabbi, and his fellow classmates acknowledge that "God can make a child without intercourse." A close reading of the story confirms that Ozzie's main intention here is to compel his rabbi in particular to acknowledge the Christian virgin birth as a *possibility;* yet, this well-meaning plea for religious tolerance gets complicated by the story's title, which evokes the end-times Christian belief that Jews will convert to Christianity at the Apocalypse. Students might also want to explore Roth's essay, "Writing About Jews," as well as such later, politically charged Zuckerman novels as *I Married a Communist* (1998) and *The Human Stain* (2000) for further insight into the author's views about fiction and politics. Of particular interest is the former novel, in which a literature professor named Leo Glucksman instructs the future novelist Zuckerman that "Politics is the great generalizer . . . and literature the great particularizer, and not only are they in an inverse relationship to each other—they are in an *antagonistic* relationship." Students might also consider comparing the stories in *Goodbye, Columbus* to more-recent story collections focusing on assimilation and its discontents, such as Asian American author Amy Tan's *The Joy Luck Club* (1989), Hispanic American author Julia Alvarez's *How the Garcia Girls Lost Their Accents* (1992), and Indian American writer Jhumpa Lahiri's *The Interpreter of Maladies* (2000).

2. Students might also confront head-on the charges of anti-Semitism and "racial self-hatred" that greeted Roth upon the appearance of "Defender of the Faith." In other words, what obligations does Roth owe to his fellow Jews, and how do these obligations conflict with his artistic freedom? Although Roth addresses these charges in "Writing About Jews," students should also explore Irving Howe's 1972 essay, "Philip Roth Reconsidered," which addresses these same charges while also providing a provocative assessment of what Howe regards as Roth's artistic shortcomings in shaping the stories that make up *Goodbye, Columbus.*

3. The novella "Goodbye, Columbus" is not only the longest piece in the collection but also its most replete. Although it clearly shares the collection's overriding theme of Jewish assimilation, "Goodbye, Columbus" complicates matters even more by adding the issue of social class. Students will find much to explore in Roth's intricate, concrete symbolism, most of which illuminates the contours of the novella's class conflict. Whereas Brenda spends her summer days sunbathing and working on her tennis backhand, Neil bides his time working at the circulation desk of the New York Public Library, where he meets a young African American boy who comes to the library every morning to look at a book of Paul Gauguin prints, insisting they can be found in the "heart" (art) section. As the novella progresses, Neil begins to associate the Patimkins' lush, affluent suburb of Short Hills with Gauguin's idealized Polynesia, thereby creating a chain of connections linking Neil, a second-generation Newark Jew, to the African American boy, a new inhabitant of "the Negro section

of Newark." In this scenario, the Patimpkins represent the post–World War II generation of Jews who "had struggled and prospered, and moved further and further west . . . pouring into Gentile territory as the Scotch-Irish had poured through the Cumberland Gap," while Neil and the boy in the library represent the next generation of working-class minorities "making the same migration," each group repeating Columbus's arrival to the New World before moving westward into the American grain.

4. But "Goodbye, Columbus" is also a story of generational conflict, as Neil and Brenda, children of the Depression who came of age during the prosperity of the 1950s, chafe against the self-denying strictures of their parents' generation. Though tame by today's standards, Neil's and Brenda's sexual freedom not only shocked much of the book's 1950s readership but also represented a genuine cultural shift that would explode in the coming decade into a full-blown sexual revolution, of which Roth's notorious 1969 novel, *Portnoy's Complaint,* was a significant emblem. Students might also explore the complexities of Brenda's relationship with her parents in this regard, particularly as this relationship exemplifies Sigmund Freud's "Electra Complex," a line of inquiry that could also encompass the novella's subtle but consistent use of mythic archetypes throughout.

RESOURCES

Primary Works

The Facts: A Novelist's Autobiography (New York: Farrar, Straus & Giroux, 1988).
A slim but provocative collection of autobiographical essays, many of which dramatize episodes from Roth's life that he later transformed in his fiction. This work includes a provocative "Afterword" from Roth's alter ego, Nathan Zuckerman, that affirms the superiority of fiction over "straight" autobiography.

Reading Myself and Others (New York: Farrar, Straus & Giroux, 1975).
A book of essays and reviews that includes "Writing About Jews," "Some New Jewish Stereotypes," "The Story of Three Stories," and other meditations on the inspirations and strategies behind the composition of *Goodbye, Columbus.*

Bibliography

The Philip Roth Society Bibliography <http://orgs.tamu-commerce.edu/rothsoc/resources.htm> [accessed 3 September 2009].
Provides a detailed listing of bibliographies, book-length studies and monographs, special issues of journals, chapters from books, journal articles, dissertations, and interviews with Roth, many with online links.

Criticism

Murray Baumgarten and Barbara Gottfried, *Understanding Philip Roth* (Columbia: University of South Carolina Press, 1990).
A comprehensive overview of Roth's major works up to *The Counterlife,* with individual chapters devoted to each book and a thorough discussion of the major themes in *Goodbye, Columbus.*

Alan Cooper, *Philip Roth and the Jews* (Albany: State University of New York Press, 1996).
A focused, accessible study of Roth's status as a representative "secular Jew" whose work returns again and again to difficulties of balancing one's ethnic identity with the desire to live as a free, unhyphenated American.

Irving Howe, "Philip Roth Reconsidered," *Commentary*, 54 (December 1972): 69–77.
A brief but influential reassessment of Roth's early stories published in the wake of the success of his scandalous best seller, *Portnoy's Complaint*.

Hermione Lee, *Philip Roth* (New York: Methuen, 1982).
An early, but also concise and formative, study of Roth's early fiction, and of *Goodbye, Columbus* in particular, before metafictional concerns took over his work.

Timothy Parrish, ed., *The Cambridge Companion to Philip Roth* (Cambridge, England: Cambridge University Press, 2007).
The most authoritative collection of essays on Roth's work, covering a wide range of issues pertinent to *Goodbye, Columbus*. The pieces include "Jewish American Identity in Roth's Short Fiction," "Roth and Gender," and "Roth and Ethnic Identity."

—Marshall Boswell

⌒⫷⫸⌒

J. D. Salinger, *The Catcher in the Rye*
(Boston: Little, Brown, 1951)

Between 1940 and 1965 J. D. Salinger (1919–2010) published thirty-six short stories and one novel, *The Catcher in the Rye*. Thirteen of these stories were collected in three volumes: *Nine Stories* (1953), *Franny and Zooey* (1961), and *Raise High the Roof Beam, Carpenters; and Seymour: An Introduction* (1963). During the four and a half decades following the publication of his uncollected final story, "Hapworth 1924," in *The New Yorker* in June 1965, Salinger remained mysteriously and conspicuously silent. *The Catcher in the Rye*, however, remains one of the best-selling books of all time, continuing to sell approximately 250,000 copies per year, nearly sixty years after its publication, and its enduring impact on American culture is no less remarkable.

Salinger's adolescence parallels that of Holden Caulfield, the protagonist in *The Catcher in the Rye*, while his early adulthood bears some resemblance to that of D. B., Holden's older brother. Salinger, too, grew up in an upper-middle-class family in New York City and lived—at least during his teenage years—on the city's affluent Upper East Side while attending private schools and vacationing in Maine during the summer. Salinger's father was not a corporate lawyer like Holden's, but he was a successful businessman, a meat importer, who hoped his son would pursue a similar line of work. Like Holden,

Salinger was an unmotivated student, and his father enrolled him in the Valley Forge Military Academy—after which Pencey Prep is loosely modeled—when his grades precluded his returning to New York's elite McBurney School. Like D. B. Caulfield, Salinger was a prolific short-story writer during the 1940s, served in the U.S. Army during World War II, and was part of the D day invasion on 6 June 1944; also like D. B. he refused to write specifically about his military experience. Salinger's first and last experience with Hollywood is no doubt responsible for Holden's resentment of D. B.'s giving up fiction writing for screenwriting. When his short story "Uncle Wiggly in Connecticut" served as the basis for the movie *My Foolish Heart* (1949), Salinger was devastated with the result and became increasingly vigilant regarding the "prostitution," as Holden would describe it, of his work, eventually demanding that no marketing tactics—cover illustrations, author photos, or reviewer blurbs—be used to attract readers. When his photo appeared on the back of the dust jacket for *The Catcher in the Rye*, he insisted that jacket be replaced with a blank back cover. The fear expressed by Holden Caulfield that the expectations of an audience can ruin an artist's creativity was a very real concern for Salinger, whose protagonist also fantasizes about moving to a rural area to live a hermit's existence. On his thirty-fourth birthday, New Year's Day 1953, in the wake of the explosive popular reception of *The Catcher in the Rye*, Salinger moved to a secluded home in New Hampshire. He continued to live there until his death, surfacing occasionally to protect his privacy and his work. His devotion to Zen Buddhism coupled with his antipathy for publicity seems to have contributed to his public silence. In 2009 the ninety-year-old Salinger successfully sued to keep a "sequel" to his novel written by a Swedish writer under the pseudonym John David (J. D.) California from being published in the United States. In *Sixty Years Later: Coming through the Rye*, published in Europe, a seventy-six-year-old Holden (referred to as "Mr. C") wanders the streets of New York City after escaping from a retirement home. Salinger died on 27 January 2010.

The Catcher in the Rye captures the restlessness of many young adults in postwar America and has become an enduring testament of teenage anxiety. Yet, it is much more than that, as it raises universal moral, aesthetic, and philosophical questions. Holden's disgust with an adult world he views as selfish, insensitive, and unimaginative presages the budding counter-culture movement of the late 1950s and 1960s, blazing the trail for disaffected protagonists in later novels such as Joseph Heller's *Catch-22* (1961) and Ken Kesey's *One Flew Over the Cuckoo's Nest* (1962). The novel has not only dominated the best-seller list but also reigned on banned-book lists and lists of the greatest novels of the twentieth century.

Study of *The Catcher in the Rye* should begin with Salinger's early uncollected stories, namely "Last Day of the Last Furlough" (1944) and "This Sandwich Has No Mayonnaise" (1945), which introduce the Caulfield family and several themes taken up in *The Catcher in the Rye*. Two other stories, "I'm Crazy" (1946) and "Slight Rebellion off Madison" (1946), are early drafts of episodes from the novel and provide a useful look into its evolution, particularly the latter, which is told from a third-person point of view. These stories may be found on the website "Free Web" <http://www.freeweb.hu/tchl/salinger/> or, with the help of a primary bibliography, on microfilm. Even more important, "A Perfect Day for Bananafish" (1948), collected in *Nine Stories*, is an essential companion piece to the novel. Ian Hamilton's slim literary biography *In Search of J. D. Salinger* (1988) provides an excellent overview of Salinger's life and work, especially considering the author's aloofness. Warren French and James Lundquist have both included excellent critical analyses of *The Catcher in the Rye* in their studies of Salinger. John Unrue's book is the best source for sound, readable criticism of the novel.

TOPICS FOR DISCUSSION AND RESEARCH

1. Salinger's short story "A Perfect Day for Bananafish," which first appeared in *The New Yorker* on 31 January 1948, marked his arrival as a significant literary author and introduced his second-most-famous protagonist: Seymour Glass, a young, recently married World War II veteran who went on to dominate Salinger's fiction after *The Catcher in the Rye*. Read this early story in an effort to better understand Holden Caulfield, as both characters personify the author's preoccupation with the plight of the hypersensitive individual in a society he finds crass and superficial. What are Seymour and Holden searching for? What makes them happy, and what depresses them? In what ways do their predicaments differ? How might the names Seymour Glass and Holden Caulfield symbolically capture the plight of each?

2. In Salinger's short story "Zooey," the title character, who is Seymour's younger brother, remarks that beauty is his "Achilles heal." And in "Seymour: An Introduction," Buddy, another Glass child, recalls Seymour throwing a rock at a twelve-year-old neighbor girl "because she looked so beautiful." Can it be argued that Holden, too, suffers in the face of beauty? Consider both his physical and emotional state. Analyze the scene in the novel's penultimate chapter where his sister Phoebe cries when he tells her she cannot run away with him. "All of a sudden I wanted her to cry till her eyes practically dropped out," he remarks. "I almost hated her." What makes Holden feel this way about the person whom he clearly cares about the most? Also consider his argument with his close friend Sally. Why does Holden suddenly turn on her?

3. On a similar note, these scenes are among dozens in which Holden displays conflicting emotions. Some of the people and ideas that repulse him are also the ones that he finds most alluring: Stradlater, for example, and the sexuality he exudes in Holden's mind. Also note how his red hat is his "people hunting hat"; yet, he flips it around in the classic style of a baseball catcher, in line with the savior role he tells Phoebe he wishes he could play. Students should delineate Holden's most dominant preoccupations and consider the reasons for his simultaneous attraction and aversion to them. Consider whether Holden is hypocritical, delusional, or actually enlightened in his moral stances. Why does he end up missing everybody, even the pimp Maurice?

4. Similarly, consider the moral worth of the novel. Does it really have the potential to corrupt young minds, as is often the claim of those who attempt to ban it? According to Buddy Glass in "Seymour: An Introduction," Seymour looked for God "in the queerest imaginable places." How might the same be true of Holden, who has nothing but scorn for Jesus' disciples? How might Holden's outlook be considered Christian despite his disregard for religion? Can the use of profanity in the novel ever be artistically or morally justified? Students should also consider the other moral concerns posed by the novel's detractors, such as Holden's drinking, smoking, and encounter with a prostitute.

5. Salinger weaves several different motifs into *The Catcher in the Rye*, and students will benefit from analyzing their significance. Many of these relate to either stasis or movement, a dichotomy central to the novel. For example, freezing and falling are two recurring images that seem to reinforce the novel's concern with spoiled innocence. Other related symbols worthy of analysis might be stairs, elevators, and the carousel, regarding movement; and death, mummies, and the museum, regarding stasis. In addition, how might the downpouring of rain in the park in the novel's final scene be interpreted? Is it a positive or a negative symbol, and in what way might it subtly foreshadow the novel's resolution?

6. *The Catcher in the Rye* is rich with literary allusions, beginning with the reference to David Copperfield, whose name is very close to Caulfield. Might this apparent association be meaningful? Consider Holden's literary tastes as well: *The Great Gatsby* (1925), *The Return of the Native* (1878), *Out of Africa* (1937), and the stories of Ring Lardner, for example. It would benefit students to discuss the relevance of any of these novels to the concerns of *The Catcher in the Rye*. Read one of Lardner's better-known stories, such as "Champion" (1916), "Haircut" (1925), or any of his Jack Keefe stories and discuss parallels between Lardner's fiction and *The Catcher in the Rye*, both of which blend criticism with compassion. In addition, students might locate Robert Burns's eighteenth-century poem "Comin' through the Rye" and consider whether the words to the poem relate to more than just the novel's title.

RESOURCES

Primary Works

Franny and Zooey (Boston: Little, Brown, 1961).
Contains two of Salinger's many *New Yorker* stories, both of which concern the Glass family, particularly Franny, a college freshman who, like Holden, laments the phoniness she encounters at school and is also recovering from a nervous breakdown.

Nine Stories (Boston: Little, Brown, 1953).
In addition to "A Perfect Day for Bananafish," contains at least two other stories that serve as useful supplements to the novel: "Teddy" and "For Esme, with Love and Squalor," which both involve child heroes.

Raise High the Roof Beam, Carpenters; and Seymour: An Introduction (Boston: Little, Brown, 1963).
Two *New Yorker* stories that provide background regarding Seymour Glass, who has much in common with Holden Caulfield.

Bibliography

Jack R. Sublette, *J. D. Salinger: An Annotated Bibliography, 1938–1981* (New York: Garland, 1984).
Provides primary and secondary bibliographic information.

Brett E. Weaver, *An Annotated Bibliography (1982–2002) of J. D. Salinger* (Lewistown, N.Y.: Edwin Mellen Press, 2002).
Updates Sublette's secondary bibliography.

Biography

Ian Hamilton, *In Search of J. D. Salinger* (New York: Random House, 1988).
The most authoritative and objective biography available, focuses primarily on Salinger's literary life with well-researched information regarding both his collected and uncollected fiction.

Criticism

Harold Bloom, ed., *Holden Caulfield* (Philadelphia: Chelsea House, 1990).
Collects excerpts from early and recent criticism with several full-length contemporary essays.

Warren French, *J. D. Salinger*, revised edition (Boston: Twayne, 1976).
Chapter 3 provides analysis and a discussion of the novel's genesis and reception as well as its reflection of and impact on American culture.

James Lundquist, *J. D. Salinger* (New York: Ungar, 1979).
Includes chapter 2, which provides incisive analysis, viewing the book as not obscene in itself but rather as a denouncement of obscenity and a subtly crafted response to profound existential questions.

Joel Salzburg, ed., *Critical Essays on Salinger's* The Catcher in the Rye (Boston: G. K. Hall, 1990).
Collects four decades of reviews and criticism of the novel.

Jack Salzman, ed., *New Essays on* The Catcher in the Rye (Cambridge, England: Cambridge University Press, 1991).
Includes five critical essays and an introduction that assesses the preceding forty years of criticism.

John Unrue, *The Catcher in the Rye* (Detroit: Gale, 2001).
Provides analysis, historical context, critical reception, and bibliographic sources.

—John Cusatis

⟨◇⟩

John Steinbeck, *East of Eden*

*   (New York: Viking, 1952)

Born in Salinas, California, at the beginning of the twentieth century, John
Steinbeck (1902–1968) returned repeatedly—in such works as *Tortilla Flat*
(1935), *Of Mice and Men* (1937), *The Long Valley* (1938), *Cannery Row* (1945),
East of Eden (1952), and *Sweet Thursday* (1954)—to the land that spawned him
in order to explore the themes he believed in and to exorcize his demons. Often
the people of Salinas and its environs did not take kindly to Steinbeck's portrayals,
and his books were banned and burned in his hometown throughout his career.
Today the area is known as Steinbeck Country. Because he poured so much of
himself, his memories of the landscape, and his family history into it, *East of Eden*
was Steinbeck's favorite of his novels. *East of Eden* contains a history, as Steinbeck
conceived it, of his family on his mother's side. Among the characters in the novel
are not only the stalwart Sam Hamilton, based on the author's maternal grandfather, but also Steinbeck's mother, Olive, and a young John Steinbeck. The novel is
a complex tale of sin and redemption, of love and innate hatred.

"God almighty," Steinbeck wrote to Pat Covici, his agent, "this is a complicated book. I wonder whether I can do it." *East of Eden,* which Steinbeck claims
to have pared down to one-fifth its original length, tells the story of the Trask
family, especially Adam Trask and what happens to him throughout his long and
stormy life. The story centers on two brothers, Adam and his stepbrother, Charles,
and eventually Adam's twin sons, Cal and Aaron. All four encounter Cathy (later
Kate) Ames, who marries Adam and is the mother of Cal and Aaron. However,
Cathy comes to represent an evil that is satanic in that it is without motive and
cannot be explained rationally. Throughout the novel each of the men faces
Cathy's perversity, and each reacts in a different way. Cal, in particular, comes to
see Cathy's evil as part of his "inheritance," something that is innate. As if to verify
Cal's conception of himself, the twins' mother opens a brothel, and in a moment
of anger Cal reveals their mother's situation to Aaron. In a modern playing out of
the Cain and Abel story, Cal sees himself as responsible for sending Aaron off to
war and believes that he is thus responsible for his brother's death. Within the plot
lines of the novel, there are important handlings of relationships: fathers and sons,
fathers and daughters, husbands and wives, wives and mothers, mothers and sons.
There are also two wise counselors, Sam Hamilton and Lee, who are Steinbeck's
mouthpieces and provide a moral center to much of the action.

Since its publication in 1952, *East of Eden* has remained at the forefront of
American literature and culture. Although the critical reception was lukewarm,
the novel was an instant best seller. In 1955 it was made into a successful film
starring James Dean, and in 1981, a popular television miniseries. In 2003 the
novel was chosen as a selection of Oprah's Book Club, causing it to return to the

number one spot on *The New York Times* best-seller list more than fifty years after its first appearance there.

Students of the novel are advised to consult *Steinbeck: A Life in Letters*, which contains twenty-seven references to the writing of the book. Another essential resource is *Journal of a Novel: The East of Eden Letters*, Steinbeck's day-by-day account of his writing of the novel. Students should also consult Sarah Appleton Aguiar's "No Sanctuary: Reconsidering the Evil of Cathy Ames Trask," and Stephen K. George's "The Emotional Context of Cruelty: An Analysis of Kate in *East of Eden*" for solid analysis of the most "evil" character in the novel. Warren French's chapter on the novel in *John Steinbeck* provides an excellent critical overview. Jack Benson's *The True Adventures of John Steinbeck, Writer* is an authorized Steinbeck biography.

TOPICS FOR DISCUSSION AND RESEARCH

1. Steinbeck said, "Caleb is my Cain principle. I am going to put the burden of experience through his eyes and his emotions. . . . And since every man has Cain in him, he will be fully well understood." After consulting Genesis 4:1–18, students might consider how Steinbeck uses Cain's story in his novel. Students might discuss how Steinbeck expands the idea that "every man has Cain in him" and modernizes the biblical story. What is the essential mixture of good and evil that goes to make up Cal's character? Finally, in considering Cal, is his judgment of himself too harsh, or is it a just perception of his own personality?

2. Throughout the writing, Steinbeck realized that there would be "a kind of delicate balance" in the novel. Consider how Steinbeck achieves this "delicate balance" in the story of the Trask family and Lee. What kinds of comparisons and contrasts does Steinbeck use in the plot; what kind of mirror images and incidents help to achieve this balance? Is one's life, according to Steinbeck, made up of balances, and what or how should one come to grips with the balances if anyone wishes to live—as far as possible—a good and moral life?

3. Steinbeck knew that the character of Cathy would garner a great deal of attention from both readers and critics. He described her as a character without a conscience. But, as with Cal, he also said that while she is a monster, "there is a little piece of monster in all of us." Cathy presents one of the single most perplexing questions in the world's philosophic and religious traditions: Are people born basically good or basically evil? Is there, then, an evil that is innate, that is the "little piece of monster in all of us"? We live in a tradition that seeks explanations; yet, Steinbeck seems to suggest in Cathy that there are individuals who are "born evil." As a means to better understanding her, students might analyze Cathy's character using *any* religious perspective. Stephen George's and Sarah Appleton Aguiar's essays will provide useful approaches to this topic.

4. Although Cathy is usually the character that, as Steinbeck rightly predicted, "fascinates people," the character that balances her is Abra. The student may wish to focus on Cathy and Abra and analyze how they "balance" each other in the narrative. How are these women portrayed? Ironically, both are strong women, but their strengths are seen in completely different ways by Steinbeck; and although

Cathy is the obvious one, Abra admits she is not perfect in her actions and decisions. Mimi Reisel Gladstein offers an interesting perspective on Abra.

5. While one central theme is the idea of good versus evil, the other central idea
Steinbeck explores is whether or not free will exists. Do the world, one's background, one's DNA, and one's environment predetermine what one will become?
If God exists and marks every sparrow's fall, has he predetermined one's life? Is
choice just an illusion? In the case of Cain and Abel, did God predetermine that
Adam would reject Cain's offering and thus deliberately determine that the first
major event this side of the Garden would be fratricide? Adam's final word in
East of Eden is *timshel*, a word central to Steinbeck's idea concerning free will and
determinism. According to the character Lee and to Steinbeck himself, the word
means "thou mayest," implying free will. Do the events in Adam Trask's life and
the lives of his two sons demonstrate that free will exists; are these characters
"free" or are they predetermined to act as they do? Read chapter 7 in Peter Lisca's
John Steinbeck: Nature and Myth (1978) to prepare for a discussion of this topic.

RESOURCES

Primary Works

Conversations with John Steinbeck, edited by Thomas French (Jackson: University
   of Mississippi Press, 1988).
Contains thirteen selections with several references to *East of Eden.*

Journal of a Novel: The East of Eden Letters (New York: Penguin, 1990).
Provides essential background information on the novel. Several of the letters
reveal how Steinbeck conceived the characters in the novel, and the letters also
reveal his thinking as he was composing the novel.

Steinbeck: A Life in Letters, edited by Elaine Steinbeck and Robert Wallsten (New
   York: Penguin, 1989).
Another excellent source, especially for Steinbeck's thoughts about the novel as it
developed and his reaction to its critical reception.

Bibliography

Michael J. Meyer, *The John Steinbeck Bibliography, 1996–2006* (Lanham, Md.:
   Scarecrow Press, 2008).
Contains 116 entries for *East of Eden.*

Biography

Jackson Benson, *The True Adventures of John Steinbeck, Writer* (New York: Viking,
   1984).
The authorized biography, a thorough study of Steinbeck's life and work.

Jay Parini, *John Steinbeck: A Biography* (New York: Holt, 1995).
A well-researched biography.

Criticism

Sarah Appleton Aguiar, "'No Sanctuary': Reconsidering the Evil of Cathy Ames Trask," in *The Moral Philosophy of John Steinbeck*, edited by Stephen K. George (Lanham, Md.: Scarecrow Press, 2005), pp. 13–144.
Argues that Cathy is a "pre-lapsarian creation" of Steinbeck's who ironically finds no place—no sanctuary—to protect herself from the "post-lapsarian" world.

Robert Demott, "'Working at the Impossible': The Presence of *Moby-Dick* in *East of Eden*," in *Bloom's Modern Critical Views: John Steinbeck*, edited by Harold Bloom (New York: Infobase, 2008), pp. 77–104.
Claims that *East of Eden* and *Moby-Dick* both try to grasp "the mass American experience." Demott sees both novels as flawed masterpieces.

Warren French, *John Steinbeck*, second edition (New York: Twayne, 1975).
A solid analysis of *East of Eden* in chapter 10.

Stephen K. George, "The Emotional Context of Cruelty: An Analysis of Kate in *East of Eden*," in *The Moral Philosophy of John Steinbeck*, edited by George (Lanham, Md.: Scarecrow Press, 2005), pp. 131–144.
Sees Cathy as a glimpse "into the origin of cruelty itself."

Mimi Reisel Gladstein, "Abra: The Indestructible Woman in *East of Eden*," in *Modern Critical Views: John Steinbeck*, edited by Harold Bloom (New York: Chelsea House, 1987), pp. 151–153.
Sees Abra as one of the major positive influences in the novel.

Barbara A. Heavlin, "'There Is One Story': Good and Evil in Steinbeck's *East of Eden* and Morrison's *Sula*," in *John Steinbeck and His Contemporaries*, edited by George and Barbara Heavlin (Lanham, Md.: Scarecrow Press, 2007), pp. 183–190).
Argues that both authors explore the existence of good and evil.

Howard Levant, *The Novels of John Steinbeck: A Critical Study* (Columbia: University of Missouri Press, 1974).
Includes chapter 9, which deals with *East of Eden*. Levant sees the novel as a flawed masterpiece, especially worthwhile for its many "moments" of brilliance and its insight into the human condition.

Peter Lisca, *John Steinbeck: Nature and Myth* (New York: Cromwell, 1978).
Deals with *East of Eden* in chapter 7. Lisca explores the Cain myth and other archetypes found in the novel.

Joseph R. McElrath, Jesse S. Crisler, and Susan Shillinglaw, eds., *John Steinbeck: The Contemporary Reviews* (Cambridge, England: Cambridge University Press, 1996), pp. 383–403.
Presents eighteen contemporary reviews of *East of Eden*.

Louis Owens, *John Steinbeck's Re-Vision of America* (Athens: University of Georgia Press, 1985).
Argues that Steinbeck "proposes the ideal of man's commitment to man and place."

Richard F. Peterson, "Steinbeck's *East of Eden* (1952)," in *A Study Guide to Steinbeck (Part II)*, edited by Tetsumaro Hayashi (Metuchen, N.J.: Scarecrow Press, 1979), pp. 63–86.
Presents background, plot summary, an explication, and a defense of the novel.

John H. Timmerman, *John Steinbeck's Fiction: The Aesthetics of the Road Taken* (Norman: University of Oklahoma Press, 1986).
Includes chapter 8, which provides analysis of *East of Eden*. Timmerman sees Cathy Ames as the "central character" in the novel.

—*Bob Bell*

William Styron, *The Confessions of Nat Turner*

(New York: Random House, 1967)

Born in Newport News, Virginia, William Styron (1925–2006) was a product of the Jim Crow South. He grew up in a segregated community and attended segregated schools, but he began to question Southern racism at an early age. Styron's parents influenced this attitude: his father was a liberal who loved the South's distinctive culture but despised its racism; his mother was a native Pennsylvanian who never became comfortable with the South.

At fourteen Styron was traveling with his high-school football team through Southampton County, Virginia, and saw a historical marker commemorating Nat Turner's 1831 slave rebellion. Styron was interested in American history and thought it was strange that he had never learned anything about the rebellion, even though it had happened so close to his home. He began to think about a way to give voice to the event. His awareness of the rebellion came just three months after the death of his mother from cancer. His mother's illness and death made Styron acutely sensitive to human suffering, a theme he traces in his treatment of slavery.

Styron joined the Marine Corps Reserve after the Japanese attack on Pearl Harbor in 1941. He entered Davidson College in North Carolina in 1942 but was called to active duty in 1943. The marines sent him to Duke University in Durham, North Carolina, for a special officers' training course. He saw no action during World War II. He was discharged in 1947 and returned to Duke, where his interest in literature blossomed.

After his graduation in 1947, Styron moved to New York City. Several aspects of this move affected his literary career. First, he chose to live in the North for the rest of his life, providing the distance he needed to examine his Southern roots. Second, in New York he met the mysterious Polish émigré who inspired his masterpiece, *Sophie's Choice* (1979). Third, his move to the city was largely financed by a legacy from his great-grandmother, who had sold a slave and had hidden the money away; thus, Styron came to feel that he had a personal connection to slavery, a feeling that influenced his lifelong obsession with the topic.

In *Sophie's Choice*, which includes many autobiographical reflections, Styron notes that he made an early decision to write a major novel about slavery. He did not, however, feel ready to deal with this subject at the beginning of his career. Instead, he wrote a novel, *Lie Down in Darkness* (1951), which earned him comparisons to James Joyce and William Faulkner. After two more novels, *The Long March* (1953) and *Set This House on Fire* (1960), Styron began preparing himself to write about Nat Turner. A careful writer and meticulous researcher, Styron worked on his Turner novel through much of the 1960s, a tumultuous period in American race relations.

Students who wish to understand Styron's intentions in writing about Turner would be well advised to read "This Quiet Dust," an essay Styron published in *Harper's* magazine in 1965 as he conducted his research for the novel. On his return to Southampton County, Styron was astonished to learn that Turner was either completely forgotten or absurdly mythologized as "a black Paul Bunyan who had perpetrated mysterious and nameless deeds in millennia past." In the midst of the growing Civil Rights movement Styron sought to bring this historical figure back to light.

TOPICS FOR DISCUSSION AND RESEARCH

1. *The Confessions of Nat Turner* is one of the most daring studies of slavery in American literature. It is also a novel about injustice, loneliness, religious faith, and an individual's desire for a fulfilling life in spite of social structures that work against him. Nat was born into a world that expected a young black person not to raise questions about slavery; many facets of Nat's status, however, made him see the cruelties of slavery in a peculiar light. As a boy Nat is taught to read by his owner, Samuel Turner, but only so that Turner can win a bet against those who believe blacks incapable of such an achievement. Nat's ability to read increases his misery by making him realize what his life could be like if he were not a slave. Students might consider how Nat's special status affects his psychological development. How does his closeness to the Turner family give him special insight into the white world?

2. Nat's sense of justice is evident in his interviews with Thomas Gray, the Virginia lawyer who comes to his jail cell to record his confession. Symbolically, Gray resembles the biblical Pharisees, strict preservers of a law that denies people justice. This symbolism is reinforced by the presence of Jeremiah Cobb, a corrupt and dying judge who is one of the signatories of Nat's confession. These characters make it clear that the laws of the Old South are in the hands of men who defend the status quo rather than seeking justice for all. How might Nat be considered a Christ figure who sacrifices himself to correct the injustices of his world? Judith Ruderman's book includes a helpful discussion of parallels between Nat and Christ.

3. In writing *The Confessions of Nat Turner* Styron made several key choices that ultimately helped make the novel controversial: he used a first-person point of view, a decision that was heavily influenced by his close friend, the writer James Baldwin; he emphasized Nat's attraction to the Bible and conviction of

having been called by God, like an Old Testament prophet; and he had Nat fantasize about love and sexual union with a young white woman, Margaret Whitehead. Each of these decisions became a source of anger for the critics who attacked the book in the 1968 volume *William Styron's Nat Turner: Ten Black Writers Respond.* The contributors, reacting in part to the assassination that year of Dr. Martin Luther King Jr., attacked Styron and his novel as racist, though Styron had received exceptional praise, as well as the Pulitzer Prize, for the novel in 1968. Several critics have responded to the complaints of the ten black critics by examining the way Styron uses history in his novel. Dawn Trouard's essay is a good example, as are two pieces in Daniel W. Ross's *The Critical Response to William Styron* (1995): Floyd C. Watkins's "The Confessions of Nat Turner: History and Imagination" and James M. Mellard's "This Unquiet Dust: The Problem of History in Styron's *The Confessions of Nat Turner.*" Mellard, for example, states that black readers are not wrong to object to aspects of the novel, but he adds that Styron uses racial stereotypes to reflect white attitudes of the time and does not endorse them. The historian Eugene D. Genovese comments on Styron's use of history in his contribution to Arthur D. Casciato and James L. W. West III's *Critical Essays on William Styron* (1982). The student might want to read the criticisms in *William Styron's Nat Turner: Ten Black Writers Respond* and some of these other essays and decide which side makes the better case.

4. Nat's ability to read isolates him from the other slaves and even makes him an object of their contempt. Many of the slaves think that Nat regards himself as too good for them; yet, he has no place in the world of white Southerners, either. Early in the novel Nat himself believes in his superiority, especially after his owner, Samuel Turner, promises him emancipation—only to rescind that offer and sell Nat to a cruel owner after the Virginia economy goes bad. Nat's extraordinary status among slaves gives him a double burden: he endures severe disappointment over his master's broken promise, while being caught in a curious social gap that leaves him feeling that he belongs to no social group at all. Students might wish to explore other ways in which Nat is isolated from his fellow slaves. For example, how does his relatively easy life as a "house slave" create resentment among those who labor in the fields?

5. Nat's loneliness and ability to read influence his sense of himself as a biblical prophet. He compares himself sometimes to Moses, enslaved by the Egyptians; sometimes to Ezekiel, the visionary of exile; and sometimes to the woodland Essene John the Baptist. Nat comes to regard his rebellion not just as a protest against injustice but as divine retribution. Through his many visions, which often come to him while he spends time in the woods, Nat comes to believe that he is an instrument of God's justice. Students might ask whether Nat's visions cause him to lose contact with reality or put him in touch with a higher reality that others cannot see.

6. For all of Nat's sense of a calling, he proves to be intensely human. He longs for the same things most people want: a chance to use his talents, to be free, and to love. John Kenny Crane discusses this idea, focusing on the importance of "human dignity" in the novel. Nat's authority in the midst of the rebellion

is questioned when his fellow insurrectionists discover that he has no stomach for the murder and rape they seek in revenge for their mistreatment. Nat's rejection of violence is one way Styron makes him an exceptional hero: though he has every reason to desire revenge, Nat longs instead for human connection. Is Nat's desire for union with Margaret Whitehead racist, or does it symbolize his desire to love and be loved? In what ways is Nat's love of Margaret a symbol of reconciliation in the midst of conflict?

RESOURCES

Primary Works
Sophie's Choice (New York: Random House, 1979).
Styron's most important novel, which includes many reflections by the autobiographical narrator on his fascination with Nat Turner.

This Quiet Dust and Other Essays (New York: Random House, 1982).
Includes many of Styron's occasional pieces. The title work is important for understanding his intentions in *The Confessions of Nat Turner.*

Bibliography
Philip W. Leon, *William Styron: An Annotated Bibliography of Criticism* (Westport, Conn.: Greenwood Press, 1978).
Though needing to be updated, an important source for finding early criticism of Styron's work.

The Society for the Study of Southern Literature Bibliography <http://www.missq.msstate.edu/sssl/view.php?wid=159> [accessed 28 July 2009].
Includes 180 entries on Styron—more than 60 of them on *The Confessions of Nat Turner.*

Biography
Biblio.com <http://www.biblio.com/author_biographies/2161815/William_Styron.html> [accessed 28 July 2009].
Includes a brief biographical sketch of Styron.

James L. W. West III, ed., *Conversations with William Styron* (Jackson: University of Mississippi Press, 1985).
Valuable interviews with Styron over a period of thirty years.

West, *William Styron: A Life* (New York: Random House, 1998).
The only book-length biography, and a superb one, written with Styron's cooperation.

Criticism
Arthur D. Casciato and James L. W. West III, eds., *Critical Essays on William Styron* (Boston: G. K. Hall, 1982).

Includes many essays on *The Confessions of Nat Turner*, representing a wide range of critical opinion.

John Henrik Clarke, ed., *William Styron's Nat Turner: Ten Black Writers Respond* (Boston: Beacon, 1968).
Unfriendly criticisms of the novel by Clarke, Lerone Bennett Jr., Alvin F. Poussaint, Vincent Harding, John Oliver Killens, John A. Williams, Ernest Kaiser, Loyle Hairston, Charles V. Hamilton, and Mike Thelwell.

Samuel Coale, *William Styron Revisited* (Boston: Twayne, 1991).
Reconsiders Styron's work after all of the major novels had been published.

John Kenny Crane, *The Root of All Evil: The Thematic Unity of Styron's Fiction* (Columbia: University of South Carolina Press, 1984).
Finds evil to be a central theme in Styron's work.

Mary Kemp Davis, "William Styron's Nat Turner as an Archetypal Hero," *Southern Literary Journal*, 28 (Fall 1995): 67–84.
Reads the novel in light of the theory of archetypes, concluding that Nat is a black Everyman searching for his own identity.

Daniel W. Ross, "'Things I Don't Want to Find Out About': The Primal Scene in *The Confessions of Nat Turner*," *Twentieth-Century Literature*, 39 (Spring 1993): 79–98.
Reads the novel in the context of Sigmund Freud's theory of the primal scene fantasy, emphasizing the trauma the young Nat endures when he sees his mother raped by a white man.

Ross, ed., *The Critical Response to William Styron* (Westport, Conn.: Greenwood Press, 1995).
Contains a broad variety of essays on all of Styron's major works.

Judith Ruderman, *William Styron* (New York: Ungar, 1987).
A good introduction to Styron's work.

Anthony Stewart, "William TurnerGrayStyron, Novelist(s): Reactivating State Power in *The Confessions of Nat Turner*," *Studies in the Novel*, 27 (Summer 1995): 169–185.
Emphasizes the way the novel contains the multiple perspectives of three figures, Nat Turner, Thomas Gray, and the author, Styron.

Dawn Trouard, "Styron's Historical Pre-Text: Nat Turner, Sophie, and the Beginnings of a Postmodern Career," *Papers on Language and Literature*, 23 (1987): 489–497.
Discusses the ways in which Styron's two most important novels use language in a Postmodernist way.

—Daniel W. Ross

John Updike, *Rabbit, Run*

(New York: Knopf, 1960)

Rabbit, Run was the second novel written by the prolific American author John Updike (1932–2009) and the first of four novels he eventually wrote about Harry "Rabbit" Angstrom, a charismatic but self-absorbed high-school basketball star from Pennsylvania who became, over the course of four decades and as many novels, John Updike's "ticket to the America all around" him.

Like Rabbit, Updike was born in 1932 in Reading, Pennsylvania (Brewer in the novel), and grew up in the small suburb of Shillington (the novel's Mt. Judge). His father, Wesley Russell Updike, taught math and science at the local public high school, while his mother, Linda Grace Hoyer, nurtured unfulfilled novelistic ambitions of her own. When Updike was twelve, the family moved to a farm located some dozen miles outside of Shillington, though he and his father continued to commute into Shillington daily for school. After graduating co-valedictorian and class president in 1950, Updike went on to Harvard University on a merit scholarship, where he flourished as a tireless contributor to the university humor magazine, *The Harvard Lampoon*. In 1954, following his graduation, he spent a year in England on a Knox Fellowship studying painting at The Ruskin School of Drawing and Fine Art at Oxford. While there, his first child, a daughter, was born, and he received his first poetry acceptance at *The New Yorker*, where he began working as a "Talk of the Town" reporter immediately following his return to the United States. After two years in New York, during which time he published a steady stream of poems, stories, and reviews in the magazine, Updike moved his growing family to Ipswich, Massachusetts, where he set up shop as a freelance writer.

Rabbit, Run, the first full-length novel Updike completed in his new home, was originally conceived as both a novella and one-half of a pair of works, the other being *The Centaur*, published three years later. Once he started the actual writing, however, the novel, according to Updike, unexpectedly "took off." At one point, Updike toyed with the idea of subtitling the book "A Movie," as a way to account for its most striking innovation, the sustained use of the present tense. The immediacy of this mode conveys Rabbit's abiding sense of *angst*, or sourceless sense of anxiety, an emotion signaled by his last name, Angstrom. Updike drew his understanding of the concept of *angst* from the Danish writer Søren Kierkegaard (1813–1855), whose ideas saturate the novel.

In the opening scene Rabbit stops while walking home from his pointless job to join a pickup game of basketball. The first touch of the basketball "makes his body go taut, gives his arms wings," such that, when he arrives home to discover his pregnant wife Janice already drunk and argumentative, he senses his current life of middle-class drudgery to be a trap and a betrayal of his best self, last accessed on the high-school basketball court. Abruptly, he leaves his wife, child, and unborn infant and drives all night, first toward the south, then back home. He soon moves in with a cynical but large-hearted prostitute named Ruth Leonard. A young minister named Eccles eventually tracks Rabbit down and begins urging him to return to Janice, but then Eccles quickly falls under Rabbit's spell. Following the birth of their second child, June, Rabbit does finally return to Janice, but tragedy follows this reunion, leaving Rabbit, in the end, still wrestling with the unresolved conflict between his desire for sexual and spiritual freedom and the threat that freedom poses to the stability of his domestic attachments.

Rabbit is a compelling, if also deeply troubling, hero, a selfish, sexually reckless adventurer who nevertheless operates under a stern conviction that "somewhere behind all this . . . there's something that wants [him] to find it." As such, *Rabbit, Run* is a story of spiritual striving, as Rabbit tries to find a balance between his duties as a husband and father and the desire to heed his inner call. Although high-school educated and firmly unintellectual, Rabbit nevertheless views the world with a lyrical sense of wonder, providing Updike with a perfect vehicle through which to exercise his own unparalleled powers of description. Students fascinated by Rabbit's character should explore the three follow-up Rabbit novels, *Rabbit Redux* (1971), *Rabbit Is Rich* (1981), and *Rabbit at Rest* (1990). Like *Rabbit, Run* each novel in the series is set in the present tense, in the final year of the decade immediately preceding its publication, while the cast of characters remains consistent throughout. Taken together, the four novels are a massive "mega-novel" covering four decades of American history as experienced by Updike's incorrigible, selfish, yet somehow lovable Everyman.

Both *Rabbit, Run* specifically, and the Rabbit novels in general, have received substantial attention from literary critics. Students interested in tracing the novel's spiritual themes should begin with George W. Hunt's chapter on *Rabbit, Run* in his *John Updike and the Three Great Secret Things: Sex, Religion and Art* (1980). David Galloway's section on the novel in his *The Absurd Hero in American Fiction: Updike, Styron, Bellow, Salinger* (1981) does a fine job of situating Rabbit within the context of the 1950s existentialism.

TOPICS FOR DISCUSSION AND RESEARCH

1. Owing to its overt indebtedness to the work of Søren Kierkegaard, *Rabbit, Run* can be read as a Christian existentialist novel, with Rabbit operating as a morally confused but intellectually compelling knight of faith. Students interested in this aspect of the novel should first consult *Frygt og Bæven* (1843; translated as *Fear and Trembling,* 1939) in which Kierkegaard meditates on the Old Testament story of Abraham and Isaac. In agreeing to sacrifice his own son, Abraham commits himself to a course of action that runs counter to every known system of ethical behavior; yet, Kierkegaard argues, in doing so he is following God's command. As such, Kierkegaard concludes that the subjective demands of faith trump the public obligations of ethical action. Rabbit's decision to leave Janice at the behest of his inner call serves as an illustration of Kierkegaard's argument. Yet, Updike does not simply resolve the story in favor of Rabbit's private search for personal salvation. As Updike once remarked, "There's a yes-but quality about my writing that evades entirely pleasing anybody." In the case of *Rabbit, Run,* he explained in a separate interview, the novel says "Yes . . . to our inner urgent whispers, but—the social fabric collapses murderously." In this regard, the novel also invokes Kierkegaard's *Enten-Eller* (1843; translated as *Either/Or,* 1944) where he outlines his concept of aesthetic versus ethical existence, with the "aesthetic" encompassing a life

of novel sensation and earthly pleasure (including sex), and the "ethical" referring to a life devoted to duty and domesticity. Rabbit moves between the two realms in a nervous zigzag; yet, students might also explore which realm best suits each of the other main characters, including Eccles, Ruth, and Janice.

2. According to his autobiography, *Self-Consciousness* (1989), Updike composed *Rabbit, Run* in the wake of a spiritual crisis that led him to the work of the German theologian Karl Barth (1886–1968). For a concise overview of Barth's thinking, consult *Das Wort Gottes und die Theologie* (1924; translated as *The Word of God and the Word of Man*, 1928), a text that Updike himself has often cited as formative. Though Barth's influence on the novel is not as significant as Kierkegaard's, students should investigate the key strains of Barthian thought in the numerous spiritual discussions Rabbit has with Eccles. Updike has also admitted that a minor character, Reverend Kruppenbach, represents "Barth in action."

3. Because of the density of its religious themes, as well as its connection to existentialist thought, the novel can be profitably read alongside several other key novels from the period that draw on similar philosophical source texts. Walker Percy's *The Moviegoer*, which appeared a year after *Rabbit, Run*, is especially pertinent, not only for its use of the present tense but also because of its own deep engagement with Kiergegaardian concepts such as despair, anxiety, and the tension between the aesthetic and the ethical. Saul Bellow's *Seize the Day* (1956) also explores such subjects as despair, spiritual renewal, and moral obligation, all within the context of European existentialism. As evidenced by the tone and voice of his much-anthologized short story, "A&P" (first published in *The New Yorker* in July 1961), Updike's early style invites comparisons with J. D. Salinger's *The Catcher in the Rye* (1951), a book that might also provide a fascinating companion piece to *Rabbit, Run*, as both books are spiritual-quest novels couched in an urbane critique of 1950s conformism and inauthenticity. Students might wish to compare Holden Caufield's adolescent critique of 1950s "phoniness" with Rabbit's more elusive resistance to middle-class bourgeois conformity.

4. For all its classic status, *Rabbit, Run* is very much a novel of its era. Students interested in this aspect of the novel might wish to explore Rabbit's rejection of his domestic obligations as a critique of the conservative Eisenhower era in general, and of bourgeois morals in particular. As Rabbit's mother says of Janice, "That girl gets no sympathy from me. She has everybody on her side from Eisenhower down." Updike has also cited Jack Kerouac's *On the Road* (1957) as exerting a negative influence. "I resented its apparent instruction to cut loose," he explains in the introduction to *Rabbit Angstrom* (1995), the single-volume edition of the Rabbit tetralogy. "*Rabbit, Run* was meant to be a realistic demonstration of what happens when a young American family man goes on the road—the people left behind get hurt. There was no painless dropping out of the Fifties' fraying but still tight social weave." At the same time, Rabbit does emerge as a prophetic figure in many ways, presaging the "turn on, tune in, drop out" ethos of the subsequent decade, a fact Updike cagily acknowledges in *Rabbit Redux* when he depicts Rabbit, in 1969, as a stodgy, stay-at-home conservative who nevertheless observes, "Everybody now is like the way I used to be." Students interested in exploring

Rabbit as a proto-Beatnik should also consider how Updike's plotting, as well as his overarching spiritual perspective, both supports and critiques the Beatnik ethos a decade later.

RESOURCES

Primary Works

Conversations with John Updike, edited by James Plath (Jackson: University Press of Mississippi, 1994).
Includes more than thirty full-length interviews with Updike spread over the course of his career.

The Early Stories: 1953–1975 (New York: Knopf, 2003).
Comprises all of Updike's stories up to 1975, organized into a series of story-cycle clusters and arranged in chronological order according the age of the protagonists. The volume includes Updike's early story, "Ace in the Hole," a brief "test run" for *Rabbit, Run.*

Rabbit Angstrom (New York: Knopf, 1995).
Includes all four Rabbit novels—*Rabbit, Run; Rabbit Redux; Rabbit is Rich;* and *Rabbit at Rest*—as well as an informative introduction by Updike.

Updike, "Rabbit Remembered," in his *Licks of Love* (New York: Knopf, 2000), pp. 177–359.
A novella-length sequel to the Rabbit tetralogy that ties up all the various loose ends left hanging at the end of *Rabbit at Rest* (New York: Knopf, 1990).

Updike, *Self-Consciousness* (New York: Knopf, 1989).
Updike's absorbing collection of autobiographical essays.

Bibliography

The John Updike Society <http://blogs.iwu.edu/johnupdikesociety/> [accessed 24 November 2009].
The official website of the John Updike Society which includes all the latest news on Updike scholarship, a complete bibliography and chronology, and up-to-date list of primary, secondary, and critical sources.

Jack De Bellis and Michael Broomfield, *John Updike: A Bibliography of Primary and Secondary Materials, 1948–2007* (New Castle, Del.: Oak Knoll Press, 2007).
The most complete and thorough Updike bibliography available, with more than six hundred pages. The book includes a CD-ROM listing works about Updike, additional appendixes, and an exhaustive gallery of color book-jacket images from throughout Updike's fifty-year publishing career.

Biography

William H. Pritchard, *Updike: America's Man of Letters* (South Royalton, Vt.: Steerforth Press, 2000).
A comprehensive but also concise examination of Updike's entire career.

Criticism

Peter J. Bailey, *Rabbit (Un) Redeemed: The Drama of Belief in John Updike's Fiction* (Madison, N.J.: Fairleigh Dickinson University Press, 2006).
Traces the evolving nature of Updike's treatment of religion in his work, with special attention to the four Rabbit novels.

Marshall Boswell, *John Updike's Rabbit Tetralogy: Mastered Irony in Motion* (Columbia: University of Missouri Press, 2001).
A book-length examination of the entire Rabbit saga, with individual chapters devoted to each book in the series.

Lawrence R. Broer, ed., *Rabbit Tales: Poetry and Politics in John Updike's Rabbit Novels* (Tuscaloosa: University of Alabama Press, 1998).
A collection of essays touching on the political ramifications of the Rabbit novels.

David Galloway, *The Absurd Hero in American Fiction: Updike, Styron, Bellow, Salinger* (Austin: University of Texas Press, 1981).
Includes a reading of *Rabbit, Run* within the context of other key texts from midcentury, all of which engage the existentialist concept of the absurd.

George W. Hunt, *John Updike and the Three Great Secret Things: Sex, Religion, and Art* (Grand Rapids, Mich.: Eerdmans, 1980).
One of the earliest and most successful attempts to tease out the Kierkegaardian and Barthian influences in Updike's early work.

Stacey Olster, ed., *The Cambridge Companion to John Updike* (Cambridge, England: Cambridge University Press, 2006).
The most current collection of Updike essays, including Donald Greiner's "Updike, Rabbit, and the Myth of American Exceptionalism," which reads Rabbit as Updike's emblem for the American experience writ large.

—*Marshall Boswell*

⟡

Kurt Vonnegut, *Slaughterhouse-Five*
(New York: Delacorte, 1969)

The funny, irreverent, and wildly inventive fiction of Kurt Vonnegut (1922–2007) has resonated with Americans, especially college students and disaffected young people, for more than fifty years. Best known for a trio of novels published in the 1960s and early 1970s—*Cat's Cradle* (1963), *Slaughterhouse-Five* (1969), and *Breakfast of Champions* (1973)—Vonnegut is the author of eleven additional novels and nearly fifty short stories, as well as many essays, plays, and autobiographical pieces. While his style tends to be simple and accessible—he uses a conversational tone, short chapters, and, at times, almost childlike descriptions—his subject matter is often quite serious. Underneath his jokes, his humorous drawings, and his descriptions of flying saucers and time travel, Vonnegut was a social critic who wrote about the suffering and atrocities human beings experienced in the twentieth century, from the effects of war and atomic weaponry to racism, social injustice, and environmental destruction. Although Vonnegut did not publish *Slaughterhouse-Five* until the height of American involvement in the Vietnam War, the novel draws on his own experiences as a prisoner of war in Dresden, Germany, at the end of World War II and remains one of the best-loved antiwar novels of the twentieth century.

Vonnegut was born in Indianapolis, where his father and grandfather were well-known architects. After graduating from Shortridge High School in 1940, he attended Cornell University for two years as a biochemistry major. He moved on to the Carnegie Institute of Technology but dropped out to enlist in the army early in 1943. (He studied anthropology at the University of Chicago after the war and earned an M.A. there in 1971.) During a visit home that Vonnegut made in May 1944, his mother committed suicide by taking an overdose of sleeping pills; her death profoundly affected the young soldier. Shipped overseas in late summer of 1944, Vonnegut's unit saw action during the Battle of the Bulge, the last major German offensive of the war. Vonnegut, who was serving as a battalion scout, was captured by the Germans and sent in a cramped boxcar with dozens of other American prisoners of war to Dresden, where he was put to work in a factory that made vitamin syrup for pregnant women. The prisoners were housed in a former slaughterhouse deep underground; the location enabled them to survive the Allied firebombing on the night of 13 February 1945 that devastated the beautiful city and killed 130,000 of its inhabitants.

The protagonist of *Slaughterhouse-Five* is Billy Pilgrim, a passive, awkward chaplain's assistant who is captured during the Battle of the Bulge and survives the bombing of Dresden as a prisoner of war. Billy's life story is not told in chronological order: he has become "unstuck in time" and shifts frequently and unexpectedly back and forth among the past, the present, and the future—his childhood; his wartime experiences; his marriage and career as an optometrist in Ilium, New York; and his kidnapping by aliens from the planet Tralfamadore, who mate him with the former pornographic film star Montana Wildhack. Often deeply funny and even cartoonlike, the work is, at the same time, a serious antiwar novel that deglamorizes violence and pleads for human beings to behave kindly in a cruel and heartless world.

While Vonnegut had been something of a cult favorite on college campuses after the publication of *Cat's Cradle*, critics thought of him mostly as a science-fiction writer and tended to dismiss his work. But *Slaughterhouse-Five* cemented his reputation as a literary artist. Christopher Lehmann-Haupt of *The New York Times* set the tone for critical reaction to the book in a 31 March 1969 review that concluded, "It sounds crazy. It sounds like a fantastic last-ditch effort to make sense of a lunatic universe. But there is so much more to this book. It is very tough and very funny; it is sad and delightful; and it works."

Students wishing to learn more about Vonnegut's work might begin by reading some of his other novels and his essays that touch on themes addressed in *Slaughterhouse-Five*. *Cat's Cradle*, about two adventurers who set themselves up as a religious prophet and a dictator in a poverty-stricken Caribbean island, captured the imagination of young people in the 1960s with its short, whimsical chapters, its invented religious rituals, and its scathing social critique of postwar America. The novel serves as a good introduction to Vonnegut's complicated views on religion and science, as well as his particular style of black humor. *Breakfast of Champions*, like *Slaughterhouse-Five*, examines the line separating art and reality. But it pushes the metafictionality of the earlier novel even further as it depicts Vonnegut as a character in his own book, who, at the end of the novel, introduces himself to science-fiction writer Kilgore Trout, one of his fictional creations. Vonnegut has also published several essay collections in which he discusses his views on topics such as science fiction, art, and Christianity, including *Wampeters, Foma, and Granfalloons (Opinions)* (1974) and *Palm Sunday: An Autobiographical Collage* (1981). Vonnegut has given many interviews about his work, the best of which are collected in William Rodney Allen's *Conversations with Kurt Vonnegut* (1988).

TOPICS FOR DISCUSSION AND RESEARCH

1. Perhaps the most heated critical debate concerning *Slaughterhouse-Five* is the issue of determinism versus free will. The Tralfamadorians do not believe in free will: in their view all moments in time exist at once; therefore, the future is predetermined, and no one can change it. The Tralfamadorians do not even try to stop one of their test pilots from blowing up the universe by pressing the wrong button on his control panel, because they argue that the moment is structured always to happen that way. While Billy eventually comes to accept the Tralfamadorian philosophy, students might want to consider whether Vonnegut is advocating such passive resignation to circumstances or whether the novel satirically undercuts this philosophy.

2. Related to the determinism/free will theme is the issue of how seriously readers are expected to take Billy's alien adventures. While some critics argue that we are to believe that he is really kidnapped by Tralfamadorians, most read Billy's Tralfamadorian experiences as a fantasy he concocts, whether consciously or not, from the Kilgore Trout novels he reads in Eliot Rosewater's library. The Tralfamadorian philosophy, with its belief that death is just another moment in time and therefore not a terrible thing, may be comforting to Billy, who has been damaged by seeing so much death and destruction during the war. What else might Billy Pilgrim find appealing about his life on Tralfamadore? What does Vonnegut gain by including these science-fiction elements in his war novel?

3. Time is another key theme in the novel. One reason that the Tralfamadorian belief that all moments in time occur simultaneously may appeal to Billy is that time, as humans experience it on Earth, is frightening: it involves an inexorable march toward destruction. In one of the key scenes in the novel Billy watches an old war movie both forward and backward. In the backward version of the film German fighter planes suck bullets and shells out of American airplanes and crews. The American bombers then fly over a German city, suck up fires on the ground, gather them into steel containers, and draw them into the bellies of the planes. When the planes return to the United States, factories work day and night to dismantle the bombs, separate the contents into minerals, and replant them in the Earth. The movie makes more sense to Billy in reverse than in forward motion. Students might explore how this scene is related to Billy's coming "unstuck in time." How else does the novel play with and upset normal conceptions of time?

4. Vonnegut's novel shows that history is shaped by the people who tell it: Professor Bertram Copeland Rumfoord's version of the Dresden bombing, for instance, is quite different from Billy Pilgrim's. The novel also asks whether human beings can learn from the past. In the first chapter Vonnegut relates the biblical story of Lot's wife, who was turned by God into a pillar of salt for looking back at the destruction of Sodom and Gomorrah. He claims that his own book is a failure because it was written by a pillar of salt: like Lot's wife, Vonnegut looks back at great destruction. While he claims that there is "nothing to say about a massacre," and while the Tralfamadorians recommend to Billy Pilgrim that he simply close his eyes and ignore the awful times in his life, Vonnegut says that he loves Lot's wife for looking back, "because it was so human." Does Vonnegut seem to believe that looking back at history is futile or that it is a human, compassionate, and necessary thing to do? Does he believe that we can we learn anything from history or not?

5. The novel focuses on storytelling itself as a main theme; the entire first chapter relates Vonnegut's difficulties in writing the book. Readers see that merely reporting about his Dresden experiences, as Vonnegut first believes he can do, will not work. The reporters he depicts at the Chicago City News Bureau are jaded and cynical, immune to tragedy and uncompassionate to survivors. On the other hand, Mary O'Hare, the wife of Vonnegut's old war buddy, warns him away from writing the type of glamorized account of war that could be made into a movie starring John Wayne or Frank Sinatra: such writing would only encourage children to go to war. Thus, Vonnegut has to find an entirely new form and structure for his book. While conventional war stories may provide roles for heroes, *Slaughterhouse-Five* presents a war fought by children and incompetents, a war in which the Allies as well as the Nazis commit appalling atrocities. Students might want to consider other ways that Vonnegut undermines traditional literary conventions in both the form and content of the novel. How is *Slaughterhouse-Five* a new kind of war novel?

RESOURCES

Primary Works

William Rodney Allen, ed., *Conversations with Kurt Vonnegut* (Jackson: University of Mississippi Press, 1988).
Interviews with the author, arranged in chronological order. Vonnegut's most critically acclaimed novels and short fiction are discussed.

Breakfast of Champions; or, Goodbye Blue Monday! (New York: Seymour Lawrence/Delacorte, 1973).
Novel that follows the separate adventures of Pontiac dealer Dwayne Hoover and science-fiction writer Kilgore Trout, who eventually meet at an arts convention in Midland City, Ohio.

Cat's Cradle (New York: Holt, Rinehart & Winston, 1963).
Novel in which, as the doomsday device ice-nine threatens to destroy the world, the residents of the island nation of San Lorenzo practice Bokononism, a religion that offers harmless untruths intended to make humans braver, happier, and kinder than they really are.

Wampeters, Foma, and Granfalloons (Opinions) (New York: Seymour Lawrence/Delacorte, 1974).
Speeches, essays, and reviews from the late 1960s and early 1970s.

Palm Sunday: An Autobiographical Collage (New York: Seymour Lawrence/Delacorte, 1981).
Speeches and essays, as well as autobiographical pieces from the 1970s.

Criticism

William Rodney Allen, *Understanding Kurt Vonnegut* (Columbia: University of South Carolina Press, 1991).
Explores Vonnegut's early science fiction, his major 1960s novels, the critical backlash against him in the 1970s, and his turn to social and political Realism in the 1980s. The book includes a biographical sketch.

Kevin A. Boon, ed., *At Millennium's End: New Essays on the Work of Kurt Vonnegut* (Albany: State University of New York Press, 2001).
Eleven essays that explore topics ranging from Vonnegut's humanism and his views on technology to the films that have been made from his novels.

Susan Farrell, *Critical Companion to Kurt Vonnegut: A Literary Reference to His Life and Work* (New York: Facts On File, 2008).
Overview and critical analyses of all of Vonnegut's works, with a brief biography and a bibliography of secondary sources.

Jerome Klinkowitz, Slaughterhouse-Five: *Reforming the Novel and the World* (Boston: Twayne, 1990).
Argues that *Slaughterhouse-Five* overturns the traditional conventions of the novel in English. The book also includes a biographical sketch of Vonnegut.

—Susan Farrell

c⟨∞⟩ɔ

Robert Penn Warren, *All the King's Men*

(New York: Harcourt, Brace, 1946)

Robert Penn Warren (1905–1989) was a towering figure in twentieth-century American literature whose energy and influence helped shape a generation. He published fiction, poetry, drama, biography, history, and criticism, and achieved the unparalleled distinction of winning Pulitzer Prizes in both poetry and fiction—the latter for *All the King's Men* (1946). In 1986 he was named the first Poet Laureate of the United States. Warren was also one of the founders of New Criticism, the dominant literary critical school during the middle of the twentieth century. Finally, his collected interviews of notable Civil Rights leaders such as Martin Luther King Jr., in *Who Speaks for the Negro* (1965), continue to offer a compelling view of the social and political struggles of African Americans and inspired a 2008 national conference titled "We Speak for Ourselves."

Born and raised in Guthrie, Kentucky, Warren graduated from high school at fifteen and enrolled at Vanderbilt University after an injury to his left eye caused him to lose his appointment to the U.S. Naval Academy. At Vanderbilt he acquired the nickname "Red," which remained with him, and connected with other writers, gaining membership in the Fugitive and the Agrarian movements. These early associations attest to Warren's attachment to traditional Southern values and classical poetic structures. While his view of the traditional South underwent profound revision over the course of his life, his pursuit of artistic excellence continued as he worked on his craft with vigor and intensity into his eighties.

In many ways *All the King's Men* represents the confluence of Warren's literary talents, comprising history, fiction, and social criticism, along with structures that are more typically the province of poetry than of fiction. In its first iteration the work was a play, *Proud Flesh*, modeled after classical Greek drama, which was produced at the University of Minnesota in 1947. From its inception to its final version, the story that drove *All the King's Men* retained the themes that had first inspired Warren. That initial inspiration came while he was teaching at Louisiana State University during the governorship of Huey "the Kingfish" Long. Long's rise to power and assassination provide the narrative arc for the central character, Willie Stark, while the details and the motivations driving Stark are Warren's invention. Equally compelling is the story of the quest for self-knowledge of the narrator, Jack Burden. Folded within the novel is a third narrative, that of Jack's ancestor Cass Mastern. The relationship of that story to the work as a whole compounds the structural complexity of the novel.

More than he did with any of his other works, Warren continued to shape and revise the stories of Willie Stark and Cass Mastern. He returned to the idea of a play, writing three dramatic versions after the publication of the novel: *All the King's Men*, written in 1947–1948 and produced in 1948; *Willie Stark: His Rise and Fall,* coauthored with Aaron Frankel, written between 1956 and 1958; and a revised version of the first play, written in collaboration with Mark Schoenberg, which was produced in 1959 and published in 1960. He had published the Cass Mastern episode that eventually found its way into *All the King's Men* in *Partisan Review* in 1944, two years before the novel appeared, as the short story "Cass Mastern's Wedding Ring"; it was republished four times during Warren's lifetime. Warren also used the story of Cass Mastern and Annabelle Trice as the central action in three dramatic versions: *The Wedding Ring* and *Listen to the Mockingbird;* the latter was revised as *An Untitled Play: A Drama of the American Civil War.* Unlike the two dramatic versions of *All the King's Men,* the stage version of the Cass Mastern story was never performed. In all, Warren spent nearly twenty-five years actively interested in the tales of Willie Stark and Cass Mastern.

TOPICS FOR DISCUSSION AND RESEARCH

1. The first key to understanding *All the King's Men* lies in understanding its structure. As John Milton wrote *Paradise Lost* (1667; revised and enlarged, 1674) to "justify the ways of God to man," Warren's intent is to make an examination of motives, which are far more important than the actions that result from those motives. The structure of epic poetry, which Warren adopts in this novel, is ideal for such an approach. He begins in medias res, with the Boss (Willie), Jack, and Sugar-Boy making their initial visit to Judge Irwin. Later, as is frequent in epic poetry, Willie's story, from his humble origins to his rise to the governor's office, is told. Warren uses this pattern of flashbacks multiple times in the novel, allowing elaboration on key plot elements—such as Jack and Anne's romance and Jack's life before Willie—when this information can lead the reader to discover what motivates the characters. Warren's insistence on retaining the Cass Mastern narrative, despite strong opposition from his editors, also has its model in epic poetry. The inclusion of parallel story lines, similar to the Finnsburh episode in *Beowulf,* allows for complex analogous relationships to be formed. Warren averred that Cass's story was crucial to understanding the main narratives of Willie and Jack. In a variation on the repetitive cataloguing found in epic poetry, Warren uses repeated scenes and statements, such as the image of Anne floating in the water, the Scholarly Attorney feeding chocolate to Jack, and Willie's statement, "Man is conceived in sin and born in corruption and he passeth from the stink of the didie to the stench of the shroud. There is always something." None of these repetitions should be seen as superfluous. Instead, Warren, in using epic conventions, creates for the reader the movement of the mind as it grows in understanding over time; as it reflects back on events again and again; as it categorizes people and experiences; and as it struggles to make meaning out of the actions of others. Students will find fertile ground for their criticism of the novel if they examine the relationship of the Cass Mastern episode to the other narratives. They might also examine the function of repetition by considering the impact on character and plot development created by returning to images and statements or by slightly varying those images and statements.

2. Another avenue of inquiry that would serve students well is a contemplation of Warren's liberal use of allusions. The allusions can be divided into several categories, any one of which would be worthy of study. The use of nursery rhymes such as "Humpty Dumpty" and "Little Jack Horner" has captivated the attention of critics. A particularly interesting approach might be to consider the nursery rhymes that Anne constructs about "Jackie-Bird" when they are dating. In all cases, Warren is illuminating aspects of his characters by using these rhymes, and students will benefit from analyzing their meaning in relationship to the narrative as a whole.

3. The novel is also filled with biblical allusions, in part, perhaps, because the real Huey Long made persistent use of such allusions in his speeches. The biblical references are most often connected to Willie and the Scholarly Attorney, and, while some are quite overt, others are more subtly drawn—for example, when the Scholarly Attorney feeds the Unfortunate by hand, he has taken to heart Christ's request to Peter: "Feed my sheep." Students might also consider why these two characters are the focal point for such allusions, examining the Scholarly Attorney as a foil for Willie.

4. The most pervasive allusions throughout the novel are literary ones, and this very pervasiveness creates the major difficulty in treating this topic. Students face the task of locating a particular grouping of literary allusions, such as those that surround Jack and Anne's romance, which are predominantly from American and British poetry, or those that surround Cass and Annabelle's romance, which are taken from classical Greek and Roman literature. Once that grouping has been determined, students might develop a thesis asserting the deeper understanding of that portion of the novel based on a dissection of the relationship between the allusion and Warren's text.

5. *All the King's Men* presents multiple competing philosophies, any one of which offers themes worthy of pursuing. Students may want to read Niccolò Machiavelli's *The Prince* (1513) and consider how well Willie succeeds in becoming Machiavelli's ideal. Students might also consider the competing philosophies presented by Jack's fathers, Ellis Burden (The Scholarly Attorney) and Judge Irwin. The Scholarly Attorney is a Christian who becomes increasingly devoted to serving others, having done as Christ suggested in giving away all that he owns and focusing his energy on following Christ. Judge Irwin, however, follows the Roman honor system, identifying far more with the Stoics than with the Christians. In the Cass Mastern narrative, Cass is the Christian and Duncan is the Stoic. In both instances a marriage is betrayed by a friend, but the reaction of the man betrayed differs markedly. Students wishing to have a greater understanding of the Cass Mastern narrative might explore the two love triangles, using the differing philosophies to understand the reaction of each of the cuckolds. Similarly, Jack's contemplation of The Great Twitch can be compared to Cass's conception of the spider web. Finally, a student wishing to do a broader cross-comparison of the competing philosophies in the novel might consider how the question of personal responsibility is addressed by each of the philosophies or by considering Jack's philosophical development.

RESOURCES

Primary Works

All the King's Men: Three Stage Versions (Athens: University of Georgia Press, 2000).
The dramatic versions of *All the King's Men*. The first play provides insight into the genesis of the novel; the later ones clarify the author's intentions.

At Heaven's Gate (New York: Harcourt, Brace, 1943).
Novel in which Sue Murdock's struggle for autonomy and love plays out against the backdrop of her father's business scandals. As in *All the King's Men,* the narrator is a character whose observations shape the reader's understanding of the novel's events.

Conversations with Robert Penn Warren, edited by Gloria L. Cronin and Ben Siegel (Jackson: University Press of Mississippi, 2005).
Warren's reflections on his life, his career, and the composition and production of the novels.

Night Rider (New York: Random House, 1939).
Fictionalized version of the Black Patch Tobacco Wars of the early twentieth century in which the protagonist, like Willie Stark in *All the King's Men,* is a flawed idealist who ultimately loses his moral center.

Talking with Robert Penn Warren, edited by Floyd C. Watkins, John T. Hiers, and Mary Louise Weaks (Athens: University of Georgia Press, 1990).
A useful complement to Cronin and Siegel's collection of interviews.

World Enough and Time (New York: Random House, 1950).
Novel in which the focus on personal responsibility, the burden of history, and the price of idealism provide a thematic connection to *All the King's Men.*

Bibliography

The Society for the Study of Southern Literature Bibliography <http://web.wm.edu/english/sssl/?svr=www> [accessed 20 November 2009].
Includes nearly 250 entries on Robert Penn Warren, more than 80 of them on *All the King's Men.*

Biography

Joseph Blotner, *Robert Penn Warren* (New York: Random House, 1997).
The only comprehensive biography.

Criticism

Maurice Beebe and Leslie A. Field, eds., *Robert Penn Warren's* All the King's Men: *A Critical Handbook* (Belmont, Cal.: Wadsworth, 1966).
Offers varied approaches to the novel and includes the author's sources and critical responses.

Charles H. Bohner, *Robert Penn Warren* (New York: Twayne, 1964).
Offers a biographical sketch and basic criticism of Warren's works up to the early 1960s.

James A. Grimshaw Jr., *Understanding Robert Penn Warren* (Columbia: University of South Carolina Press, 2001).
Excellent critical overview of Warren's work, with a detailed analysis of *All the King's Men*.

Robert S. Koppelman, *Robert Penn Warren's Modernist Spirituality* (Columbia: University of Missouri Press, 1995).
Includes chapter 2, *"All the King's Men:* The Experience, Language, and Concentric Circles of Conversion," which looks at Jack's spiritual and philosophical development.

James A. Perkins, ed., *The Cass Mastern Material: The Core of Robert Penn Warren's All the King's Men* (Baton Rouge: Louisiana State University Press, 2005).
Comprises Perkins's insightful introduction and the various forms of the Cass Mastern material.

Harold Woodell, All the King's Men: *The Search for a Usable Past* (New York: Twayne, 1993).
Clear, detailed analysis of the novel.

—*Rhonda McDonnell*

c⟨∞⟩ɔ

Tennessee Williams, *Cat on a Hot Tin Roof*
(New York: New Directions, 1955)

In his *Memoirs* (1975) Tennessee Williams (1911–1983) admits that if he had to choose his favorite play, it would be *Cat on a Hot Tin Roof;* and since its opening on Broadway on 24 March 1955, it has remained, through all its permutations, one of Williams's most popular. *Cat on a Hot Tin Roof* is among Williams's "big three," which also includes *The Glass Menagerie* (1944) and *A Streetcar Named Desire* (1947). While Brian Parker points to several biographical parallels in the play, he states that "real life models remain problematic." The seed of the play comes from a short story Williams published in 1952, "Three Players of a Summer Game." The short story has little in common with the plot of the play, but it does contain a husband named Brick who is an alcoholic and his take-charge wife, Margaret.

Williams, who was born Thomas Lanier Williams III in Columbus, Mississippi, and moved to St. Louis, Missouri, in 1919, won his second Pulitzer Prize for *Cat on a Hot Tin Roof,* having won the first for *A Streetcar Named Desire.* The inspiration for the title of the play comes from an expression Williams's father liked to use: "You're making me as nervous as a cat on a hot tin roof." Critics have also noted the influence of Williams's father in his creation of the domineering character of Big Daddy.

Cat on a Hot Tin Roof is one of Williams's most tightly wrought efforts. The action of the play primarily unfolds through the dialogue; the play occurs mostly in one setting, Brick and Maggie's bedroom; and it takes place in real time. The first act belongs to Margaret, or "Maggie," as she confronts Brick regarding his lack of sexual drive, their childless marriage, the knowledge that Brick's father Big Daddy, though he does not yet know it, has terminal cancer, and the problem of Brick's older brother Gooper and his wife May preparing to take Big Daddy's plantation and wealth from him. Maggie has had a brief liaison with Skipper, Brick's former friend and teammate in professional football, who has committed suicide after confessing his homosexual attraction to Brick. The second act belongs to Big Daddy as he confronts Brick with his drinking and his relationship with Maggie and Skipper. During their argument, Brick reveals that Big Daddy has been lied to and is going to die. In the third act, these elements come together as the family meets to discuss the crisis. Gooper, who has children who are potential heirs of the plantation, wants Big Daddy to sign everything over to him; and Maggie, then, lies, claiming she is pregnant with Brick's child. In the end Big Daddy refuses to give up his plantation, wanting to spend his remaining days touring his land; Maggie and Brick go to bed attempting to produce an heir.

In terms of human emotions and motivation, the play is more complex than can be captured in a brief summary. The play concludes with an uneasy resolution: Big Daddy decides to spend the remainder of his days on the land he loves and feels he belongs on while there is an uneasy peace between Maggie and Brick. Whether or not they have taken care of all of their problems is left unresolved, since their only act of resolution is going to bed together. There is also the unresolved situation with Gooper and May and how they fit into the future Big Daddy bequeaths to his family.

Modern criticism of the play tends to center on the issue of homosexuality in the relationship between Brick and Skipper, but other studies of the play may prove more worthwhile. These studies include Jordan Y. Miller's "The Three Halves of Tennessee Williams's World" (1977), Benjamin Nelson's *Tennessee Williams: The Man and His Work* (1961), and Roger Boxill's *Tennessee Williams* (1988). Signi Flack and Felicia Hardison Londre provide useful overviews of the play in their critical surveys of Williams's work, and Donald Spoto's biography, published shortly after Williams's death, is a fine resource. Not to be missed is the 1958 film version of the play with Elizabeth Taylor as the definitive Maggie the Cat and Burl Ives as Big Daddy.

TOPICS FOR DISCUSSION AND RESEARCH

1. Williams said of the play, "The bird that I hope to catch in the net of this play is not the solution of one man's psychological problem. I'm trying to catch the true quality of experience in a group of people, that cloudy, flickering, evanescent—fiercely charged!—interplay of live human beings in a thundercloud of a common crisis." Students might analyze how each of the major characters

in the play approaches and reacts to the "thundercloud of a common crisis." Which of the characters comes away with dignity and honor, and which of the characters fails to meet the challenge of the crisis of the moment? Loomis's essay will be a useful starting point in answering these questions.

2. It would be beneficial for students to begin with the play's most celebrated characters: Big Daddy and Maggie. Both have a great deal in common, especially their backgrounds. Students might explore the common backgrounds of these two characters. In what way do their early lives prepare them for the crisis that pervades the play? How does each face the crisis in his or her own life? It is interesting in this regard to compare Williams's version of the play with Kazan's acting script, which is included in *Tennessee Williams: Plays, 1937–1955* (2000).

3. Maggie is also one of the play's most interesting characters. In the first act she describes herself: "One thing I don't have is the charm of the defeated, my hat is still in the ring, and I am determined to win!" She continues, "What is the victory of a cat on a hot tin roof?—I wish I knew. . . . Just staying on it, I guess, as long as she can. . . ." Remembering Williams' description, what does this say about Maggie's character, and does the play reveal what she says is true? Finally, students will find it helpful to compare and contrast Maggie with Stella in *A Streetcar Named Desire*. While both women are openly and delightfully sensualists, how else are they similar, and how are they different? Concentrate especially on their marital situations.

4. At one point in the play, as they are talking about Maggie and May, Big Daddy tells Brick that the two women are "like a couple of cats on a hot tin roof. It's funny that you and Gooper being so different would pick out the same type of woman." Although they hate each other, May and Maggie have the same goal in mind. In what way does this make them "cats on a hot tin roof"?

5. Of all the characterizations in the play, the most debated is Brick. Several lines of inquiry will help you to begin to understand Brick. First, there is the problem of Brick's seeming indifference throughout the play. At one point Maggie says, "Your indifference made you wonderful at lovemaking—strange?—but true. . . ." Is Brick's indifference an attempt to distance himself from the crisis that is gripping the family, or is it part of his personality? Through all the indifference that Brick shows toward others, why does everyone (except May and Gooper) love Brick even though the love may not be returned? When they are breaking the news of Big Daddy's cancer to Big Mama, she wants Brick by her side. When Gooper is getting ready to present the papers that will give control of the plantation to him, Big Mama says, "Brick! Come here, Brick, I need you. . . . Oh, Brick, son of Big Daddy, Big Daddy does so love you." Big Mama, Maggie, and Big Daddy all love and are devoted to Brick. Why isn't this love returned? Or is it? Read Williams's account of writing act 3 in his *Memoirs* as you attempt to answer this question.

6. Mendacity, the deceiving of others or oneself, is a major theme in Williams's work. Brick claims that he drinks due to his disgust with mendacity. In what ways does mendacity manifest itself in the play? In what ways does it inform

other Williams plays such as *The Glass Menagerie* or *A Streetcar Named Desire?* Judith Thompson's book addresses the theme of mendacity in Williams's work.

RESOURCES

Primary Works
Cat on a Hot Tin Roof (New York: New Directions, 2004).
Williams's "final" dramatic version of the play, completed in 1974.

Conversations with Tennessee Williams, edited by Albert J. Devlin (Jackson: University of Mississippi Press, 1986).
Contains two dozen selections with numerous references to *Cat on a Hot Tin Roof.*

Tennessee Williams: Plays, 1937–1955, edited by Mel Gusson and Kenneth Holditch (New York: Library Classics of the United States, 2000).
Contains both the complete reading version and the acting version of act 3 of the play, which incorporates changes based on suggestions by the director, Elia Kazan.

Memoirs (Garden City, N.Y.: Doubleday, 1975).
Details the rewriting of act 3 and explains why the play was Williams's favorite.

"Three Players of a Summer Game," in *Tennessee Williams: Collected Stories* (New York: New Directions, 1994), pp. 303–325.
Contains characters who appear in *Cat on a Hot Tin Roof:* Brick, an alcoholic husband, and Margaret, his domineering wife.

Bibliography
George W. Crandell, *"Cat on a Hot Tin Roof,"* in *Tennessee Williams: A Guide to Research and Performance* edited by Philip C. Kolin (Westport, Conn.: Greenwood, 1998), pp. 109–125.
A bibliographic essay that covers all aspects of the play from autobiographical references to individual characters and symbols. The work contains an extensive bibliography.

Crandell, *Tennessee Williams: A Descriptive Bibliography* (Pittsburgh: University of Pittsburgh Press, 1995).
Contains thirty-six entries for *Cat on a Hot Tin Roof.*

Biography
Benjamin Nelson, *Tennessee Williams: The Man and His Work* (New York: Obolensky, 1961).
A literary biography that sees the play as a series of dualities: "a world of mendacity, avarice and hypocrisy" paired against a world of "nobility and dignity and tenderness and love and courage" in some of the characters in the play.

Donald Spoto, *The Kindness of Strangers: The Life of Tennessee Williams* (Boston: Little, Brown, 1985).
An excellent biography of Williams, which includes discussion on the background and history of *Cat on a Hot Tin Roof.*

Criticism

Roger Boxill, *Tennessee Williams* (New York: St. Martin's Press, 1988).
Sees the central issue of the play as the "subject of the loss in time." Big Daddy and Brick are relics of the past who have no place in the world of a "modern corporate nation."

George W. Crandell, ed., *The Critical Response to Tennessee Williams* (Westport, Conn.: Greenwood Press, 1996).
Contains Walter F. Kerr's review of the original production of the play (1955), a John Simon review of a revival of the play (1974), and a Frank Rich review of yet another revival of the play (1990). The section concludes with Paul J. Hurley's 1964 analysis of the play.

Signi Flak, *Tennessee Williams* (Boston: Twayne, 1978).
Reviews the major action of the play and the critical responses to it at the time of its first performance.

Felicia Hardison Londre, *Tennessee Williams* (New York: Ungar, 1979).
Analyzes the play and discusses its reviews and revivals.

Jeffrey B. Loomis, "Four Characters in Search of a Company: Williams, Pirandello, and the *Cat on a Hot Tin Roof* Manuscripts," in *Magical Muse: Millennial Essays on Tennessee Williams,* edited by Ralph F. Voss (Tuscaloosa: University of Alabama Press, 2002), pp. 91–110.
Reviews the different versions of the play, noting how each affects the differing perspectives about the play, its meaning, and its characters.

Jordan Y. Miller, "The Three Halves of Tennessee Williams's World," in *Critical Essays on Tennessee Williams,* edited by Robert A. Martin (New York: G. K. Hall, 1997), pp. 209–220.
Compares and contrasts Maggie and Brick with Stanley and Stella in *A Streetcar Named Desire.* Contends Maggie and Brick's struggle ends happily.

Brian Parker, "Swinging a Cat," in *Tennessee Williams' Cat on a Hot Tin Roof* (New York: New Directions, 2004), pp. 187–192.
An excellent introduction to the play with several important biographical connections and commentary concerning the different versions of the play.

Judith J. Thompson, *Tennessee Williams' Plays: Memory, Myth, and Symbol* (New York: Peter Lang, 1989).
Sees the themes of the play as "life's inherent corruption and 'mendacity.'" Brick withdraws to a "psychological Death," while Maggie "embraces Life."

—Bob Bell

Part IV
Annotated Bibliography

Thomas P. Adler, *American Drama, 1940–1960: A Critical History* (New York: Twayne, 1994).
Traces the history of American drama from the later work of Eugene O'Neill to the early work of Edward Albee, providing a cultural context and also covering the work of Lillian Hellman, Arthur Miller, William Inge, Tennessee Williams, Lorraine Hansberry, and several lesser-known postwar dramatists.

Jonathan Baumbach, *The Landscape of Nightmare: Studies in the Contemporary American Novel* (New York: New York University Press, 1965).
Explores the psychological crises of several postwar protagonists, in which Baumbach traces a pattern of collapse and redemption. The book includes close readings of nine major postwar novels, including Robert Penn Warren's *All the King's Men* (1946), J. D. Salinger's *The Catcher in the Rye* (1951), Ralph Ellison's *Invisible Man* (1952), and Flannery O'Connor's *Wise Blood* (1952).

C. W. E. Bigsby, *A Critical Introduction to Twentieth-Century American Drama*, volume 2: *Williams, Miller, Albee* (Cambridge, England: Cambridge University Press, 1984).
An examination of the works of three dominant playwrights of the postwar years.

Harold Bloom, ed., *Contemporary Poets* (New York: Chelsea House, 1986).
Critical essays on nearly thirty postwar American poets, as well as a helpful introduction by Bloom and critic David Bromwich.

Bloom, ed., *Modern Black American Fiction Writers* (New York: Chelsea House, 1995).
Biographies, criticism, and primary bibliographies for eleven American postwar black novelists and short-story writers, including James Baldwin, Ralph Ellison, and Ann Petry.

Bloom, ed., *Modern Black American Poets and Dramatists* (New York: Chelsea House, 1995).
Biographies, criticism, and primary bibliographies for twelve American postwar black playwrights and poets, including Amiri Baraka, Gwendolyn Brooks, Lucille Clifton, Lorraine Hansberry, and Robert Hayden.

Robert Boyers, ed., *Contemporary Poetry in America: Essays and Interviews* (New York: Schocken, 1974).
Essays on postwar American poets and poetry by leading critics and poets of the generation. The book also includes interviews with such figures as John Ashbery, Galway Kinnell, W. S. Merwin, Sylvia Plath, and Theodore Roethke, as well as critic M. L. Rosenthal's essay "American Poetry Today."

Matthew J. Bruccoli and Judith S. Baughman, eds., *Modern Women Writers* (New York: Facts On File, 1994).
Discusses the impact of such writers as Willa Cather, Carson McCullers, Joyce Carol Oates, Flannery O'Connor, and Eudora Welty on assumptions regarding women's roles in literature and on American fiction in general.

David Castronovo, *Beyond the Gray Flannel Suit: Books from the 1950s That Made American Culture* (New York & London: Continuum, 2004).
Focuses on the literature of the 1950s, which the author believes has left a permanent mark on American culture.

Bruce Cook, *The Beat Generation* (New York: Scribners, 1971).
A detailed and intimate look at the Beat movement, based largely on interviews Cook conducted with both its key and its minor figures.

James Dickey, *Babel to Byzantium: Poets and Poetry Now* (New York: Farrar, Straus & Giroux, 1968).
Essays and reviews by one of the most prominent poetic voices of the postwar years on the work of nearly seventy American and British poets of the 1950s and 1960s. The book also includes critical essays on earlier poets, as well as a critical look at some of Dickey's own work.

William Everson, *Archetype West: The Pacific Coast as a Literary Region* (Berkeley, Cal.: Oyez, 1976).
Examines the American West and its archetypal association with freedom, spontaneity, and possibility as represented in the works of West Coast authors in the first half of the twentieth century, as well as the postwar literature of writers such as Allen Ginsberg, Robinson Jeffers, Jack Kerouac, Ken Kesey, and John Steinbeck.

Edward Halsey Foster, *Understanding the Beats* (Columbia: University of South Carolina Press, 1992).
Traces the development of the Beat movement, with chapters on the work of the four original East Coast Beats: Jack Kerouac, Allen Ginsberg, Gregory Corso, and William S. Burroughs. The book also includes a thorough primary and secondary bibliography.

Foster, *Understanding the Black Mountain Poets* (Columbia: University of South Carolina Press, 1995).
Traces the development of this experimental group of writers, focusing on its three major proponents: Robert Creely, Robert Duncan, and Charles Olson. The book includes thorough primary and secondary bibliographies.

Warren G. French, *The Fifties: Fiction, Poetry, Drama* (De Land, Fla.: Everett/Edwards, 1970).
Essays on several American authors who wrote during the 1950s, including James Agee, William Faulkner, Flannery O'Connor, and Tennessee Williams.

French, *The San Francisco Poetry Renaissance, 1955–1960* (Boston: Twayne, 1991).
A thorough introduction to this West Coast movement, including discussions of all of the major Beat poets.

David D. Galloway, *The Absurd Hero in American Fiction*, revised edition (Austin: University of Texas Press, 1970).

Treats the existentialist notion of the absurd as essential to understanding the plights of the protagonists in the fiction of Saul Bellow, J. D. Salinger, William Styron, and John Updike.

Richard J. Gray, *A History of American Literature* (Malden, Mass.: Blackwell, 2004).
Devotes a lengthy, detailed chapter to the literary developments of the postwar years. The book also includes a lengthy secondary bibliography.

Charles B. Harris, *Contemporary American Novelists of the Absurd* (New Haven, Conn.: College and University Press, 1971).
Explores the philosophical proposition that humanity is trapped in a world devoid of meaning and purpose as depicted in the work of John Barth, Joseph Heller, Thomas Pynchon, and Kurt Vonnegut.

Ihab Habib Hassan, *Contemporary American Literature: 1945–1972* (New York: Ungar, 1973).
A thorough survey of the major fiction writers, poets, and dramatists of the postwar period.

Josephine G. Hendin, ed., *A Concise Companion to Postwar American Literature and Culture* (Malden, Mass.: Blackwell, 2004).
Fifteen essays that discuss the various literary genres and movements, including established and emerging ethnic literatures and the works of gay and lesbian writers, as well as popular music and movies in postwar America.

Peter G. Jones, *War and the Novelist* (Columbia: University of Missouri Press, 1976).
Analyzes the war novel, using key works such as Norman Mailer's *The Naked and the Dead* (1948), James Jones's *From Here to Eternity* (1951), Joseph Heller's *Catch-22* (1961), and Kurt Vonnegut's *Slaughterhouse-Five* (1969) for illustration and tracing the influence of such earlier American war novelists as Stephen Crane, John Dos Passos, and Ernest Hemingway.

Robert F. Kiernan, *American Writing since 1945: A Critical Survey* (New York: Ungar, 1983).
Delineates and discusses the major postwar movements and schools in fiction, drama, and poetry.

Adam Kirsch, *The Wounded Surgeon: Confession and Transformation in Six American Poets* (New York: Norton, 2005).
Considers the poetry of John Berryman, Elizabeth Bishop, Randall Jarrell, Robert Lowell, Sylvia Plath, and Delmore Schwartz, contending that the label "confessional" belies the complexity and uniqueness of the work of each.

David Krasner, *American Drama, 1945–2000* (Malden, Mass.: Blackwell, 2006).
Chapters 2 and 3, "Money Is Life" and "Reality and Illusion," deal with the work of postwar dramatists.

David Lehman, *The Last Avant-Garde: The Making of the New York School of Poets*
    (New York: Doubleday, 1998).
A detailed study of the creative outpouring that developed out of the friendship
of the poets John Ashbery, Kenneth Koch, Frank O'Hara, and James Schuyler
between 1948 and 1966. Lehman traces the influence of the Abstract Expressionist painters on these writers, proposing that the New York School may have had
a more lasting impact than other 1950s literary movements.

Vincent B. Leitch, *American Literary Criticism from the Thirties to the Eighties*
    (New York: Columbia University Press, 1988).
Thorough discussions of thirteen major critical approaches and the historical and
cultural contexts in which they developed.

Roger Luckhurst, *Science Fiction* (Malden, Mass.: Polity, 2005).
A history of the evolution of science fiction since the late nineteenth century,
with particular attention to the blossoming of the genre in the post–World War
II years. Luckhurst analyzes several major works; he views the genre as a chronicle
of the effects of technological advancement on both the world and the human
imagination.

Jerome Mazzaro, *Postmodern American Poetry* (Urbana: University of Illinois
    Press, 1980).
Traces the origins of Postmodernist poetry in the work of the English poet W. H.
Auden and analyzes the works of Postmodernist American poets Randall Jarrell,
Theodore Roethke, David Ignatow, John Berryman, Sylvia Plath, and Elizabeth
Bishop.

Brian McHale, *Postmodernist Fiction* (New York: Methuen, 1987).
An essential study that traces the development of Postmodernism with regard to
its Modernist roots. The basic difference, McHale contends, is in the Modernist concern with knowing, as opposed to the Postmodernist preoccupation with
being.

James F. Mersmann, *Out of the Vietnam Vortex: A Study of Poets and Poetry against
    the War* (Lawrence: University Press of Kansas, 1974).
Analyses of the anti–Vietnam War poetry of Robert Bly, Robert Duncan, Allen
Ginsberg, and Denise Levertov.

Raymond M. Olderman, *Beyond the Waste Land: A Study of the American Novel in
    the Nineteen-Sixties* (New Haven, Conn.: Yale University Press, 1972).
Explores the dark-comic works of novelists such as John Barth, John Hawkes,
Joseph Heller, Ken Kesey, Thomas Pynchon, and Kurt Vonnegut, who portray
alienated characters in a world grown increasingly elusive and sinister.

David Perkins, *A History of Modern Poetry: Modernism and After* (Cambridge,
    Mass.: Belknap Press of Harvard University Press, 1987).
A meticulously researched, highly readable, and exhaustive survey of American
and British poetry after World War I.

David R. Pichaske, *A Generation in Motion: Popular Music and Culture in the Sixties* (Granite Falls, Minn.: Ellis Press, 1989).
A detailed history of the counter-culture movement that traces its origins, development, and key events, paying special attention to the response of writers and musicians to the political, social, and cultural atmosphere of the era. The book includes a helpful bibliography and photographs.

Pichaske, *The Poetry of Rock: The Golden Years* (Peoria, Ill.: Ellis Press, 1981).
A literary analysis of the themes and style in lyrics of such 1960s rock artists as The Doors, Bob Dylan, The Jefferson Airplane, Phil Ochs, and Paul Simon.

Sanford Pinsker, *Jewish-American Fiction, 1917–1987* (New York: Twayne, 1992).
A concise yet thorough study of the development of Jewish American fiction, focusing mainly on postwar fiction writers.

George Plimpton, ed., *Beat Writers at Work:* The Paris Review *Interviews* (New York: Modern Library, 1999).
Interviews with the major figures in the Beat movement, as well as major writers whose work is often associated with that of the Beats.

Dannye Romine Powell, *Parting the Curtains: Interviews with Southern Writers* (Winston-Salem, N.C.: Blair, 1994).
Interviews with nearly two dozen writers, including postwar novelists such as James Dickey, Walker Percy, William Styron, and Eudora Welty. The book includes many photographs.

Charles Ruas, ed., *Conversations with American Writers* (New York: Knopf, 1985).
Interviews with fourteen American authors, including Truman Capote, Joseph Heller, Gore Vidal, Eudora Welty, and Tennessee Williams.

Louis D. Rubin Jr., ed., *The History of Southern Literature* (Baton Rouge: Louisiana State University Press, 1985).
Detailed examinations of the work of such postwar Southern writers as James Agee, Truman Capote, Ralph Ellison, Carson McCullers, Flannery O'Connor, Walker Percy, William Styron, Robert Penn Warren, and Eudora Welty.

Richard H. Rupp, *Celebration in Postwar American Fiction, 1945–1967* (Coral Gables, Fla.: University of Miami Press, 1970).
Assesses the life-affirming outlook of ten postwar writers: John Cheever, John Updike, Eudora Welty, Flannery O'Connor, James Agee, J. D. Salinger, James Baldwin, Ralph Ellison, Bernard Malamud, and Saul Bellow.

David Seed, *American Science Fiction and the Cold War: Literature and Film* (Chicago: Fitzroy Dearborn, 1999).
Traces the impact of such Cold War concerns as nuclear holocaust, government surveillance, and computer technology on the development of science fiction after World War II.

Tony Tanner, *City of Words: American Fiction, 1950–1970* (New York: Harper & Row, 1971).
A thorough discussion of the American novel and the representative works of twenty-five authors who dominated the 1950s and 1960s.

Matt Theado, *The Beats: A Literary Reference* (Detroit: Gale, 2001).
A thorough overview of the East and West Coast origins of the Beat movement with lengthy discussions of its major figures. The book includes a chronology, reviews, interviews, photographs, and extensive primary and secondary bibliographies.

Gordon Weaver, ed., *The American Short Story, 1945–1980: A Critical History* (Boston: Twayne, 1983).
A collection of essays that trace the stylistic and thematic evolution of the American short story after World War II. The pieces treat major figures of the form such as Donald Barthelme, John Cheever, Bernard Malamud, Flannery O'Connor, Joyce Carol Oates, and John Updike, as well as less-prominent writers.

Part V
Glossary

American dream The notion that America provides the freedom and opportunity for all of its citizens to prosper—an idea that seemed increasingly credible after World War II. This idea is challenged in such works as Arthur Miller's *Death of a Salesman* (1949) and Ralph Ellison's *Invisible Man* (1952).

Antihero Originally referred to a hero whose vices outweighed his virtues; but in postwar literature it tends to indicate a flawed but morally conscious character who becomes disillusioned with authority, such as Holden Caulfield in J. D. Salinger's *The Catcher in the Rye* (1951) or John Yossarian in Joseph Heller's *Catch-22* (1961).

Automatic writing A style of writing based on the uninhibited flow of language with little regard to plan or revision. This approach was popular among Beat writers such as Allen Ginsberg and Jack Kerouac and New York School writers such as Frank O'Hara.

Bildungsroman German term (now taken into English) for a novel that traces the coming-of-age or individual growth and enlightenment of its protagonist, such as Harper Lee's *To Kill a Mockingbird* (1960). Novels such as Ralph Ellison's *Invisible Man* (1952) and Jack Kerouac's *On the Road* (1957) fall into this category, as well, but are more specifically examples of the *Künstlerroman*, which traces the development of an artist.

Black Aesthetic movement An artistic separatist movement that emerged among African American writers during the 1960s in response to racial discrimination, producing such works as Amiri Baraka's play *Dutchman* (1961) and Eldridge Cleaver's autobiographical essay collection *Soul on Ice* (1968), and effecting a dramatic change in the poetry of Gwendolyn Brooks.

Black comedy A fictional or dramatic work in which a hapless character struggles to maintain dignity in an absurd world. These works, such as Joseph Heller's *Catch-22* (1961) and Kurt Vonnegut's *Slaughterhouse-Five* (1969), use an ironically light-hearted, often detached, tone to underscore the gravity of their moral concerns.

Containment An effort on the part of the U.S. government to contain the spread and influence of communism. The policy brought on the Second Red Scare in the 1950s and triggered American involvement in the Korean and Vietnam Wars, the latter serving further to unify the American counter culture.

Consumerism The tendency to purchase excessive goods and conveniences, which are often viewed as a measure of success. This tendency, which was exacerbated after the shortages imposed by World War II, is the subject of much postwar protest writing by the Beats, J. D. Salinger, Edward Albee, and others.

Existentialism A philosophical outlook that views free will as the human being's only redeeming value in a world that has no inherent meaning. In existential literature the freedom to create a meaningful existence is both burdensome and liberating, as can be seen in novels such as Ralph Ellison's *Invisible Man* (1952). Many postwar writers espoused Christian existentialism, which does not render the world meaningless but still places an emphasis on the individual's responsibility to determine his or her fate.

Grotesque literature   Fiction that employs bizarre characters and situations as a way of conveying moral concerns. In Flannery O'Connor's fiction, for example, physical impairments often symbolize spiritual shortcomings, and strange, violent incidents induce moral awakenings.

Indeterminacy   The tendency of much Modernist and Postmodernist literature to resist a definitive interpretation. A novel such as Thomas Pynchon's *The Crying of Lot 49* (1966), for example, is purposely open-ended.

McCarthyism   Named for Republican senator Joseph McCarthy of Wisconsin, who conducted intense investigations of suspected Communist sympathizers during the Second Red Scare. The term has come to refer to the interrogation of those suspected of subversive behavior without regard to significant evidence. Arthur Miller indirectly attacked McCarthyism by comparing it to the 1692 Salem, Massachusetts, witch trials in his play *The Crucible* (1953); Ray Bradbury extrapolated it into the future in his novel *Fahrenheit 451* (1953); and Bob Dylan mocked it in his song "Talkin' John Birch Paranoid Blues."

Metafiction   Fiction that draws attention to its own illusory qualities. Examples of metafictive tactics can be seen in novels such as Kurt Vonnegut's *Slaughterhouse-Five* (1969), in which the author is a character, and Richard Brautigan's *Trout Fishing in America* (1967), in which the narrator discusses the cover of the book.

Naturalism   A literary movement popularized at the beginning of the twentieth century by writers such as Jack London that continued to influence postwar writers such as the playwright Edward Albee and the novelist James Dickey. Naturalism emphasizes the reality of the human being's animal nature and the dominance of the survival instinct in a universe portrayed as indifferent to humanity.

New Criticism   An approach to understanding literature, popular during the postwar years, that views the work as an autonomous entity, independent of its author's life or intentions and made meaningful by the interrelationship of literary devices such as irony, tone, diction, figurative language, and symbolism.

Nihilism   A philosophical outlook that views the universe as having no inherent meaning or value. It is captured in Friedrich Nietzsche's *Die fröhliche Wissenschaft* (1882, The Gay Science; translated as *The Joyful Wisdom*, 1910) and *Also sprach Zarathustra* (1883–1885; translated as *Thus Spake Zarathustra*, 1896) by the expression "Gott ist tot" (God is dead).

Organic form   A form of poetic composition thought to grow naturally in accord with the content of the piece, as opposed to the more calculated, mechanical form often associated with Modernist writers. Modern Primitive poets such as Robinson Jeffers and Theodore Roethke saw the creation of a poem as analogous to the growth of a plant.

Pastoral   Originally referred to bucolic poetry but in reference to postwar literature describes a work that is nostalgic for a vanished simplicity. Richard

Brautigan's *Trout Fishing in America* (1967) can be seen as a sort of pastoral parody.

Philosophical materialism A philosophical outlook that views the universe as composed solely of matter and, thus, denies the existence of a soul independent of the body. Hazel Motes in Flannery O'Connor's *Wise Blood* (1952) futilely attempts to maintain this outlook.

Primitivism A predilection among certain writers to view the natural world as superior to the civilized, human-made world. Primitivists such as James Dickey rely heavily on natural imagery and tend to emphasize the primacy of unconscious impulses.

Realism A literary movement popularized in the late nineteenth century by writers such as Mark Twain that continued to inform the work of post–World War II authors. Realism tends to emphasize the harsh, unacknowledged realities of everyday life, such as the pervasiveness of human cruelty, and the individual's inability to control many aspects of his or her fate.

Red Scare A period of intense scrutiny of American citizens suspected to have Communist sympathies. The Red Scare of the Cold War period was the second of two in American history; the first occurred after World War I. The careers of many American artists were negatively affected by these investigations, and many, such as Ray Bradbury, Bob Dylan, and Arthur Miller, vented their anger in allegorical literary works.

Regionalism A literary approach that aims to capture the culture and character of a particular area of the country, such as the American West or South, as seen in the work of John Steinbeck and Flannery O'Connor, respectively.

Southern Gothic A literary style, epitomized in the work of William Faulkner and in postwar novelists such as Carson McCullers and Flannery O'Connor, that features mysterious and often sinister settings inhabited by grotesque characters who struggle amid oppressive social and moral circumstances.

Stream of consciousness A narrative style that attempts to mimic a character's unrefined thought processes. It is prominent in postwar novels that often aimed to convey the psychological crises of their protagonists.

Surrealism An artistic movement that rejects conventional aesthetic, moral, and social restraints and defies a rational perception of reality. It was popularized in the 1920s but continued to affect the novels of such postwar writers as Thomas Pynchon, William S. Burroughs, and Richard Brautigan and the mid-1960s songwriting of Bob Dylan.

Theatre of the absurd Theatrical movement, originating in France with the lays of Samuel Beckett, Jean Genet, and Eugene Ionesco, that portrayed characters grasping futilely for meaning and order in a seemingly senseless world. Much of the work of the American playwright Edward Albee can be classified as part of this movement.

Index